Harvest of Rage

HARVEST OF RAGE

Why Oklahoma City Is
Only the Beginning

JOEL DYER

WestviewPress
A Division of HarperCollins*Publishers*

Copyright © 1997 by Westview Press, A Division of HarperCollins Publishers, Inc.

Published in 1997 in the United States of America by Westview Press, 5500 Central Avenue, Boulder, Colorado 80301 2877, and in the United Kingdom by Westview Press, 12 Hid's Copse Road, Cumnor Hill, Oxford OX2 9JJ

A CIP catalog record for this book is available from the Library of Congress.
ISBN 0-8133-3292-3

The paper used in this publication meets the requirements of the American National Standard for Permanence of Paper for Printed Library Materials Z39.48-1984.

10   9   8   7   6   5   4   3   2   1

For Ellen Ramsey

In memory of Bill Dyer and Brad Northcott

Contents

Acknowledgments

I would like to thank all the folks at Westview Press who have made this project possible. I'll never be able to express my full appreciation for your encouragement, enthusiasm, and friendship. Thanks for having faith in my abilities and realizing the importance of this project.

Going back a little further, I would like to thank my brother, Paul, whose unwavering belief in me, though most times unfounded, has been my strength for thirty-nine years. And of course there's Mom, who told me I could do anything I put my mind to. She's wrong about that, but I have no doubt that hearing those words through the years has made many of my dreams come true. Thanks to all of my siblings, Jeff, Toni, and Christie, and to Ron Beeson.

A very special thanks to Glen Wallace who made this book possible. In many ways this is Glen's story. Any understanding I have of the rural crisis is because of Glen and his amazing compassion for the people who live on the horizon of our nation.

Thanks to my staff and friends at *Boulder Weekly*—Kathy, Greg, and Jeff—who made it possible for me to disappear for over half a year. Thanks to Stewart and Lon for holding my job as editor until my return.

Wes Moses, you are a tremendous friend and researcher. Thanks for all the help and letting me run up several hundred dollars' worth of library fines in your name. I can't forget my friends at Tortugas who encouraged me, fed me, helped me with research, and often let me bend their ears for hours at a time.

I need to thank journalist, fiction writer, and friend Kevin Burke, who inspired me to be an investigative reporter, as well as his very significant other, my dear friend Debra, who has always been able to calm the seas that surround me. I'll be calling you soon.

Thanks to Nanci Griffith, whose words kept me company, who kept me sane, and who never let me lose sight of the souls of the people on the back roads. And thanks to all the people who allowed me to pry into their lives even though they were hurting and I was a stranger.

And lastly, thanks to the unknown Washington potato farmer who left a message on my answering machine asking me to tell the world how hard life has become in rural America. I hope that I succeeded. This book exists through grace.

Joel Dyer

Introduction

On April 19, 1995, a Ryder truck filled with fertilizer and racing fuel exploded outside the Alfred P. Murrah Building in Oklahoma City. The murderous blast killed 168 innocent people and forever changed the emotional and political landscape of America. In the bloody aftermath of that single event, we realized that there are people and organizations that will stop at nothing to demonstrate their hatred for the federal government, even if innocent children have to be blown to bits to make their point.

While the smoke was still clearing from America's most infamous terrorist attack, all eyes looked across the ocean for answers. The national media began to explore which faraway terrorists were likely culprits. After all, this was Oklahoma City, the middle of the American heartland, and only the mind of some foreign murderer could have conceived such a bloodthirsty plot.

But in Oklahoma and around the nation, FBI agents were looking across our own oceans of wheat, corn, and barley for their answers. They weren't raiding the homes of Palestinian nationals or people born in Iraq and Iran. Within hours of the blast, they were questioning men and women who had attended meetings on how to stop farm foreclosures or on how to return the country to a constitutional republic. They raced to question those who run the agriculture hot lines that assist stressed-out farmers when they become suicidal or violent or just need to talk to someone who understands what losing the family farm means.

While a shocked nation sat glued to its television sets and watched the Oklahoma City body count rise, government agents were questioning people who had attended a meeting held at an Oklahoma City motel just two weeks before the explosion. The meeting was advertised as an effort to address the issue of farm foreclosures. But instead, it turned out to be a Christian Identity crash course in antigovernment theology. The guest speakers at the meeting were from Decker, Michigan—the place where James Nichols has his farm, the place where his brother Terry and his friend Timothy McVeigh had been spending a lot of time.

The speed with which the FBI moved to question attendees of the meeting demonstrated that although the victims had been caught completely off guard by the bloodbath in Oklahoma, the government had not. The intelligence community had been concerned with the politics of people in places like Decker long before the Murrah building became a bombed-out tomb. Agents may not have known who struck the match, but they knew the bomb's fuse had been lit somewhere in the economically devastated landscape of rural America.

In the late 1990s, after a decade and a half of crises, the people who live in the nation's hinterland have finally reached the edge of the abyss. The fertilizer and diesel fuel that once enriched the soil and powered the machines that plant and harvest will now be used to destroy their perceived enemies, primary among them, the federal government. Like the agents who had been waiting and preparing for this inevitable day, many in the pockets of poverty that dot the back roads of the United States heard and understood the message of the bomb: "I hurt, so you're going to hurt." But for the rest of us, it was maddeningly well encrypted. The only sounds we heard were the screams of the innocent children and the wailing of the thousands whose families had been destroyed.

Nine years before that bomb ripped through the Murrah building, another tragedy took place. It was much smaller in scope and only whispered the message that the Oklahoma City terrorists later shouted to the world. Katherine Copeland, a fifty-four-year-old kindergarten teacher, mother of three, and farmwife, died violently. Copeland and her husband, Eugene, lived in the small town of Chattanooga, Oklahoma, near the Texas border, where they raised cotton and cattle on their farm.

Like thousands of other towns in America's backwaters, Chattanooga was in trouble in the mid-1980s. It was a place composed of farm families and those who ran the small businesses that relied upon the area's agricultural incomes for survival. The Copelands, like everyone else in town, had become the victims of powerful forces far beyond their control. A destructive combination of high interest rates dictated by the Federal Reserve, low prices for farm products due to the multinational food monopolies' control of the market, and new, smaller government subsidies that caught farmers by surprise in 1985 had sealed their fate. The Copelands were facing foreclosure.

On July 9, 1986, Katherine Copeland's life became unbearable. The small-town farmwife who could have passed for anyone's grandmother walked out to a burning trash heap and killed herself by crawling onto a flaming barrel of garbage. Eugene Copeland tried to explain his wife's demise to the *New York Times* (August 17, 1987): "You learn all your life that if you work hard, things will get better. But in this business it just doesn't work that way. She just couldn't see any escape. She got desperate."

Katherine Copeland hurt so much she wanted to kill someone. But unlike the Oklahoma City terrorists, she chose herself as the victim—as would many in farm country during the 1980s and 1990s. Suicide has become the number one cause of death on America's farms.

It's hard to imagine that slowly incinerating yourself could be preferable to losing a farm. In fact, choosing a violent and painful suicide over foreclosure is a decision that few can comprehend, outside of the 2 percent of Americans who still work the land or the hundreds of thousands of farm families that have lost their farms since 1980. The message contained in the self-destructive actions of people like Katherine Copeland is really this: Farmers and others in rural America aren't like those of us who make our way in the cities and suburbs. For these rural people, the loss of their land and their way of life creates an incomprehensible despair, more severe even than the death of a loved one. It's as if all the family members who had worked that soil before them and all the children and grandchildren who should one day inherit that opportunity had suddenly been murdered by an unseen assailant: You don't just lose a farm. You lose your identity, your history, and, in many ways, your life.

If you can understand the pain that can cause someone to burn to death in an effort to avoid facing foreclosure, you can understand the power and the awesome potential for violence that exists in much of today's antigovernment movement. Although most of us in America don't see—and don't want to see—the common threads that run through this culturally and economically driven violence that ranges from farm suicides to the Oklahoma City bombing, there are those who do.

Dr. Glen Wallace, former director of rural mental health services for the state of Oklahoma, and a number of his peers who specialize in rural psychology have been watching this metamorphosis in rural attitude from anger turned inward (farm suicide) to anger turned outward (antigovernment beliefs) for nearly fifteen years. In 1989, long before incidents such as the Weaver tragedy in Ruby Ridge, Idaho, the raid on the Branch Davidians in Waco, Texas, and the bombing in Oklahoma City turned our focus to the militias, Wallace was testifying before a congressional subcommittee about the state of rural America. He warned those in power that the economic policies and food monopolies that were bringing ruin to the nation's agricultural areas were also creating feelings of anger and distrust among the rural population, feelings directed toward the federal government. At the time, Wallace could only have guessed what form this anger would eventually assume, but he predicted accurately that it would be a force in America for decades to come.

I first worked with Glen Wallace in 1989. He was counseling farmers and doing suicide interventions for Ag-Link, a crisis hot line in Oklahoma City, and I was documenting the plight of farmers facing foreclosure. A few weeks after the Oklahoma City bombing, we spoke on the phone. He caught me off guard when he said: "I don't even know if I should say this, but the minute that bomb went off, I suspected it was because of the rural crisis. These people [farmers] have suffered so much."

Several studies conducted by rural psychologists and sociologists in farm states have uncovered shocking evidence of the suffering to which Wallace refers. These studies show that more farmers died from suicide than from any other unnatural cause from 1981 to 1988. In some areas of the country, equipment accidents, which had long been listed as the number one cause of farm deaths, were being outpaced by suicides at a staggering ratio of 5:1. As a group, farmers were—and likely still are—killing themselves at least three times as often as the general population. It is here, in this self-inflicted violence, that rural psychologists find the connection between suicides and the antigovernment movement.[1]

Losing a farm is a slow process; it often takes several years from the time a family first gets into financial trouble. Psychologists have determined that by the end of this painful process, these families are the victims of chronic long-term stress. Once they reach that point, there are only a few things that can happen.

People suffering from long-term stress either get help or get violent. If they choose the latter route, there are only two directions to go, depending on whom they blame for their pain and suffering. If they blame themselves, they commit suicide. If they blame others, they turn their violence outward. Wallace points out that it's the outwardly violent group that often ends up threatening or even killing the lenders, the perceived enemy. He also says the people in this group are the most susceptible to the violent antigovernment message.

People who have turned their anger outward continue to look for the support they need to function in day-to-day life. Unfortunately, the rural mental health network that once offered them their best hope has been systematically dismantled all across America. State- and federally funded programs have been replaced by a few HMO facilities that require insurance—something few in rural America who are experiencing economic hardship or foreclosure can afford. And these privately owned facilities have created ridiculously short timetables for treatment.

Patients who once received months of intense counseling or long periods of inpatient care now get, at best, a few days of therapy. The goal of mental health has been replaced by the quest for profit. And this not-so-subtle shift toward profit affects us all. Antigovernment teachings have become the salve for the depression and other mental wounds of rural America. No one knows how many of the millions of rural people who have lost their land or their jobs since 1980 or how many of the tens of thousands more who are still holding on under extreme duress have fallen prey to the antigovernment gospel. But the number is large—and growing every day.

When Wallace told me that he immediately thought of the rural crisis when he heard about the Oklahoma City bombing, he wasn't saying that the bombers were farmers. Rather, he meant that the ongoing problems in rural America—which started with the farm crisis and the changing global economy—are fueling the growth and volatile nature of the movement. The revolution that began in the wheat fields in the middle of the country has now spread through many other sectors of the population. The one thing these sectors all have in common is a lousy economic future that they blame on the federal government.

Over the last several years, while researching this book, I've had the opportunity to interview literally hundreds of farmers facing foreclosure and a lot of people now involved in the antigovernment movement. My travels have taken me from armed compounds near the Mexican border in Texas to ranches in Montana. I've talked religion over dinner with Christian Identity believers, whose doctrine is at the heart of the white supremacist movement. I've spent time holed up in an already-foreclosed-on farmhouse, where the owner and some of his militia buddies were refusing to give up the land. While staring at the business end of a .45, I conducted a five-hour interview with a man involved with the issuance of several "common-law court" death sentences on FBI informants. And I've shared the floor of a hotel room in Kansas City with delegates to the "Third Continental Congress," a gathering where the representatives of groups from thirteen states met to create a new provisional government to replace our current one.

I interviewed one farmer in 1989 while he was going through the foreclosure on his family farm. He didn't know what a militia was back then. When I next talked to him in the early 1990s, he had lost his wife and kids and was attending common-law courts and antigovernment meetings. He had joined the underground world of the landless farmer, moving from one part of farm country to another, spreading the news of the one-world government controlled by Jewish bankers. The last time I interviewed him was in 1996—in prison, where he's serving a hefty sentence for filing "Freemen-style" liens against the banker he blamed for the loss of his farm years earlier. His was a painful seven-year process that had taken him from farmer to inmate. And this is a process being repeated all across the land.

There is one question I always ask the people I meet in the antigovernment movement: "What was it that finally made you stop and say, 'This isn't right; I've got to do something about it'?" The answers they have given are varied, yet in one sense, the same: "They took my farm." "The IRS took everything I owned." "Environmentalists wouldn't let me run my cows cause some damn little sparrow they said was endangered lived on my place." "They were going to put me in jail because I didn't have the money to pay my tickets." "They took away my kids because I can't pay my child support. I only make five bucks an hour. How can I pay child support?"

Different answers, one theme. Simply put, those who cannot financially afford to live in our system are taking up arms. The economic gap between rich and poor can no longer be bridged by our dwindling middle class. We have once again, as at other times in our history, reached a turning point.

It's not enough to say that Oklahoma City was the result of the antigovernment movement. It's not enough to generalize and say this movement is made up of hate groups, racists, and right-wing religious zealots, even though these are, in some ways, accurate labels. We must determine why a rapidly growing number of people are scrambling to accept this new gospel of hate and violence. What are the elements in our rural culture that have made this "anti" message so palatable?

America's innocence lay in the rubble of the Murrah building as surely as the crumpled bodies of the victims. The deadly Oklahoma City bomb was just the first shot in the collective suicide of the nation. Some Americans—some of them our neighbors—have declared war on the powers that be, and those of us who stand unknowingly in between these warring factions are paying the price. And we will continue to pay the price—one building, one pipe bomb, one burned-down church at a time—until we come to understand, first, that the nation is holding a loaded gun to its head and, second, why so many among us are struggling to pull the trigger.

Part One
Fertile Ground

1

The Myth

The only thing new is the history we don't know.
—Harry S. Truman

Blue states went for Clinton, red went for Dole—at least that was network news anchor Peter Jennings's explanation of the two-toned map shown to TV viewers on election night 1996. Later in the evening, newly reelected President Bill Clinton pronounced his victory to be an overwhelming vote of confidence from all across America. But the red and blue were not distributed in a pattern that reflected the normal boundaries of our two-party system. The map told a different story.

There was a gap in Clinton's victory. In the middle of all those blue states was a wide band of red that stretched from Mexico to Canada. Those big square states in America's heartland had voted against the president. Although analysts reported that Bob Dole had won in the red areas, it would have been more accurate to say that those were states where Bill Clinton and the federal government had lost.

I'd spent much of 1996 crisscrossing the middle of the country doing interviews and talking politics, stopping at farms, gas stations, restaurants, and nursing homes. Believe me, Dole was hardly popular. Most farmers and rural Americans saw little difference between the Republican and his Democratic foe. As far as they were concerned, Washington politicians were all cut from the same cloth.

The same map Jennings used to show the election results hinted at another story. It could have been used to explain to viewers where today's antigovernment revolution has become a powerful force. Red wasn't for Dole. Red was anti-Washington. But it's a mistake to think the states that voted for Clinton are immune to this radical government backlash. Underneath the map's blue—in those areas that fill the space between cities—is a layer of disenfranchised and angry red. At best, Clinton had won the election in varying degrees of purple.

A Lesson from the Geographic Center

The highway winding north through the countryside from Bob Dole's hometown of Russell, Kansas, to the Nebraska border is devoid of traffic. The tumbleweed towns that the highway pierces from time to time are on the verge of being lost in the landscape; houses are boarded up, mills and industrial complexes are stalled forever, businesses are hollow. Signs hanging in storefronts announcing going-out-of-business sales have long been bleached by the sun, their original color lost to time. The people who, for whatever reason, remain in these towns wander about like ghosts, mowing their crabgrass lawns in the fading light of day or sitting on the porch thinking about how the town was in the old days, before the people all moved away.

I blow through these towns in a cloud of dust, slowing only because I can never be sure there isn't some remnant of a law enforcement structure lurking in the potholed alleys. As evening draws near, I coast into Lebanon, Kansas, a small farm town only a stone's throw away from the exact geographic center of the United States, a hollow town in the middle of the sea of red where Clinton had lost on election night. If ever there was an accurate portrait of rural America in the 1990s, this is it. Lebanon could serve as a metaphor for many of the subjects that cry out for discussion in our nation's capital—the gap between the rich and poor, the place of religion in politics, disdain for the federal government, and the failed economy of the heartland.

For twenty years, in places like Lebanon, the American economy has been acting like a giant cassette tape when it comes to the distribution of wealth. This cassette starts out with equal amounts on either side. Then someone hits the fast forward button of money-controlled politics. At first, both sides of the tape seem to move at about the same speed. You can hardly notice that one side is getting bigger as the other shrinks. As the redistribution continues, the growing side actually seems to slow down, almost to a crawl. If you look only at the side now holding most of the tape, you get the feeling that the transfer is happening very gradually and calmly. But a glance at the shrinking side gives a different impression. It spins faster and faster, actually beginning to whine as it nears the end. And then, "pop"—everything comes to a violent halt. The end of the economic tape can seem like the end of the world to the millions of people at the bottom.

Government bureaucrats have a thousand different ways to interpret economic statistics in their eternal effort to figure out who's doing well and who isn't. Not surprisingly, come election time, incumbents tell us everyone is doing better now than they were a few years ago, a stance that relegates their challengers to the "whole-place-has-gone-to-hell" position. The truth is, they're both right: Of late, rich folks always seem to be doing better and poor folks are always doing worse, and that's particularly true in rural places.

After spending a little time talking to residents of Lebanon, Kansas, I realize that poverty, unemployment, and a feeling of political helplessness have done what even the awesome power of plate tectonics couldn't manage: These forces have pushed the geographic center of the United States a considerable distance to the right. At a time when its failing economy has actually resulted in a shrinking population, north-central Kansas has become a hotbed of antigovernment activity.

I ask Lebanon resident Pam Burt, who has to drive thirty miles one way just to keep her minimum-wage job as a trainee at a gas station, what message she would like to send to Washington politicians. She answers:

> It's so hard to get by here. You have to drive real far to get any decent job, and that's if you're lucky. Grand Island is the nearest jobs that pay and that would be an extra sixty miles. The economy here is going down these days and we could use some help. The big farmers are doing fine but it's getting harder and harder for the smaller ones. If the president came here for a week and looked around he'd do something.

She may be right, but presidents don't come to the middle of America to look around. They only visit places like Lebanon to look wholesome in their attempt to garner the nostalgia vote. Unfortunately, they believe their pollsters, who tell them that the measly number of votes controlled by rural Americans will mean little, come election time.

Pollsters and politicians may know how to count, but they seem to know very little about the consequences of pushing people too far. The story of rural America's economic and political disenfranchisement does not show up in the polls—it shows up in the news. It takes the form of suicides, child and spousal abuse, farm foreclosures, substance abuse, and, more and more often, pipe bombs and increased antigovernment activity.

On the northern outskirts of town, I turn left and head for the park that pays homage to the exact center of the United States. The old road that leads to the site is straight and lonely, and I get the feeling that its grass-infested asphalt is rarely disturbed by out-of-towners. The park itself has been carved out of the pasture of a nearby dairy farm.

The sun is just sinking below the horizon as I begin to explore this place. A rock pyramid bearing the U.S. Geological Survey seal with a tattered American flag flying overhead marks this literal and symbolic center of our country. At the back of the park is a boarded-up, six-room motel. It stands above the silent prairie like a memorial to the countless rural citizens whose American dreams have died amid a changing global economy and the consolidation and restructuring of the rural landscape.

A few feet away from the rock pyramid is a tiny chapel, perhaps eight by ten feet in size. Inside are four wooden seats and a small podium. On the back wall hangs a red, white, and blue plaque that merges a map of the United States and a cross into a single icon. It contains the words "Center of the United States Prayer Chapel." Apparently those who live in the center of America are unfamiliar with the American Civil Liberties Union. I'm pretty sure they prefer it that way.

On the podium is a Bible. Its yellow, worn pages are open to Psalm 106. Maybe the wind swirling through the open door made the selection of text, or maybe it was an anonymous passerby—either way, the message is clear. Over and over again, the psalmist describes how the nation of Israel had forgotten its past, the place it had come from, and the trials it had been through. Each time it forgot, there was a corresponding human tragedy.

The analogy is clear. We, too, have forgotten where we came from. We no longer seem to remember the way of life that has made us who and what we are as a nation. To dismiss rural America lightly in the name of progress and a profitable global market is an invitation to a tragedy of monstrous proportions, filled with human suffering and increasing violence.

How Bad Is It?

Norman Rockwell's version of rural America is dead, if it ever really existed. What's left in the 90 percent of the landmass that is designated "rural" is massive poverty and despair. For decades, men, women, and children in our small towns and farms have cried out for help. But their pleas for assistance have gone unanswered, as if they couldn't be heard over the noise of the city. Rural residents are drowning in a tumultuous sea of circumstances beyond their control. The millions of rural Americans still trying to tread water are being pulled under by the callous decisions emanating from corporate boardrooms and the nation's capital. Unable to be heard or to rescue themselves, they've grown angry.

Depending on how you define the term "farm," rural America has lost between 700,000 and 1 million small- to medium-sized family farms since 1980.[1] These losses have resulted from several causes. In the 1970s, the Department of Agriculture, bankers, and university extension offices told farmers that they must either get big or get out. The rate of inflation was running several percentage points above interest rates, so banks and government lenders, such as the Farm Home Administration (FmHA), were encouraging farmers to borrow as much money as possible to buy additional farmland. As a result of all this "new" money entering the system, the price of farmland skyrocketed as farmers tried to outbid each other for available property. Lenders would actually call farmers and ask them if they could please take more money. And why not? Many lenders at the time were being paid bonuses based on how much money they could loan.

But that all changed in 1979. Federal Reserve Chairman Paul Volcker decided that inflation was out of control. Volcker made the decision to shrink the money supply by raising interest rates to unheard-of heights. His decision succeeded in halting runaway inflation, but there was a side effect: the farm crisis. Property values collapsed at the same time the interest rates on the farmer's loans climbed out of sight. The men and women who had listened to the experts and had done exactly as they were told lost everything.

At the peak of this crisis in 1986–1987, nearly 1 million people were forced from their land in a single twelve-month period. Other years before and since have been much the same, with 500,000 forced from the land here, 600,000 there. It's true that the numbers are not as big these days—but only because there aren't as many farmers left to fail. As a percentage of the remaining farm population, the farm failures are as bad today as at any time in the 1980s. In Oklahoma alone, the 1996 drought was expected to cause the loss of 10,000 family farms. That's one-sixth of all the farms in the state.[2]

For the roughly 20 percent of the U.S. population that live in rural America, this continuing loss is a crisis that compares to the Great Depression. For the rest of us who gauge the health of farm country by the amount of food on supermarket shelves, the farm crisis is a barely remembered headline from the last decade—but not for long.

And it's not just farmers and ranchers who are being affected. Rural America as a whole is collapsing under the weight of a rapidly changing world. Industries such as mining, oil, and timber have been hit hard in recent decades. Increasing government regulation and dwindling resources at home have made it more profitable for today's multinational corporations to mow down the forests and rip the minerals from the earth in distant Third World countries. These mega-companies now prefer to operate in places like Burma and Brazil, where workers can be exploited with poverty wages and horrific working conditions, places where less than democratic governments can be controlled for a pittance. Take Nike, for example. It was bad enough when the corporation was operating in Taiwan and South Korea to avoid paying the U.S. minimum wage of $4.25 an hour to workers. But then democratization in those countries gave workers the right to organize, and wages there jumped from a slavish $4.00 a day to a quasi-slavish $12.00 a day.[3] Consequently, in 1988 Nike moved its Asian production facility to Indonesia, where the minimum wage was 86 cents a day. Corporations now go wherever the labor is cheapest, and that's no longer rural America.

The rural South has watched helplessly as its textile jobs have been shipped to Asia, Haiti, and Guatemala. These lost jobs and farms have in turn destroyed the small businesses that once prospered in rural towns. One by one they have withered away, taking with them the last hope of their communities. More often than not, large areas—areas that once encompassed several small towns with a hundred different businesses—are being served by a single Wal-Mart or other large discount store. This trend of consolidation has thrust rural America into an economic hell filled with depression and anxiety.

In 1990, the Intergovernmental Health Policy Project of George Washington University reached the following conclusion:

> The restructuring of rural America has exacted a tremendous human toll. Studies have shown that adults and adolescents in rural communities have significantly higher rates of mental disorder than those in urban areas. Other studies have shown moderate to large increases in the

numbers of dysfunctional adults; exceptionally large increases in the incidence of child abuse, spouse abuse, and substance abuse; and as well an increase in cognitive impairment, depression, and anxiety disorders.[4]

Our leaders in Washington and at the state level are well aware of these problems. In 1986, Senate Agricultural Chairman Patrick Leahy (D-VT) warned: "Rural America is hurting. The changing global marketplace closed the door on economic growth across rural America. Small manufacturing plants succumbed to foreign competition. Farms and farmers disappeared. Oil wells stopped pumping and mines closed."[5] Why does Washington remain silent in the face of this rural catastrophe? The answer is cold but practical. Our nation's politicos realize that the collapse of rural America is an inevitable result of a global economy, and as such, it would be a waste of time and money to bail it out.

In 1979, only 5 percent of the 2,040 nonmetropolitan counties in the United States had an unemployment rate of over 9 percent. By 1984, over 50 percent of rural counties fell into that category. And these figures don't include the millions of people who lost their farms. Even if you're one of the lucky people who has a job in rural America, the news is still not good. Thirty-five percent of the workers in these places are underemployed and have to take on a part-time job. In other words, nearly one-half the workforce in rural America has either no job or an inadequate one.[6]

The competition for these low-paying jobs has increased because of dwindling profits in agriculture. The United States Department of Agriculture reports that nearly two-thirds of farm families have been forced to seek off-farm incomes. Nearly 60 percent of the net income now realized by farm families comes from off-farm jobs.[7] A report by the National Mental Health Association notes that most often, these jobs are in maintenance or in the restaurant trade. Even low-paying jobs like cleaning motel rooms are disappearing as investment in rural America dwindles.

Between 20 and 25 percent of the U.S. population live in rural areas, but 38 percent of all people now living in poverty live there. Sixty-seven percent of the nation's substandard housing is rural, and 27 percent of the children in rural America are growing up hungry, forced to live in poverty even though the parents of most of them work.[8]

Part of the problem is that the rural economy has always been heavily dependent upon commodities, and that dependence has left it more vulnerable now than ever. The difference today is that those commodities are controlled by a few vertically integrated multinational corporations that have made American agricultural and natural resource businesses subject to global pressures. Our farmers, miners, lumbermen, and other rural workers now compete on an even playing field with their counterparts in the Third World.

The same six grain monopolies that buy almost all of the U.S. wheat also purchase the majority of wheat in the global marketplace. American farmers are therefore forced to compete with growers in places like Argentina, where only a few landowners control the country's grain belt and pay low wages to their workers. In order to compete in the global market—the final destination of over 40 percent of U.S. wheat—American growers must accept artificially low prices for their product.[9]

The face of America is changing once again. As happened during the Great Depression of the 1930s and the Industrial Revolution of the nineteenth century, today's restructuring—a combination of postindustrial society and the new realities of the global economy—is of historic proportions. It's the final push that will bring our rural population once and for all into the cities, leaving behind fewer and fewer large corporate farms and only a few factories.

In his book *New Rules: How to Succeed in Today's Post-Corporate World*, John B. Kotter explains that we have entered a new economic era. Kotter believes that this new era of globalization can be traced to a specific date and business transaction. On October 16, 1973, the oil producers in the Persian Gulf joined together to raise prices, which culminated in the first Arab oil embargo. It was the first shot in the global war for market share and increased profits. Technological advances in global communications have made it possible for a Chicago-based company to run a manufacturing plant in China—where cheap labor is abundant—as easily as it could in Shreveport, Louisiana. Kotter is right: A new era has begun, but when and how will it end?

Modern communications, multinational corporations, and a quickly approaching global monetary system have made this final chapter in the history of rural America inevitable. But it's not going to be a smooth transition. Those who oversee such monumental cultural transformations have made a grave miscalculation. Our leaders have based their plans for a united world economy on the false presumption that all of us are the same and that everyone shares in their quest for progress. Perhaps those who greet these plans with skepticism remember that history has shown us that for those in positions of power, the words "progress" and "profit" are often synonymous and that for the few to prosper, the many must pay the price.

The federal government has failed to realize and take into consideration the fact that urban and rural peoples are truly different and that they will perceive and react to this global restructuring in unique ways. When factory workers in the city lose their jobs, they tend to go across town to get another—albeit these days, probably for less money and fewer, if any, benefits. When farmers lose their land, they don't retrain and get a new job. They have lost much more than their livelihood. Farmers' ties to the land are their ties to their family, their history, and their God. Rural farmers would often rather die than lose their land. Many will kill before they give it up.

This difference between urban and rural peoples is not imaginary. It has been well documented in dozens of studies.[10] The rise in antigovernment activity as a result of the economic restructuring of rural America was inevitable, considering the distinct cultural and psychological makeup of the people who live there. It should have been predicted and dealt with accordingly.

Research all across rural America has reached the same conclusion: The stress associated with the rural crisis has been transformed into violence and abuse. In Minnesota, a study of 3,600 rural adolescents conducted in 1988 found that "a change in parents' finances" was commonly associated with the onset of stress, depression, and attempted suicide. In Colorado, twenty-four rural mental health centers reported significant increases in child and spousal abuse between 1979 and 1986. An Iowa study showed that rural child abuse increased by a staggering 43.6 percent from 1982 to 1986 due to the stress of the farm crisis. In 1985, Iowa had 1,620 cases of rural spousal abuse, but by 1987, that figure had risen to 4,500. A midwestern mental health–care clinic found that its alcoholism diagnosis among farmers doubled between 1981 and 1983.[11] And the bad news just goes on and on.

It would be easy to spout statistics to demonstrate the sad shape of our rural places. Many volumes have been written on the subject, only to find their way to the dusty back shelves of university libraries. In any case, hearing about the rural plight from the people who live there offers a better appraisal of the situation. It provides insight into more than just the economics of disaster. It offers glimpses into the cultural and spiritual differences of the rural world and demonstrates how and why the federal government is so often the focus of rural America's discontent.

During 1989–1990, several years after the farm crisis had dropped off the radar of media coverage and several years before the antigovernment movement appeared in the news, the state of Oklahoma discovered that there was a high rate of suicide among its rural population. In an effort to determine why, the state requested input from the very people who were suffering. As part of that effort, Governor Henry Bellmon created a task force charged with holding regional meetings to discuss the problem.

The following letters and task force testimony tell the story of what was happening in Oklahoma and all across the rural United States during that time. In many ways, these testimonies are like the "missing link" in the theory of evolution. They provide evidence of the connection between economic stress and depression and the resulting disdain directed toward government and bankers. A few years ago, references to justice, suicide, bad banking practices, and a dispassionate federal government permeated these task force letters. If written today, many letters would no doubt be filled with references to common-law courts, violence directed at the federal government, and conspiracy theories about Jewish bankers and the new world order.

No corrections to grammar or spelling were made to these letters, though some were edited for length. The names of those testifying were withheld at some task force meetings (for example, at the Tonkawa, Oklahoma, meeting) because of fear of reprisal by the participants' lending institutions. In those instances, the speaker has been assigned a number.

Voices of Despair

I am writing this letter to let you know why so many farmers are shooting themselves. One year ago I had a gun to my head and was going to end it all. I called the hotline to see if I could find help. A very nice lady who had lost her husband the same way was very understanding and helped me see there was light at the end of the long tunnel of misfortune. I owe my life to Mrs. Mona Lee Brock and the hotline people.

Two years ago I was forced to turn my land back to the Federal Land Bank. I had made payments on it for 15 years. It was my whole life that I had worked hard and saved to buy and pay on.

Then one year ago FHA [Farm Home Administration] sends out notice they are going to take my machinery that I am farming rented land with, and my cow herd. FHA accused me of fraud and bad faith. And would not refinance my loan. I appealed their allegations to the appeal office. The decision on fraud and bad faith was reversed, for I had done nothing wrong. Just trying to make a living for my family by working hard and farming.

All this time my family and I don't know from one day to the next what's going to happen or when this mental harassment is going to end. It's very hard on us not knowing and dragging it on and on. We can not make any plans cause we don't know where we will be tomorrow.

Why can't somebody see what is going on and do something about it. They are just trying to do away with as many farmers as they can. Now can you see why farmers are blowing their heads off! Please, somebody do something to help us.

—Cletus Blabough, Ponca City, Oklahoma

I wish I could tell you that we haven't had a suicide in our part of Okla., but I can't tell you that because we've had several. Some are definite confirmed cases, some listed as accidents. One of our neighbors, Mr. White, shot himself in the head, a couple of years ago, after becoming despondent over the stress of things going bad after years of doing well. His family still can't talk about the trauma of the experience.

We had a neighbor lady that shot and killed herself, then a young man has a strange hunting accident. The wound was in a place that made an accident questionable. We've had several one car accidents, with no apparent reasons for the accident, no alcohol, drugs, etc., and the person alone. Are they really accidents?

Then there are those that have the heart attacks, strokes, ulcers and so on. Suicide, no, but the body turns on itself from stress and worry causing death. And death is death, no matter how it's caused. And people in rural Okla. are dying, maybe not all by personal violence, some die a little each day.

I guess we caused too much trouble, for in June of 1983 (I think, I try not to remember) we received our foreclosure paper, so did several other farmers in the area. We stayed and fought and fought and fought. Some others lost their farms, their wives, their husbands and their lives. One farm wife had a heart attack the day they received their notice. Another neighbor's husband abandoned her at the grocery store. Just left her there with no good-bye, no nothing, just gone, leaving her to deal with all the FmHA mess alone.

We feel like a leaf left twisting in the wind for months, no years, wondering what's going to happen, what to do, how to fix things. Can it be fixed? Does anyone care, especially anyone in a position of authority, the leaders, those that are supposed to be in control.

So many of my neighbors are working so hard, some living in overcrowded conditions; 8, 10, 12 people in a small house just trying to make it to the next paycheck. Some just can't take the pressure and take their own lives. People are hurting, hungry and cold.

There are a lot of words written and spoken. The TV reporters go on and on about things happening in China, Germany, Poland and all over the world, while America, our homeland, slowly, painfully is falling apart. Please do something.

—**Maureen Wade, Jay, Oklahoma**

I am a farmer who has been through the lack of legal foreclosure by the FmHA. I personally know over one hundred that have watched their past being destroyed by rumors, false statements, lack of correct business action and threats of personal harm and law-breaking by the loan agencies themselves or their employees.

We have gone to U.S. Senators, U.S. House of Rep., Inspector General's Office, U.S. Dept. of Agri., A. G. Office state of Okla. and local and District judges to find out why they will not or can not investigate or have covered up and squashed vital facts about our cases.

—**Alan Early, Alex, Oklahoma**

I am a 46 year old mother of three children. We have lost two farms since 1980, my mother-in-laws farm as well as our own. We were forced to sell 160 acres of land that was very special to us. It was homesteaded by my husbands great grandfather and for years had served as home to our cow and calf operation which we were forced to sell just a few months before we sold the land.

My husband became completely consumed by our circumstances caused by the farm crises. He left me. Our family continued to deteriorate and our marriage ended in divorce. We had been through natural crises before, drought, flood, crop failure, these we accepted and went on.

But when the threat of losing everything comes to your doorstep because of the bad economy, low commodity prices and high interest on your base notes has left you hopelessly in debt, your faith is sometimes shaken. No one likes to consider that their life has been pointless.

When you are confronted with these kinds of thoughts, along with circumstances out of your control that destroy the things you cherish, I believe one might consider taking their own life.

In many cases the intimidation techniques are ruthless. Lending institutions call meetings on Thanksgiving or Christmas Eve, robbing them of what little joy might have been allowed them during the holiday season.

So why wouldn't a farmer want to finish it. He has been judged and sees nothing left of his life's work. He's empty financially, physically and spiritually. All that is left is anger, denial, doubt, fear, hostility and paranoia.

—Speaker #2,
town meeting on rural stress,
Tonkawa, Oklahoma, 1991

About one and a half years ago my family lost its farm. I had many losses before we lost our farm. Like my horse died, that hurt me a whole lot. I didn't stop crying for two days. Then my dog got ran over and I thought he was going to die, but he lived. Then we had to give away our cat and kittens.

It was a lot of pressure when we lost our farm. It was sad to lose . . . after the farm was repossessed. It was very, very hard to change schools, since I went to school there my whole life. When I went to the new school I cried almost every day.

—Nine-year-old girl,
town meeting on rural stress,
Tonkawa, Oklahoma, 1991

A couple came to see me at a loss as to why their four and a half-year-old son changed from a happy disposition toddler to a child who often went off alone rather than play with his cousins. He even refused to go with his granddaddy fishing, which had been a frequent happy activity since being a toddler.

He was described as having crying spells and temper tantrums over nothing. The parents recognized that the changes had been coming over the last year, but worsening in the last few months. The parents were seen as healthy, caring, with good parenting skills.

Not until the third session did they begin to speak of the crisis they had experienced over the last two or three years in trying to keep their farm business going. And now they were making the decision on whether to give it up.

I shall never forget that determined, confident young man dropping his head and weeping as he spoke of the agony of the decision as he woke each morning and put in another 15 hour day, knowing not whether it was going to make a bit of difference in the outcome.

To say it briefly, as far as their son, they were successful. It was their own depression that was to blame.

—Edna Brown, rural counselor,
town meeting on rural stress,
Tonkawa, Oklahoma, 1991

I have read that in the House of Representatives, standing from the speaker's desk and looking over the main entrance, one's eyes meet the piercing eyes of Moses, the original law giver. Psalms 106:3 reads; Blessed are those who keep justice and they who do righteousness at all times.

A decade of extreme hardships have come our way. I have written letters to Washington D.C. on brown paper food bags, as I had no other paper to write on. My sisters would send me postage stamps. I have written letters to the U.S. Dept. of Agriculture, Senators, Congressmen and the President of the United States.

Neverless, the greedy Farmer's Home Administration foreclosed on our only source of livelihood. Our farm and ranch was not only of sentimental value, it was our way of life. We put pride in our work. We had love and respect for our neighbors.

Taxes kept soaring higher each year on our land and home. Why can't anybody rescue the taxpayers.

I was raised from early childhood to work and earn an honest living, to hold fast to a good family name as it was our most valuable heritage. Why have 160 farmers or farm wives committed suicide recently? I surely understand! Who will answer?

—Dorothy Cunningham,
Paul's Valley, Oklahoma

The whole damn problem is the price. I'm getting tired of taking what they want to pay me for my product. It's time we started telling them what we need to make a profit.

It makes me mad to see my neighbors, my friends, my relatives and myself go through this crap. We don't know what the solution is other than raise the price of wheat down here. And how are we going to do that when we have people up there going to the best restaurant every night and driving fancy cars, spending $50 to $60 for a meal. How can we deal with things like that?

It's just pretty difficult for us to sit out here and maybe get to go to the Sonic for a hamburger once in a while or go to the Blue Moon and splurge for 7 or 8 bucks. It makes you plum sick. When you hear about people like that woman whose family lost their feed business, it shows me that there is a lot more stress than just on the farm. I've even talked to bankers who are scared to death.

—Speaker #5,
town meeting on rural stress,
Tonkawa, Oklahoma, 1991

This is a typical sampling of the thousands of letters and hundreds of hours of public testimony that poured into the task force. As noted earlier, the contents reveal all the ingredients of today's antigovernment movement, though more subdued and internalized.

The task force concluded that the problems in rural Oklahoma indeed constituted an emergency. Governor Bellmon requested that the federal government investigate the actions of the farm lenders and provide additional money for rural mental health. But once again, a voice from the hinterland—this time, Bellmon's—fell on deaf ears inside the beltway. No investigation was initiated, and the money for rural mental health quickly evaporated all across the nation, leaving those in need to seek help wherever they could find it, if they could afford it.

But the months of work put in by the task force were not in vain. The record that survived has provided a way of tracking rural America's descent into the antigovernment abyss. In recent times, I've been able to link the names of people appearing in news stories about antigovernment activity to some of the names appearing on task force letters from years earlier. Reading about a farm family's desperate situation and seeing that their cry for help preceded their enlistment in this heartland war makes it easier to understand how people can arrive at the idea that overthrowing the government makes some sort of sense.

In their world, the long-held rural myths that spoke of a tranquil and stable lifestyle have been replaced by paranoid conspiracy theories. As a result, the rural sector of the nation is being transformed, not only into a part of the global economy but also into a wildfire of rage, fueled by its perceived losses and blown by the winds of hate-filled rhetoric. Men and women who were once the backbone of America have been pushed into the ranks of this "anti" phenomenon, some finding their way into the most violent layers of the movement.

Although detractors of the "anti" factions correctly blame these groups for everything from the Oklahoma City bombing to influencing Pat Buchanan's 1996 populist campaign rhetoric, few have attempted to explain why this apocalyptic antigovernment ideology is so palatable in rural places. Lousy economics is one explanation. The psychological makeup of those who live in the boarded-up towns and farms along the washboard roads of our backcountry is another.

To understand the antigovernment movement, we must understand what "rural" means. We must realize that many people outside our cities are, in fact, part of a distinct subculture, as are blacks, Hispanics, Asians, and Native Americans. And as such, rural people will continue to respond uniquely, often violently, to the overwhelming pressures of their rapidly changing world.

2

Two Kinds of Anger

It's just like the deal where the captain goes down with the ship. It's not like they wanted to. I just think the ship's captain after 30 or 40 years at sea, they kind of take their ship as seriously as we take our farm. Telling a guy after his ship goes down that, well, you can get you a job somewhere else. Don't worry about it. I don't think they'd go with that. The captain of the USS Oklahoma shot himself after Pearl Harbor. Even though his ship was tied up right where it was supposed to be. He went ahead and shot himself because he lost his ship. He didn't have nowhere else to go.

—Speaker #8, town meeting on rural stress,
Tonkawa, Oklahoma, 1991

As he topped a hill on the sandy road southeast of Gracemont, Oklahoma, school-bus driver Jimmy Reeves could see smoke rising above the blackjack trees. "It must be near the Stalder place," he thought to himself. But he'd find out soon enough. Bill Stalder's farm was the last stop on his new route. It was August 19, 1986, the first day of school.

On the previous Friday, Reeves had made a mandatory practice run. The idea was to meet the kids who would be riding his bus and familiarize himself with the often unmarked back roads that composed his route. It was a rehearsal that was hardly necessary in a place like Gracemont, population 503; everyone knew everyone. On Friday's rehearsal, Reeves had been greeted at the gate of the Stalder farm by ten-year-old Jeremy, his sixteen-year-old sister, Jamie, and the ever-present family dog; but today would be different.

As Reeves neared the Stalder house, the bus went silent. The children's chatter about the new school year turned to gasps and moans.

Where the house had stood, only smoldering rubble remained. Reeves wheeled into the drive to look for signs of life. There were none. The cars were still in the drive, but there was no activity—not even from the dog.

With a busload of kids, Reeves felt his best course of action was to head for the school, drop off his young passengers, and notify someone about what had happened. After all, the Stalders were probably all right. Maybe a neighbor had taken the family to town.

But that was not the case. When two men from the school returned to the smoky scene, they discovered a gruesome scene that would emotionally scar the small town of Gracemont for years to come. Inside the gutted house, they found the remains of Bill Stalder, his wife, Susan, the two children, and the dog. The bodies were badly burned. Investigators could only identify the young girl because of the melted braces on her teeth. But it was the presence of the dog in the house that gave the first clue that this macabre event was no accident. Like most farm dogs, it was never allowed inside the house. Why was the animal there in the ashes with the rest of the family?

As the investigation progressed, the chain of events that had transpired on that warm August morning became clear, though its meaning remained a mystery. Bill Stalder had killed his wife, his son, and his daughter; he had shot the family pet and carried it into the house; and only then had he set the place on fire and, finally, entered the burning building and turned his shotgun on himself.

Local residents were stunned. This was the kind of thing that happened in faraway big cities, not places like Gracemont. What on earth could have driven Bill Stalder, a church-going school board member and good family man, to such madness? The forty-year-old Stalder was the son of a prominent banker. Yet despite his connections, he was in financial trouble. He was facing foreclosure on the land his family had accumulated over many years. And just as it would for thousands of others devastated by the farm crisis, the fear of the auctioneer's gavel became a death blow.

Nonetheless, there were strange nuances in the Stalder case that made it stand out from the tidal wave of economically induced suicide that started in the early 1980s and still thunders over the plains today. First, Stalder died with money in the bank. And second, why had he turned on his family? Most farmers commit suicide because they believe they have failed their loved ones, or they do so in an attempt to collect life insurance and save the farm for the surviving family. What was Stalder's reason for destroying those he loved?

"Responsible"

I first read about the Stalder case in 1986, but it was ten years later that I arrived in Gracemont to look for answers to those nagging questions. I was afraid too much time had passed, but I was wrong. Small towns aren't like cities. The slower pace of rural living lends itself to remembering events, good or bad. In Caddo County, Oklahoma, it was as if the Stalder tragedy had happened yesterday.

At the court clerk's office in Anadarko, the county seat, the woman behind the desk told me I wouldn't find any records because there had been no criminal investigation. But she asked me what I wanted to know. She had been a neighbor of the Stalders and had driven past their place for years going to and from work. By the time I left her office, I had the names and telephone numbers of all the Stalder relatives still living in the area, as well as the names of the investigators who had pieced the terrible puzzle together a decade before. Most important, I heard about life in the Stalder home: "They were great kids." "Bill and Susan were wonderful parents." "Their kids played basketball and the parents attended every game." "Things were great until the money problems started, then they died."

Bill Covey had been the pastor of an Assembly of God church in Gracemont for thirteen years prior to the tragedy and knew the Stalders well. He said, "I think that Bill just couldn't face losing his entire way of life . . . He was able to sell off the place and pay everything off before they foreclosed. So I don't think it was just the money. I think he'd lost the thing he loved most." Stalder's brother-in-law, a farmer named Max Tally, told me the same thing: "It wasn't the money problems. He'd sold that north farm for a pretty good price. Bill had over a hundred thousand dollars when he died."

Stalder's economic status at the time of his death is important. It shows that for farm families, the loss of their land goes well beyond the financial realm. Even though Bill Stalder still had money, he had lost his identity. He had lost his family history, which existed through his connection to the land. I've met countless farmers like Bill Stalder, who in all sincerity have told me they would rather live in poverty on their own farm than make a comfortable living at a city job.

It's understandable that the surviving family still chooses to believe that someone other than Bill murdered Susan and the kids. But the law enforcement officers who worked the case say it was open and shut. Bill Stalder had snapped and killed them all—that they knew. But they had only one clue as to why he had done it, and it didn't seem to make much sense.

While going through the barn that had survived the hellish flames, an investigator found Bill Stalder's diary. The last entry read like a page out of Stephen King's novel *The Shining,* in which the main character had repeatedly typed the words "All work and no play makes Jack a dull boy." As the final entry to his journal, Bill Stalder had written the word "responsible" over and over again, until the entire page was filled.

It may not have made sense to the cops that found it, but the diary's final repetitive message was perfectly clear to the rural counselors who so often work the aftermath of failing farms. For every lost chunk of American farmland, someone must be blamed. A farmer can blame himself the way Bill Stalder did, in which case the anger is turned inward and the result is often suicide. Or the blame can be put at the feet of a lender or the government, in which case the anger and subsequent violence are turned outward, often resulting in antigovernment behavior.

As I stood looking at the brown, dry grass that now covers the old foundation of the Stalder home, my mind raced as I tried to imagine the rage of that morning a decade earlier—the desperation and confusion the family must have felt as they were herded into a room filled with screaming and gunshots, the vision of Bill Stalder carrying his bleeding dog into the house and laying the pet near his dead children and wife. Had he written that final diary entry before he exploded? Or had he slipped into the barn after the others were dead and scribbled out "responsible, responsible, responsible," his mind locked in a painful knot?

After ten years there was no hint of the hellish heat and flames that had swallowed the family. The old metal barn stood creaking in the cold December wind, a silent witness to the terror of that day. It offered no clue as to why an apparently loving father and husband had turned on his family instead of just killing himself. I left the skeleton of the Stalder place and drove the four and one-half miles into Gracemont.

The town sits atop a hill overlooking the fertile wheat fields to the west. It looks a bit old and tired but, on the whole, seems neatly kept. Gracemont is close enough to the county seat for commuting and, consequently, is in much better shape than other farm towns its size—their downtowns boarded-up empty shells whose only purpose now is to spur conversations that begin with the words "Remember when."

I stopped at the aptly named Hilltop Cafe for lunch. The Hilltop could have been a cafe in Anywhere, U.S.A. It had the requisite friendly waitress with more to say to locals than to a stranger, two farmers who looked to be in their late fifties sitting at the center table and talking about commodity prices, and a couple of greasy-looking kids plugging quarters into a pinball machine crammed in the corner by the john. Through the order window that connected the kitchen to the dining room, a thirty-something woman paced back and forth, staring at me through the small opening as if, given enough time, my name would rattle loose from her memory. Big burgers, weak coffee, and a good dose of apprehension about strangers—Gracemont is a typical place in rural America.

After finishing my burger and onion rings, I carried my coffee over to the farmers' table and joined them. I figured I'd take a shot in the dark. I asked if they remembered the Stalder tragedy and why it had happened. They did, and they seemed eager to talk about something other than the price of wheat: "He was a good man." "It was a terrible thing." "He was having money trouble like all of us, but I didn't know it was going that bad for him." "The tragedy is those kids. They were sure good kids."

It sounded like the other stories I'd been hearing. That is, until the man on my left paused and said, "I heard he got messed up in the Bible. I mean the way he understood it. He thought we had started that end time. What do you call it?" The other farmer interjected, "Tribulation." "Yeah, that's it, tribulation. That's why he killed his whole family. He didn't want them to have to live through the tribulation." The farmer on my right had heard the same story.

I wasn't completely surprised by this strange disclosure. In my experience, people in the antigovernment movement commonly believe that the period of tribulation is about to begin or has already begun. Tribulation is the final few years that lead up to the Battle of Armageddon. The Bible describes it as a time so terrible—filled with pestilence, natural disasters, and persecution of Christians—that it would be better not to have been born. Believing that this horrible time has begun is one of those unique ideologies fostered by the decaying rural way of life and its centuries-old belief system. It's also one of the reasons that the potential for violence in the movement is so great. If the world is ending, there's not a lot to lose.

Rural psychologists who have been battling the mental devastation resulting from the farm crises since 1980 are also familiar with this idea. The belief that foreclosure and tribulation go hand in hand is something they've been hearing all along. If Bill Stalder truly believed that the horrible events described in the Book of Revelation were at hand, he no doubt felt he was committing an act of mercy for Susan and the kids. It seemed I had found my answer.

Although tribulation, suicides, the farm crisis, antigovernment groups, rural economics, and small-town culture may seem unrelated to most of us, in reality, they are separate parts of a larger whole. Understanding their interconnections can give us insight into why the Bill Stalders of the rural world react the way they do.

Suicides

It's two in the morning when the telephone rings and wakes Dr. Glen Wallace, a psychologist in Oklahoma City. The farmer on the other end of the line has been drinking and is holding a loaded gun to his head. The distressed man tells Wallace that his farm is to be sold at auction within a few days. He goes on to explain that he can't bear the shame he's brought to his family and that the only way out is to kill himself. Within hours, Wallace is at the farm. This time the farmer agrees to go into counseling; this time no one dies.

Unfortunately, as the Stalder case so dramatically illustrates, that's not always the case. Of the hundreds of on-site suicide interventions Wallace has handled through Ag-Link, a farm crisis hot line based in Oklahoma, not too many have been successful.

According to Mona Lee Brock, another former Ag-Link counselor, therapists in Oklahoma alone have been making over 175 on-site suicide interventions each year since the mid-1980s. And Oklahoma has only the third-highest number of farm suicides in the nation, trailing both Montana and Wisconsin.[1]

In 1989, at Oklahoma State University, researcher Pat Lewis was examining death certificates from across the state in his effort to determine the leading causes of death on family farms. What he found was shocking. Until Lewis's investigation, equipment accidents had always been listed as the biggest culprit, but the records were about to break with tradition. Lewis found that suicide had taken over as the leading cause of death, and not by a small margin. The study showed that farmers took their own lives five times more often than they were killed by equipment accidents, now the second leading cause. The suicide rate among farmers was a staggering three times the rate of the general population.[2]

"These figures are probably very conservative," Lewis says. "We've been provided with information from counselors and mental health workers that suggests that many of the accidental deaths are, in reality, suicides." Wallace, who was one of those mental health workers, agrees.

> The known suicides are just a drop in the bucket. We have farmers crawling into their equipment and being killed so their families can collect insurance money and pay off the farm debt. They're dying in order to stop a foreclosure. We've had farmers stage car wrecks and hunting accidents. This one older couple decided they were going to hit the abutment on the side of a bridge. They went out to the spot and made several practice runs to make sure they could get enough speed up to do the job. Fortunately, they called the hot line and we were able to get them some help.

Many of the suicides in rural America are a reflection of its unique culture and belief system. Psychologists believe that rural suicides often fall into the category they refer to as altruistic suicide, a suicide in which a society's customs or rules sanction or even require the death. In these cases, self-inflicted death is considered honorable. An example would be the Japanese practice of hara-kiri, ritual disembowelment in response to being disgraced for any reason. In the same way, a farmer who kills himself to allow his family to collect insurance money and save the farm is often thought to be honorable in the subculture of rural America.

The Oklahoma State study is not alone in its findings. Dr. Paul Gunderson, former director of the Minnesota Center for Health Statistics, conducted a study in five midwestern and northern Great Plains states and found similar suicide increases as in Oklahoma. Other research studies in Iowa and South Carolina came to the same conclusion: People in farm families were dying at an incredible rate by their own hands.

These studies help to further illustrate that people in rural America are different from their city counterparts. Urban research conducted during the last one hundred years has also concluded that suicides increase during times of economic duress, though nowhere near the increased rates uncovered by the rural studies.

A good example of this difference can be observed by comparing the collapse of the energy industry with the farm crisis; both occurred in the early and mid-1980s in the same geographic locations. In places like the Dakotas, Kansas, Oklahoma, Texas, and Louisiana, oil workers often worked the same fields as farmers. During the oil bust, rigs were stopped in mid-drilling. Graveyards filled with the skeletons of multimillion-dollar rigs sprang up all over the country. Many of these steel giants sat idle so long they rusted to uselessness. This was a time when people in the energy industry were laid off with little hope of finding work. Their homes were foreclosed on, cars and trucks repossessed. The oil bust had all the qualities of the farm crisis, except one: There was no corresponding increase in suicides among the energy workers. Whereas the oil workers reacted by trying to find new jobs, the farmers began killing themselves.

Rural people react differently. And unless that fact is taken into consideration in the policymaking process, they will continue to be a thorn in Washington's side as it plots the restructuring of the rural economy.

The Rural Mentality

Most Americans don't understand farmers. We ask, "Why don't farmers just get new jobs? Why does losing a farm cause someone to kill himself or someone else?" Part of the answer concerns the farmer's connection to the land and the role that plays in his long-held spiritual and cultural beliefs. And part of it lies in the unique personality makeup of these people.

Rural psychologist Dr. Val Farmer has often written on this subject. In an article that ran in the *Iowa Farmer Today* in 1989, Dr. Farmer explained why farm loss affects its victims so powerfully.

> To lose a farm is to lose part of one's own identity. There is probably no other occupation that has the potential for defining one's "self" so completely. Those who have gone through the loss of a family farm

compare their grief to a death in the family, one of the hardest experiences in life.

Like some deaths, the loss may have been preventable. If a farmer blames himself, the reaction is guilt. Guilt can stem from a violation of family trust. By failing to keep the farm in the family, he loses that for which others had sacrificed greatly. The loss of the farm also affects the loss of the opportunity to pass on the farm to a child. Guilt can also arise from failing to anticipate the conditions that eventually placed the farm at risk: government policy, trade policies, world economy, prices, weather.

On the other hand, if the loss is perceived to have been caused by the actions and negligence of others, then the farmer is racked with feelings of anger, bitterness and betrayal. This feeling extends to lenders, government, the urban public or the specific actions of a particular individual or institution. In the end they're just grabbing for straws.[3]

To make matters worse, folks in agriculture are subjected to a mental double whammy of sorts. During the farm failure and the subsequent foreclosure process, they are simultaneously experiencing anticipatory grief (grieving the loss before it actually occurs). In other words, their stress over the inevitable outcome is compounded by the additional stress of trying to stop the threatened loss from taking place. They work fifteen-, then twenty-hour days trying to stave off foreclosure. In the end, they become not only mentally beaten down but also physically sick.

Farmers, more than the rest of us, have a specific need to blame someone for the pain and suffering they experience as their world collapses around them. This observation is borne out by at least four studies on rural personality types that shed light on why they feel the way they do.

James T. Horner and Leverne A. Barrett of the University of Nebraska conducted two of these studies.[4] In their most recent research in 1989, they used the widely accepted Myers-Briggs Type Indicator to measure the personality makeup of 500 farm couples. They found the perfect ingredients for a rural Molotov cocktail.

The study showed that farm men and women are indeed different from the mythical "average" and that there are many significant personality type differences. The Myers-Briggs Type Indicator is made up of sixteen distinct personality types. The average farm man was an introverted, sensing, thinking, judging type, whereas the typical farm woman was introverted, sensing, feeling, and judging. What all this means is that of the known sixteen personality types, farm people scored as the most conservative and hardworking. The study concluded:

> These types are strongly devoted to the family and its traditions and accept the obligation and responsibility to maintain the family farm at all costs.
>   Because of their strong devotion to the farm family and its traditions, any threat to the family heritage, such as foreclosure, can cause an unusual amount of anxiety. When threats to the family heritage and hard work that ends in failure are combined, the farm couple may begin to believe there is little hope. As the sensing type farm couple begin to lose what they view as reality, they begin to imagine, with the aid of their inferior intuition, the worst possible scenario. This strain is much more severe for these two types because of their very make-up.[5]

The subtle differences found between the women and men in this study also provided bad news. In times of high stress such as during foreclosure, farm couples are more likely to become volatile toward each other, further threatening their family stability.

The situation is like a whirlpool spinning out of control. Economics that threaten a farmer's way of life pull him down through the loss of his farm and the collapse of his family, which in turn sucks all hope out of him, leaving him shattered and only able to explain it all by imagining the worst possible causal scenario. And what could be a worse scenario than the message of the antigovernment movement, which teaches that all of this pain and destruction was avoidable and, worse, that it was intentionally planned and orchestrated by an evil force that has taken over the government.

Stress-Related Illness

Although suicides take the lives of stressed-out farmers at an alarming rate, they don't account for as many deaths in the rural population as stress-related illnesses such as heart attacks and cancer. There's been an avalanche of research in recent years that confirms the direct connection between stress and such physical problems. For example, a study of deaths caused by stress-related illness in the general population during the recession of 1974–1975 determined that the nation's normal mortality rate increased by 2.3 percent as a direct result of that economic downturn.[6]

Taking into consideration the psychological makeup of farmers, mental health–care professionals believe it can be assumed that, as with suicide, their rate of stress-related illness is well above the national average. And just as is the case with financial failures, rural personality types often feel the need to blame someone for these stress-related illnesses and deaths. Not surprisingly, considering the dark cloud of depression and the influence of the antigovernment philosophy that hang over much of rural America, these natural deaths are often treated as murder by surviving loved ones who blame outside forces for creating the situation. Many of the antigovernment movement's common-law courts have convicted bankers and judges, who are often seen as the instigators of financial stress that leads to heart attacks and other illnesses, of murder and have sentenced them accordingly—to death by hanging.

Natural Murder

While meeting with antigovernment adherents in a farmhouse in western Oklahoma in early 1996, I had the opportunity to observe a scenario in which the government is blamed for a death due to heart attack. I watched as the loss of a loved one to a stress-related illness became a launching pad for the movement's message. The scene is played out like this:

"They murdered her," Sam Conners says. The room goes silent as the gray-haired sixty-year-old stares out the window of his soon-to-be foreclosed-on farmhouse. In his left hand, he holds a photograph of his wife, who died of a heart attack in 1990. "She fought 'em as long as she could," he continues, "but she finally gave out. Even when she was lying there in a coma and I was visiting her every day—bringing my nine-year-old boy to see his mamma every day—they [government lending institutions] wouldn't cut me no slack. All they cared about was getting me off my land so they could take it. But I tell you now, I'm never gonna give up. They'll have to carry me off feet first and they probably will."

There are several other men in the room. They sit quietly as they listen to Conners's story, their eyes alternating between their dirty work boots and the angry farmer. The conversation comes to a sudden halt with a "click" from a nearby tape recorder. Conners looks clumsy as he tries to change the small tape in the microcassette recorder. His thick earth-stained fingers seem poorly designed for the delicate task. "I apologize for recording you," he tells me. "We just have to be careful."

With their low-tech safeguard back in place, one of the other men begins to speak. Tim, a California farmer who looked to be in his early thirties, describes his plight: another farm, another foreclosure, more antigovernment sentiment. Only this time, the story is filled with the unmistakable religious overtones of racist Christian Identity teachings: one world government, Satan's Jewish bankers, the Federal Reserve, a fabricated Holocaust, a coming holy war.

"This kind of injustice [death and foreclosure] is going on all over the country," Tim says.

> It's what happened to the folks in Montana [referring to the antigovernment group called the Freemen, who were involved in an eighty-three-day standoff with the FBI in 1996], and it's what happened to me. That's why LeRoy [LeRoy Schweitzer, the leader of the Freemen] was arrested. He was teaching people how to keep their farms and ranches. He was showing them that the government isn't constitutional. They foreclose on us so they can control the food supply. What they want to do is control the Christians. They'd like to kill us all.

The FmHA agent who dealt with Conners and his wife prior to her death has been found guilty of murder by a common-law jury, currently operating in western Oklahoma. The death sentence, up to now, has not been carried out.

Chronic Long-Term Stress

Like the fuse on a time bomb burning shorter and shorter, the stress a farmer feels intensifies with each new setback. At first it's the failure to maintain the cash flow. Then it's the pain and embarrassment of not being able to pay the bills. The farm couple seeks help from the lending institutions that once encouraged them to go more and more heavily into debt, only to be turned away. They're told that they're a bad risk and poor managers.

In the next phase, with no money for food or gasoline, they become prisoners in their own home. Every day they walk to the mailbox, only to receive another stack of legal documents telling them that they will lose the farm, will be sold out. Then the foreclosure notice arrives and, inevitably, after years of dreaded anticipation, the farm auction is scheduled. As the final blow, they are forced to look on as strangers and sometimes friends and neighbors bid pennies on the dollar and walk away with their life's work, which includes their parents' and grandparents' life's work.

All the while, the family has been falling apart. Family members are in poor health, but they can't afford a doctor. The adults and often their teenage children have been drinking more to dull the pain. They argue constantly. Parents hit their kids and each other. In the end, they don't recognize themselves or anything in the world around them. Death makes sense—it would be easier.

Why do they stay? Perhaps it's like the frog experiment with boiling water. Drop a frog in boiling water and it immediately jumps out. But place the frog in cool water and only turn up the heat a small increment at a time and the frog will actually stay in the pan and boil to death.

Financial failure comes one increment at a time. By the time a rural family loses the home or farm to foreclosure or files for bankruptcy, the struggle has likely gone on for several years. Rural counselor Glen Wallace believes that by the end of the failure process, most families will have become the victims of chronic long-term stress. This would explain why stressed-out rural people so often fall prey to outward-turned anger or inward-turned anger. The reality is, they really have no other choice. Wallace explains it this way:

> There are basically four escape hatches that can blow from chronic long-term stress. One, a person seeks help—usually through a church or the medical community. Two, they become dysfunctional. Three, they can't take the pain and they turn their anger inward, becoming physically sick, or they hurt themselves by committing suicide. And last, they become depressed or psychotic and turn their anger outward. They decide that since they hurt, they're going to make others hurt. These are the people that wind up threatening or even killing their lenders or FmHA agents. They're also the ones that are the most susceptible to the antigovernment message.

A North Dakota study conducted in 1988 sheds some light on what percentage of farmers blame themselves for their farm loss and what percentage blame others such as the government. The study found that 64 percent of those surveyed claimed that outside forces, rather than their own actions, would ultimately determine their fate.[7] That means there is twice as much outward-turned as inward-turned anger, and that translates into trouble.

I Hurt, So You'll Hurt

I'll tell you about a thing I had to deal with in the last year. I had a neighbor come by and he had a gun with him. He said, "I'm on the way to see my lender and I've got this gun. I plan to use it." I did everything I could to keep that gun there at my place. But he took it with him.

—Speaker #5,
town meeting on rural stress,
Tonkawa, Oklahoma, 1991

Victims of the rural crisis have largely been ignored. If their precarious situation has been discussed at all, the emphasis has been on the economic causes, with no attention paid to the consequences—the suicides and heart attacks, the mental health problems, the shift to radical politics. We can easily ignore people we don't know in places we've never been, so long as their problems remain internal. For most of society, farm suicides and other rural problems like child abuse, wife battering, and substance abuse are no more cause for alarm than the black-on-black violence that has devastated American inner-city communities. The American creed has been "If it doesn't touch me personally, it doesn't matter."

But that was before Ruby Ridge, Waco, the Freemen standoff in Montana, the bombing that rocked the Atlanta Olympic Games, the arson fires at black churches, the violence at abortion clinics, and the Oklahoma City bombing. Now that we have been touched, we will never be the same. We've started to experience the wrath of those who fall into Glen Wallace's "I hurt, so you'll hurt" category—those whose need for support has been redirected into rage under the influence of the antigovernment movement.

"Any group," Wallace points out, "can fill the need for support. Not just good ones. Identity, militias, or any antigovernment group can come along and fill that role. Add their influence to a personality that is already violent toward itself or others and you have an extremely dangerous individual."

Time Bomb

Nebraska farmer Arthur Kirk was one such individual. Like a lot of farmers in the mid-1980s, Kirk had borrowed a huge amount of money against his farm—in his case, $300,000. With the booming agricultural markets of the 1970s long gone, it was impossible for him to repay the debt. What started as a fight with the bank evolved—with the help of a Christian Identity–influenced antigovernment group—into a holy war with real bullets.

Kirk had been in desperate financial straits for quite a while before he became involved with the Posse Comitatus, one of the most successful of the "anti" groups in rural America. Many, though not all, Posse devotees are Christian Identity believers, and among other things, they think that Jews are the seed of Satan and now control the world's banks and governments. They also believe that minorities are subhuman, that white people are the true nation of Israel, and that they are at war with what they call the "Zionist Occupied Government" (ZOG).

In 1984, two sheriff's deputies arrived at Kirk's small white farmhouse to serve him legal papers concerning his dispute with the bank, but they got more than they had bargained for. When the first deputy was about fifteen feet in front of him, Kirk pulled a revolver and pointed it at the deputy's head. The deputies had no intention of dying over bank papers, so they backed off and called in a Nebraska police SWAT team.

A standoff ensued, and for several hours, Kirk made his uncompromising position known to the law enforcement officers who had surrounded his home. This was it. Kirk had been pushed as far as he was going to go. He would die before he gave up his farm to the evil forces that had taken control of the government.

After several hours of fruitless negotiations, Kirk made his move. With a gas mask over his shoulder and holding a machine gun, the farmer flew out his back door en route to the barn a few yards away. He never got there. The SWAT team mowed Arthur Kirk down in a hail of bullets.

A search of the farm turned up a total of twenty-seven weapons, along with something more telling. On the kitchen table of the Kirk home, authorities found piles of literature. There were brochures describing conspiracy theories of all kinds, Posse publications warning members to arm and defend themselves against the evil government, and a copy of the *Protocols of the Elders of Zion*, a book that purports to describe the actual plan for world domination created by Jewish elders at a mysterious meeting held in Poland in the early 1800s.

I suspect that Kirk's transformation from farmer to soldier was typical of other conversions resulting from conditions in rural America. As the transcription that follows shows, his desire to be left alone so he could farm his land, coupled with his disdain for the bank, permeated his final conversations with police. Kirk's venomous language to authorities exemplifies the mind-set of a farmer whose interpretations of justice, government, banks, and lawyers have been run through the grinder of the conspiracy-laden teachings of the antigovernment movement.

All of the outward-turned anger, frustration, and hatred felt by Arthur Kirk were conveyed in a telephone conversation he had with officials during the standoff. The transcript of that conversation reads like an Oklahoma task force letter on steroids. Following are some excerpts from that transcript:

> Kirk: This is my home . . . I'm a German Irish, but I'm a mixed up mongrel but by God I've been learning how to shoot my whole life, defending myself my whole life. I've climbed the wall my whole life and, damn you, I'm not stopping now. You ain't going to walk over me until I'm cold and if you want to make me cold I ain't afraid of it. I've led a damn good life and I'm not ashamed of nothing I ever done. . . . Why don't you let me try and make a living?
>
> Police: Art, I don't have anything to do with what's—
>
> Kirk: God damn fuckin' Jews, they destroyed everything I ever worked for. I've worked my ass off for 49 God damn years and I've got nothing to show for it. By God, I ain't putting up with their bullshit now. I'm tired, and I've had it, and I'm not the only God damn one, I'll tell you that. . . . Farmers fought the revolutionary war and we'll fight this son of a bitch. We were hoping to do it in court but if you're going to make it impossible, then damn you, we'll take you on your own terms.
>
> Police: Yeah, but nobody wants to do that Art. . . . basically what they want, they want you to go to court.
>
> Kirk: Jesus Christ, I've been trying to get them in court for years. They squirm and bellyache around like a typical God-damned Luciferized bastard. I'm not afraid to meet 'em in court, but by God I'll have my PPK [Walther 9mm semiautomatic pistol] on my hip. You son of a bitches are armed so will I be, and if you want to shoot me, go ahead, but I'll carry that bastard into the courtroom. If you can carry 'em, so can I. Got to protect myself someway.
>
> Police: Art, that's part of our job is to protect people.
>
> Kirk: That's right, and you sure in the hell ain't doing a very good job for me. Norwest Bank and the Jews are doing fine. You broke every damn right I got.

Why did you come up on posted property without any authorization? Wouldn't even step back and explain to me what you done. That's all I ask. I was told to quit pointing the gun—dammit, he pointed the gun at me first. I got a right to defend myself and by God you tell me different. . . .

Until you can tell me what kind of papers you're serving and what you're up to like a man and then leave me alone, quit harassing me.

Police: Art, first of all, I don't serve papers; the second thing, the papers were there to deal something with you going to court, and that's all I know, Art.

Kirk: I've been trying to get the court for—Jesus Christ—ask Jan Steeple how long ago he told me to hire a lawyer. It did me one hell of a lot of good. You know what that son of a bitch did? He lied to me, every turn in the road. Filthy lying member of the bar, outlaw bastards. I filed a suit against the God damn bank that's been misusing me for years and years and years, unbeknown to me until I started reading the laws myself because there was no other way to do it. . . .

I found out them dirty rotten son of a bitches have done everything despicable that they can think of to me. Everything you can think, it's unimaginable, it's covered by the U.S. Constitution and U.S. titles passed by Congress, the highest law-making body in the land, and they tell me that my suit is meritless. I'm going to tell you something; if the Constitution and the laws Congress passes are meritless, them son of a bitches are completely discredited. . . .

You bring my wife up here and you put your God damn gun in the mailbox, let me search you and we'll talk. I ain't taking none of your damn tricks. . . . you know what I am? I'm an Israeli.

Police: You're a what?

Kirk: I'm a son of Abraham. Just what Lucifer claims—he claims my birthright and that's a dirty rotten lie. He's born a king. I'll have none of his shit. Norwest Bank is run by—where did they get all the power, who's got power of the world, how come the God damn Jews stink and go and farm other people's nuclear plants and we just sit and say, "Now boys, now boys, mustn't do that." Who runs this world? You tell me. Think about it a little bit. Open your eyes and smell the coffee.

Police: Art, it's obviously . . .

Kirk: You're just egging, son—you know who the Massad is?

Police: What's a Massad?

Kirk: Most ruthless son of a bitches the world has ever known. . . . They're more ruthless than Stalin's NKVD and the Gestapo put together ever thought of being. It's the people who are running the whole damn show, that's who it is. . . .

There's a big move to try to subvert the Constitution, to change the whole thing. Communism—that isn't communism, it's Judaism. . . . Rockefeller and all the big shots running the whole damn thing. Well, I can tell you, they ain't running me. We're going to have to make some better arrangements and I'm in the process of trying—and if this harassment is supposed to deter me, I'm telling you it has the opposite effect. And it ain't going to change, nothing is going to change.[8]

Arthur Kirk was not alone in his beliefs. At a Nebraska farm auction held a few days after his death, hundreds of rural people showed up at the sale wearing black armbands in memory of the man the authorities had killed.

No one knows for sure how many rural Americans have been transformed into Arthur Kirks by the misguided support of the antigovernment movement. The best estimates range from tens of thousands to hundreds of thousands. It is known for sure that the number is growing and that the outward-turned anger and its subsequent violence is on a grander scale today than it was a few years ago. It may well be that the popularity of the antigovernment message in rural America owes much to a lack of competition. With hope seemingly lost in the rural world, only the haters of government offer a message of support, or perhaps that could be more accurately defined as an "invitation to live."

3

An Invitation to Die

Now comes the invitation to die from others in our lives. A spouse strikes out because of heavy stress, the equipment dealer repossesses the equipment, and the land bank forecloses on the land. The lenders announce publicly in the newspapers that you have failed. Embarrassed and humiliated, you withdraw from all community activities and go into hiding.

Where can you go and what can you do? There doesn't seem to be at this point but one thing to do. Suicide.

—Dr. Glen Wallace, rural psychologist

"Consciously or unconsciously, as individuals or as symbols of society, we can invite a person to live or die." So says renowned psychologist and suicidologist Sidney M. Jourard. "Let us inquire into this phenomenon of invitation, since it appears to affect physiology, experience, behavior, and—in the long run—life and death."[1]

The idea that what goes on in the environment around us will affect our behavior is nothing new. This idea has been a mainstay of modern psychology for decades. Jourard's thesis is simple and sheds light both on suicides and, ultimately, on the recent success of the antigovernment movement's recruiting efforts.

Jourard believes that our lives are made up of "projects," which could be described as occupations, families, spiritual beliefs, hobbies—in sum, anything of interest that we value. When individuals reach the end of a "project," they must turn their attention to a new one in order to remain healthy. People who reach the end of a project with no new project on the horizon begin to die, as they now have no reason to justify their existence.

As Jourard puts it, "A person lives only as long as he experiences his life as having meaning and value, and as long as he has something to live for: meaningful projects that will animate him and invite him into the future." Without such an invitation, death will come, either slowly, from stress-related illness—our bodies give up the fight to survive—or quickly, by way of suicide. Jourard points out that a person who has no reason to exist will begin to suffer from some type of psychosis.

As a society, we send messages that determine how an individual will view this loss of a project. If we encourage the person to pursue new interests, we are offering that individual an invitation to live and move forward into the future. But if all the messages in the individual's life are negative, we are extending an invitation to die to that person.

Perhaps the best illustration of Jourard's theory can be found in the farmer facing foreclosure. As a result of his very personality type, a farmer views his work as his main project, his identity. As the farm begins to fail, society begins to send its messages: Creditors demand payment, lenders become more hostile, every day the mail brings a dozen negative invitations; family relationships turn sour at the same time a farmer is beginning to withdraw from the social activities that once gave him support. And then there is the foreclosure, the final and loudest invitation to die.

A research proposal from Texas Women's University described the likelihood that a direct correlation between the issuance of foreclosure notices and suicides exists.[2] The Oklahoma task force and the agricultural hot lines may also have inadvertently stumbled across evidence of the "invitation" scenario. The counties where farmers had lodged the highest number of complaints against the way they were personally treated by their FmHA supervisors—complaints about such behavior as callousness toward the farmer's economic situation and seemingly cavalier attitudes—were also the counties with the highest suicide rate among farmers.

Jourard is convinced that we can either "inspirit" or "dispirit" other individuals.

> To inspirit a person is to augment and confirm his values and purposes, to increase his experience of meaning in his existence, and—I believe—render him more resistant to both "physical" and "mental" diseases.
>
> Conversely, to dispirit a person is to disconfirm him, to reduce his hope, to diminish the value he invests in his aims and purposes—in short, to accelerate his rate of dying.

Think of the persons, for instance, who kill themselves after the loss of money, status, work, a limb, their beauty, their sexuality or a loved one, and those persons who, on reflection, discover that they no longer are the persons they believed themselves to be. By killing themselves they are saying, in effect, that they believe there is only one way to live and be, only one incarnation is possible for them. When the value of their existence is eliminated, so is their existence.[3]

When Jourard's theory is considered in conjunction with the findings of the studies regarding the personality types and the long and painful process of farm failure and foreclosure, it becomes clear why farmers are killing themselves three times as fast as the rest of us: They have been given an "invitation to die."

Invitation to Live

In the late 1980s, rural counselors and local clergy offered the best hope of providing an "invitation to live" to stressed-out rural residents. In their effort to stop the flood of suicides, they searched for creative new "projects" to offer individuals. Projects ranged from turning a farmer's focus to his faith in God and love of family to entering retraining programs at area vocational-technical centers or joining organizations like the American Agricultural Movement.

Even my own effort to document the farm crisis was used on occasion as a symbolic "project" by psychologist Glen Wallace. During one suicide intervention, in which a farmer with a shotgun had been drinking heavily, Wallace persuaded the man to talk to me instead of blowing his own head off. He convinced the farmer that telling his story to the world would help save other farmers from going through the pain he was experiencing. The new project worked long enough for the farmer to sober up and agree to enter inpatient treatment.

At the height of the rural effort—when funding for hot lines and rural counselors was readily available—the results were successful and impressive. Mental health–care workers had almost reached a 100 percent success rate in stopping the suicides that came to their attention through the hot lines. The "invitation to live" was working. But unfortunately, as often happens, Washington decided it was time for a new "problem of the day." Despite the magnitude of the rural crisis, rural mental-health funding dried up. The words "farm crisis" no longer appeared in newspaper headlines, so job-conscious politicians ceased to feel compelled to provide money for something that would likely fail to translate into votes.

Common sense would tell us that health workers at the local level should determine what problems exist in their areas and then seek financial support from the federal government to help alleviate those problems. But common sense can be a rare commodity these days. Under the current system, federal bureaucrats sitting around a big table in the rarefied air of Washington, D.C., determine what they believe to be America's most pressing health-care needs. More often than not, these "needs" are whatever happens to be making headlines in the big city daily papers at the time (it should be noted that rural problems have been almost invisible in these papers since 1990 and, consequently, so has rural funding). After deciding what it thinks the problems are, Washington makes funds available specifically for those needs. Aware of how the system works, local health organizations— usually in the person of grant writers—have little choice but to fly to Washington to figure out what problems are being funded. They then return to their local areas to look for those problems.

Heroin on the Prairie

I heard a good example of this topsy-turvy health-care focus during a candid conversation with Glen Wallace about his experiences in Oklahoma.

> We would go to Washington and look at the federal register to figure out where the money was, then we'd come back and see if we could find the problem to fit the money. We knew we had a lot of pressing needs like rural mental-health care, but there wasn't any money appropriated for it.
>
> This one year, all the money was for setting up methadone programs. So I had to come back and try to find a heroin problem. It's amazing what you can find when there's a pot of money sitting there waiting to be spent. I hate methadone. The stuff's just as bad as the heroin. It just trades one addiction for the other. But we needed funds, so methadone it was.
>
> They [federal government officials] not only tell you what the parameters are for getting the funds, they use the system to pay back their campaign contributors. On the methadone deal, this one senator made it a requirement that the program had to be audited by a particular consulting company that had supported his campaign. The way it was writ-

ten in the register, if you wanted a grant, the consulting firm had to get a third of the $300,000 for the audit. Those lousy people only spent one day at our program and took $100,000. I almost got in a fistfight with that guy.

What we'd try to do is write the grant in such a way that we could use at least some of the money for real problems that existed. Push come to shove, you could still get a farmer into inpatient treatment under the methadone program. You just had to pretend he was a heroin addict.

A Window of Opportunity

Though the image of rural America is pastoral and bucolic, the real rural America is graying faster, losing its young people, its economic base, receiving less employer-based insurance, paying more of its discretionary income on less insurance coverage. The rural worker is at greater risk of job-related injury, has less access to emergency medical services, has less regulatory safeguards and is very subject to national and international pressures that are well beyond his or her control. The need for mental health care is present in rural America, and services need to be more affordable and available.[4]

—Kim Sibilsky, National Rural Health Association

All across the nation, rural health care—which has always played second fiddle to its urban counterpart—has disappeared. Rural hospitals and clinics have shut down. Rural physicians and mental-health workers have moved to the cities where they can make substantially more money. The regional hospitals that are left have become a part of the managed health-care system, in which profit-motivated insurance plans with their short hospital stays are the rule. Impoverished rural Americans, who are the most in need of help in the country, have been effectively shut out of the system.

Norma C. Harms of the Nebraska Friends of Mental Health notes:

One hour of counseling costs the entire profit of 60 head of butchers [hogs], and I know because I have helped buy the breeding stock and I have given those pigs the shots. And believe me, when it takes 60 head of butchers that have to be bred, raised and sold, and the profit will pay for one hour of counseling, we have different priorities. It also takes the full profit from 10 acres of field corn, or six acres of alfalfa.[5]

This makes it clear that without financial support, struggling rural citizens are not going to seek the help they know they need.

A 1990 Intergovernmental Health Policy Project report noted that "at the same time that mental health and behavioral problems are on the rise, the system of mental health services in rural areas shows signs of serious impairment. Communities have had unusual difficulties in providing services, because of high rates of poverty; the difficulty of making services accessible over large geographic areas; and the dearth of health professionals willing to locate in remote areas."[6]

In 1989, a congressional subcommittee sought testimony from rural health-care workers concerning the condition of the system. Lou Northcutt, a registered nurse, was one of those who testified passionately about the double standard imposed on rural health care:

> We in rural health care have been trying diligently to take care of our people. Rural people believe in taking care of their own, and we have done that faithfully and well. It is not until now, when the system is disintegrating, that we raise our voices in concern and frustration.
>
> 33.75 percent of billed charges at our hospital for fiscal 1989 are uncollectible. 26.16 percent are uncollectible due to government regulations. If our hospital had been in Dallas or even in a county adjoining the urban area, Medicare would have paid us $500,000 more for the same patients. [Only 25 percent of the rural poor qualify for Medicaid, compared to 43 percent of the inner-city poor.]
>
> Do the elderly, the unemployed and medically indigent in the rural areas deserve less because they are rural? Do you believe that we pay less for our equipment and supplies than they do in Dallas, Texas?
>
> The only thing that is cheaper in the rural areas is the cost of labor. Nurses with my training and expertise make at least twice as much money as I do because they work in the city. If the only way you can see to keep rural hospitals alive is by paying the people who work there significantly less, then let it die. That is not an acceptable solution. I am not a third-class nurse and my doctors are not third-class doctors. You will get what you pay for eventually and that will be nothing or substandard care as more and more capable, caring professionals give up the fight and move to the city.
>
> Our patients are young single mothers and their children who work for $3.50 an hour at the clothes factory. Their male counterparts are making $4.00 at another factory. Our patients are the small business men and women who are striving to keep their businesses open in an unfavorable economic climate.
>
> Our patients are the farmers and their families who are in great despair because they cannot make a living. Many have lost their farms and

their homes and others are in danger of just that. These people are killing themselves with guns, machinery accidents, worry and hours of hard work without any thought of taking care of their bodies until they can not work anymore.

Who is going to take care of these people? Once the care has vanished from the scene it will not return. It is not a matter of years. It is now that something must be done to empower rural people.[7]

Something was done, all right. The funding for rural health care was withdrawn. Counties that once had ten physicians and several mental-health workers now have one or none. To make things worse, the network of hot lines that had handled hundreds of thousands of desperate calls so successfully became part of the Department of Agriculture. Now, stressed-out rural people who often blamed the government for the loss of their way of life, their loved ones, and their land were supposed to call and be comforted by their perceived enemy.

Northcutt had asked Congress, "Who is going to take care of these people?" If members of Congress had known the answer to that question, perhaps their actions would have been different. The federal government had exited rural America at its greatest moment of need, forgetting to close the door behind it. The government's lack of concern about rural America's future made it possible for anyone to walk in and set up shop. If the government's system could no longer offer the needed "invitation to live," then someone else would, and that "someone" was the antigovernment movement. Glen Wallace sees it this way: "When these groups come along and tell a struggling person that it's not his or her fault, it's the government's fault, they're more than ready to listen. These groups are preying on sick individuals. They're offering them the hope that the system can't, or won't."

Support, a.k.a. the New "Project"

Psychology textbooks tell us that individuals only exist in one of three states: natural, supportive, or protective. The natural state is that of the healthy personality. The supportive state occurs when an individual needs the support of others such as counselors or doctors in order to remain functional. At this stage, the type of "project" (invitation to live) that is presented will determine an individual's behavior. The protective state is that in which a person needs to be confined in a hospital or institution.

Unfortunately, many of those suffering from depression due to the restructuring of the rural economy and the overall poor outlook for the future are now in a supportive state. Studies conducted in several states have found that between 20 and 35 percent of the rural population showed signs of depression.[8] That means there are potentially 25 million people who are, at some level, vulnerable to the antigovernment movement's "invitation to live" because other alternatives have all but disappeared.

Common-law courts, militia groups, anti-tax organizations, and sovereignty organizations are springing up in every nook and cranny of the rural landscape. Their evangelical approach to recruitment has allowed them to far outpace their dwindling competition in the business of "support." Go to any farm auction or tax sale and you'll find antigovernment proponents working the crowd, offering encouraging words and easy answers to complex problems in the form of conspiracy theories.

People who believe they have lost everything that had meaning in their lives eagerly embrace any scenario that can explain why it happened. More often than not, the antigovernment movement can provide an explanation that fits a person's particular circumstance like a glove, and more important, a hurting individual can find a group of empathetic supporters who help him hang on.

The movement offers converts the "new project" of restoring order and justice to the confusing world around them. It reaches them at the very roots of their rural belief system, invoking God, patriotism, family values, anticommunism, and a nostalgic view of American life. It tells them that they are not to blame for their predicament. The movement provides them with a scapegoat for their rage in the form of Jews and government, the IRS, and international bankers.

In a somewhat prophetic report titled *State of Mental Health in the Heartland*, rural counselor Mona Lee Brock describes a plan that she believes would revitalize the dying rural communities:

> Dr. Sidney M. Jourard, in his writing about the "invitation to live and invitation to die," documents the best way to help a person with strong suicidal ideation is by giving the individual a "new project." Certainly the empowerment of a local support group can become a "new project."
>
> The motivation, adrenaline, anger, guilt, blame and withdrawal can be channeled into a worthy "new project" by a self-help group. There should be one strong support group in each community of the heart-

land. Yes, a "new project" may require activism during the empower-
ment process of these support groups. But, this activism is saving lives
of individuals and the quality of life of the communities.

We must alleviate the farm stress in the heartland by not letting
lenders, politicians, bureaucrats, the Chicago Board of Trade, Tyson
Chicken, Cargill Beef, City Bank of New York, the IRS or anybody else,
take our joy out of the heartland.[9]

Brock's design for saving rural communities reads like the blueprint
that the antigovernment movement has used to swell its ranks all
across rural America. The support groups turned out to be militias,
common-law courts, sovereign townships, and any number of other
"anti" organizations.

I've attended a number of antigovernment meetings in different
parts of the country. In many ways, they have become the center of
social activity in their respective communities. Meals and casual conversation are often part of the experience. Women gather in the back
of the room to talk about children, schools, and recipes (antigovernment groups are not generally on the cutting edge of women's issues), while the men exchange hunting stories or talk about crops and
weather. You would be hard-pressed to tell the difference between
one of these meetings and a Kiwanis Club get-together, that is, until
the meeting is called to order. Then things get deadly serious.

Ironically, Brock's prediction that "activism" would save lives has
probably turned out to be true. I've spoken to several rural counselors who, as a last resort to prevent a suicide, have actually encouraged troubled individuals to join their local antigovernment groups.
They have told me that suicide was avoided in each case. But one has
to wonder what the long-term implications are for sending an in-
wardly violent personality to a place where he can have his anger
redirected, while being programmed to hate and distrust the federal
government.

A Case in Point

In May 1996, authorities, including the FBI, made their move on a
southside Oklahoma City motel room and arrested farmer Gideon
Cowan. The fugitive the television showed being pulled from the
low-budget motel complex looked more like Robinson Crusoe than
the man I had met some six years before. Cowan's thick beard and

ratty appearance told the story of a man on the run—in Cowan's case, a man running from the system he blamed for destroying his life.

I first met Cowan in the basement of a small church in Watonga, Oklahoma, in 1990. The smell of chili and cherry Kool-Aid filled the stuffy air of the below-ground structure. Small groups of people congregated throughout the large room and the kitchen area, sometimes smiling but mostly shaking their heads and looking somewhat shell-shocked. The occasion was a wake—a wake for the death of a farm.

Gideon Cowan's four-thousand-acre farm operation was going on the block. His equipment was being auctioned off the next morning. And as has become the practice in small towns across the plains, hot-line workers, rural counselors, local preachers, neighbors, and friends had gathered with the family to show their support and remember the good times that had come before.

After the chili dinner, the hundred or so people took their seats around the long folding tables that filled the room. One at a time, they stood up and told their favorite stories about the Cowan family and farm. Some tales were humorous recollections, though the laughter was subdued and forced. Others recalled memories of how the Cowans had helped them out. One man stood and, through tears, recounted how Gideon, his wife, June, and their two children had helped other farmers in the area survive the tough times of the mid-1980s. He related how the Cowans had shared their food and labor to try and keep their neighbors from losing their farms. There was a lot of sadness that night but no talk of militias or mention of other antigovernment themes. People in Watonga were not happy with how things were going, but they still trusted their government to some degree.

The next day, at the equipment sale, Gideon Cowan was absent. He couldn't bear the sight of seeing the tractors he had worked a lifetime for being sold for next to nothing. As I walked through the crowded auction with Gideon's two young boys, all they could say was, "What will we do now?" The mood of the other farmers who had come to see their friend "sold out" was equally somber. They knew that they could be next. If a good farmer like Gideon Cowan could blow away in the wind, anyone could.

But Cowan didn't believe he had just blown away. He was sure he had been pushed out by the local banker, the judge, and the attorneys involved in his case. Cowan believed he was just the latest victim in a national movement to reduce the number of farms in rural America. And he may well have been right.

During his long battle to keep the farm, Cowan wound up suing the local banker. A jury of Cowan's peers found the banker liable of fraud. But the joy of the Cowan family was short-lived. According to Gideon, at the same time the judge announced the jury's verdict of liable against the banker, he also announced that the bank would still be allowed to foreclose on the four-thousand-acre Cowan spread. It was a hollow victory, and justice seemed far away.

The Cowans had the right to an appeal, but the day after the trial, according to Gideon, their attorney informed them that he would need an additional $20,000 to start the appeal process. The family that had spent its life's savings fighting the bank was only able to raise one-fourth of that amount. This would not be the last time that money would erect a barrier between Gideon and a fair legal process.

At that point, the Cowans were forced to make a decision they had hoped to avoid. Gideon recalls, "The only alternative we had left to save the farm was to file Chapter 12 bankruptcy, and this was totally against my upbringing." Despite his heartfelt reservations, Cowan filed for bankruptcy and created a financial plan that he believed was workable. But after a short while, the plan failed. Cowan believed that those who were in control of his bankruptcy were out to get him, despite their claims that they had done all they could for the farmer. According to Cowan, "Once we filed for bankruptcy, the banker started to persecute my family and I. He tried to have us removed from the Chapter 12."

In small towns where judges, bankers, and local lawyers play on the same golf course, funny things can happen. Cowan claims that the judge abruptly decided to remove his farm from Chapter 12, requiring him to make 100 percent of the principal and interest payment immediately. As Cowan recalls, "I had enough to make all of the interest payment and half of the principal payment. By the standards of the judicial system, this should have been enough to continue the Chapter 12. But the banker must have gotten to the judge. We had to have the full amount or get off the property. They moved us off."

The Cowans had nowhere to go and no money to get there. They stayed in their car or with friends. And as often happens in such difficult circumstances, the family began to disintegrate. June and the kids left, leaving Gideon to face the world of the landless farmer alone.

The desperate and depressed Cowan moved around from farm to farm doing what he could to survive. All the while, his state of mind was deteriorating. He became a regular caller on the Ag-Link hot line. In particular, he turned to counselor Mona Lee Brock for guidance and support. The next few years of Cowan's life were filled with thoughts of self-destruction and the struggle to find a reason to live. The one thought that kept Cowan going was the ever-present hope that one day justice would be done and he would get his farm back.

Mona Lee Brock shared Gideon's hope. She had seen thousands of farmers lose their land under questionable circumstances. If there was even a prayer of Cowan getting his place back, Brock would find it. In 1992, Brock heard about a meeting in Enid, Oklahoma, that might just be the ticket. The word was that some people had figured out a way to use the system so that farmers like Cowan could win back their farms. And the whole thing was perfectly legal, so the story went. Brock called Gideon and told him about the meeting. Maybe he would find his miracle. Gideon remembers that

> Mona Lee called me and told me of a meeting that might shed some light on how we could retrieve our farm and our ranch and our property. I attended the meeting along with hundreds of other people from across the state. It was an informative meeting, but not at first, because I didn't believe what I was being told. But as I began to look into what I was being told, I found it to be accurate. And that began my journey of how they took my property and why it's being taken.

"Journey" is a good word to describe Gideon's next few years. He attended meeting after meeting, always being diligent about researching the information he was being given.

> Most of what I was being taught was coming from the Library of Congress and the Federal Register. I was alarmed to say the least at what I was finding out as opposed to what I had been taught in school—what my kids were being taught in school. People would be shell-shocked to find out what's in the library and the Federal Register.
>
> People are so busy today—through a most intelligent design—trying to raise a family and keep up with their expenses through the Federal Reserve and the IMF. They don't have time to do the research I'm talking about. As time goes by, more and more people are being dispossessed of their property, so naturally more and more people are getting the time to find out what is happening to them and their families. Until our public schools start teaching the truth, people won't know they're being pushed over a cliff, so to speak.

Cowan's observation is accurate. As more and more people lose their property and way of life to the global economic restructuring of rural America, they are turning to the only people who seem to have an explanation, those in the antigovernment movement. In the effort to regain his farm, Cowan began to learn and absorb the basic radical beliefs of the antigovernment movement, beginning with the conspiracy theory: The Illuminati, a centuries-old secret society whose goal is nothing short of world domination, has taken over the American government, banks, and legal system. The secret group's main purpose is to own all of the land and wealth of the world, relegating everyone else to slavery in one form or another. It just so happens that this secret and evil group is composed of wealthy Jews.

Cowan had found his new "project." His desire for suicide had been replaced by a struggle for what he saw as a holy war for justice. Cowan had been given an "invitation to live" by people who seemed to understand what he was going through. He had become a convert.

But Cowan learned about more than just the great conspiracy. He was taught how the Uniform Commercial Code (UCC)—which contains the procedures governing how banks do business—could be used to legally get his farm back. Groups like the Freemen in Montana have used the UCC to justify their billions of dollars' worth of liens and bank drafts. Cowan explains the process this way:

> After going to these meetings and about three years of research, I found that I had a remedy and recourse to retrieve my property or recompense for my property in terms of creditory monetary value—which could be used to repurchase my property, livestock and house. . . . The remedy I found in the UCC was a nonjudicial private security agreement in which you file a UCC-1 against whoever has caused you harm and damages and loss of property.

Cowan once again had hope for regaining his farm. He filed his documents against the banker who he felt had wronged him during the process of losing his land. But the system didn't see things quite Gideon's way. As Gideon left the courthouse after filing the lien, the banker and the sheriff were waiting for him. Cowan was arrested and charged with filing false or forged documents.

Gideon went to court, and as he had been taught, he represented himself. Time after time during the trial, Cowan tried to present the jury with evidence to justify why he had filed the documents, to show how the judge and bankers had conspired against him. He tried to explain his years of research and why the documents he had filed were legal. But as often happens when a judge is presiding over a case considered to be antigovernmental in nature, much of the evidence was disallowed. With no defense, the jury had little choice but to find Cowan guilty.

Gideon Cowan was sentenced to eight years in prison, an incredibly harsh sentence, considering the crime. Like many people arrested today for infractions perceived to be antigovernmental, Cowan had the book thrown at him. Antigovernment adherents believe the justice system is trying to send a message through the harsh sentences it imposes on their peers, which, as they see it, relegates many of those now serving time to the category of political prisoners. Cowan will likely serve more days behind bars than a convicted rapist for his filing of a lien in a courthouse. The political prisoner idea would seem to have merit.

But Gideon still maintained his hope for justice through the appeal system. With the help of other farmers who raised the money he needed, Gideon was released on an $80,000 appeal bond. While he was out on bail, the forty-seven-year-old Cowan sought justice through the antigovernment movement's common-law courts that were meeting almost weekly at various locations around the state. This time, Cowan prevailed. A common-law jury found Gideon "not guilty" of the same charges he had been convicted of when his defense had been disallowed. Cowan, like most participants in the antigovernment movement, believes that the U.S. Constitution has established common-law courts as the highest court in the land.

Cowan then took the jury's finding of fact along with the liens they had issued and filed them according to the regulations of the UCC. They were filed at the county level and, subsequently, at the state level. In addition to the filings, Cowan ran public notices in the newspaper as required. In his mind, he did everything possible to adhere to the law.

Armed with the success of the common-law findings, Cowan was confident he would win his upcoming appeal. Unfortunately, he'd forgotten that justice is rarely for the poor. On the day he was required to file his appeal, Cowan was told that he had to provide a complete transcript of his original trial in order to proceed. According to a friend of Cowan's, the transcript would have cost at least $700. Cowan had nowhere to turn for the money. Consequently his transcript-absent appeal was disallowed, and the State of Oklahoma issued a warrant for his arrest. Once again, the system had denied Cowan an appeal because he could not afford it.

Cowan wondered why something so basic as "justice" was so elusive for him. All he wanted was to get back the farm and family he had worked his whole life for. But then he realized why: He'd been telling people about the evil forces that were trying to take over the world, and now those forces were going to silence him by having him rot away in prison. Cowan believed he had no choice left but to tell others about his situation.

Cowan became a teacher. He traveled and told his story to large crowds that listened intently to his message of the Illuminati and the injustice that the system had doled out to him. He told people that the courts were trying to keep them from finding out about the "recourse" that was available to those whose homes, cars, and furniture had been repossessed. "They don't want the people to become aware of the deception going on," he would tell them, pointing to the seal on a dollar bill that contains the pyramid and the all-seeing eye, the symbol he believed proved that the Illuminati had taken control of the monetary system. As part of his speech, Gideon would place a Bible on one of his shoulders and a *Black's Legal Dictionary* on the other and then announce, "Choose ye today whom you will serve, God or man." Gideon had become an apostle of the new faith.

But all this came to an end in May 1996, when Cowan was arrested in the rundown room of the southside Oklahoma City motel. He was taken into custody and placed in the prison at Taft, Oklahoma, to begin serving his eight-year sentence. It was in the Taft prison that I conducted my last interview with Cowan in November 1996.

Ironically, Gideon is once again working the land with his hands, doing what he loves most in the world: farming. But the joy isn't there as he plows the fields of the prison farm, fields in the gently rolling hills that surround the razor wire and guard towers of the place he now lives.

After going through the requisite security procedures, I'm led to a small waiting room with dingy baby-blue furniture. There are several people in the area but no one who looks familiar, so I settle into an overstuffed chair to wait for further instructions. "Mr. Dyer?" asks a soft voice in front of me. I look up at the clean-shaven grey-haired inmate who has been sitting six feet away the whole time. "Gideon?" I respond. I didn't recognize him, given the toll of the last few years. I suddenly go blank. What can I say? The normal greetings like "How are you?" or "How have you been?" seem an inappropriate icebreaker to use with a man rotting away in jail. "It's good to see you" finally finds its way out of my mouth, just as the prison's press liaison arrives to take us to a room where we can talk.

As we walk through the prison with barred doors clanging and locking behind us, everything becomes a bit surreal. We make our way down a hallway filled with gang-bangers and crudely tattooed arms pushing brooms. The gentle, soft-spoken farmer beside me seems more out of place in this cold world of steel and concrete than I do. I can't stop imagining what life must be like in this hellhole for a grey-haired farmer from Watonga.

The conversation is a bit sterile at first. Cowan has become more than a little skeptical of media after seeing himself appraised as a criminal and lunatic in the newspapers. But after a while, we laugh and talk about the old days. Cowan can sense that although I don't agree with a lot of his beliefs, I at least have an understanding of the real circumstances that have led him to this dreadful place. The hours fly by in conversation until the press liaison—who had sat there and listened through the entire interview—announces that we only have ten minutes left. Gideon tells me that the system is afraid of him because it doesn't want the truth to get out. He says that he's a political prisoner because he was telling people what's really going on with the government and the world. As proof, he offers what he says is the district attorney's offer of a plea bargain. According to Cowan, "They told me if I'll, one, drop the liens and two, drop my appeal, then I can walk out of here. But I refuse because I am not wrong. I am 100 percent truthful, honest and right in what I did." It is clear to me that Cowan is sincere in saying this. As much as he wants to get out of prison, his desire for what he perceives as justice and the return of his beloved farm are more important.

The liaison woman signals that time is up. Gideon extends his hand and firmly shakes mine. We are led back through the depressing halls of the prison and, to my surprise, out into the parking lot, where my car is waiting. The woman finally leaves us to speak in private. Gideon points to a stark-looking brick building and says he has to go and check in for the night. Once again, I'm at a loss for words. I find myself apologizing for being able to just drive away and leave him behind.

Gideon looks at me, and for the first time, his emotions get the better of him. With tears filling his eyes despite his valiant effort to hold them back, this normally stoic farmer murmurs, "I just have to get out of here, it's so bad. If you know anyone who can help me, I'd appreciate it. I have to hurry now. If I'm late for my check-in they'll add time to my sentence, and I couldn't take it." With that, Gideon turns and walks quickly back to his place in hell. I drive away.

Gideon Cowan is a peaceful man. He's lost everything he ever loved: his family, his neighbors and friends, his land, and his freedom. He has fought through the urge to end his life by turning his attention to his quest for justice—a quest made possible by the teachings of the antigovernment movement. Has he broken the law in the process? Perhaps. But he doesn't believe that he has, and he never intended to do so.

Cowan is a perfect example of the plague that has befallen rural America. Economic hardship and the subsequent depression nearly tortured him to death. The inward-turned anger that nearly drove him to suicide has been redirected by the new "project" of the antigovernment movement.

Gideon Cowan just wanted to be a farmer, but no one would hear him. What Cowan needs is a system with someone in authority who can understand who he is and what he's been through. He neither needs nor deserves to be in prison. He's a victim of the global restructuring of the rural world—one of the millions of people who have fallen prey to the inevitable.

4

Like a Disease

As the local storefronts are being boarded up, as the rural institutions such as schools, hospitals, churches, and banks are being closed, whole communities develop the same symptoms as a depressed individual. They become angry, withdrawn communities whose guilt gives them the need for someone to blame. They have paranoid feelings toward money lenders and the county, state, and federal government.

—Mona Lee Brock, rural counselor, 1990

I've heard the argument made that the Oklahoma City bombing could not have been tied to the radical movements in farm country because the accused, Timothy McVeigh and Terry Nichols, aren't farmers. This is an interesting but somewhat oversimplified notion that fails to take into consideration how the growing rural crisis—and subsequently the antigovernment phenomenon—spreads its effects through entire communities and regions. The farm crisis was only the detonator of the rural crisis, which in turn has affected almost every rural setting in the United States, including places like Decker, Michigan; Kingman, Arizona; and Herington, Kansas—places where Nichols and McVeigh spent a lot of time prior to the Oklahoma bombing.

Terry Nichols grew up on a farm and, according to Phil Morawski, James Nichols's next-door neighbor and friend, watched his father struggle to keep his land from being repossessed by the bank on more than one occasion. According to those who know him, Terry used to travel to farm auctions, where he, his brother James, and a neighbor would attempt to stop the foreclosure sales by bidding $25.00 in silver coins—one of the early ploys attempted by rural activists in an effort to stop farm sales by the banks. And as for Tim McVeigh, he made his feelings clear in a letter he wrote to his hometown newspaper in Lockport, New York, declaring that "the American dream of the middle class has all but disappeared, substituted with people struggling just to buy next week's groceries."

McVeigh and Nichols may not be farmers, but they have been affected by the same disease that has engulfed the state of mind of rural America. At various times in their lives, they have clearly been involved and motivated by the economically induced radicalism that exists throughout the rural United States. It is a moot point that they aren't farmers. What's important is that their exposure to the powerful forces that started in and continue to flow through rural places allegedly carried them to Oklahoma City.

Communicable Anger

Antigovernment behavior can spread from person to person, from group to group, and even from community to community. Like the effects of a violent storm, it began by flooding the fields and closed-down factories, but now it has swept through entire populations, and it's still raining. This monsoon called the antigovernment movement owes its success to a phenomenon some psychologists are calling "community depression."

Like any communicable disease, depression and anger can spread from one person to another. This is a very common occurrence in families, where the depression of one family member is ultimately transferred to the others.[1]

Many rural psychologists believe we are now experiencing the results of this second-hand psychosis, just as occurs in a family. Large portions of entire communities are beginning to show the same symptoms as a depressed individual: anger, paranoia, and a distrust of government. These pockets of collective depression have become the perfect breeding ground for the antigovernment movement.

Community depression is not bound by physical properties such as a specific locality. "Community" is defined as a group of people who share a common religion, occupation, or other belief. Technology such as the Internet has made it possible for community depression to affect a group of people spread out over a large geographic area. Members of any group who draw their support from one another through a shared ideology may be considered a community. Glen Wallace believes that community depression can lead to a community psychosis and that in some cases this psychosis can create a cult mentality among the members of the community. Wallace says that in many respects, individual antigovernment groups may, in fact, be functioning as cults.

As far back as 1989, Glen Wallace was beginning to see the birth pangs of today's heartland revolt. In his testimony before a congressional subcommittee examining rural development, Wallace warned that

> many debt-ridden farm families will become more suspicious of government as their self-worth, their sense of belonging, their hope for the future deteriorates . . . these families are torn by divorce, domestic violence, alcoholism. We see a loss of relationship with their peers, they do not go to the coffee shops anymore, they do not belong to the co-op boards. There is a loss of relationships of these communities to the state and federal government. . . .
>
> Farm-dependent rural areas are suffering what I could call community depression. We have communities that are made up now of collectively depressed individuals, and the symptoms of that community depression are similar to what you would find in someone that has a long-term chronic depression.[2]

Wallace went on to tell the congressional committee that if the rural economic system continued to remain fragile, which it has, the community depression could turn into a social and cultural psychosis that Wallace described as "delayed stress syndrome. There are regions of the country where the rural crisis has created pockets of poverty in whole communities and where large numbers of individuals are suffering from this syndrome."[3] Wallace believes this transition is now a reality in many places such as Tahlequah, Oklahoma; St. Mary's, Kansas; and Sand Springs, Idaho.

He also warned Congress that even if the government were to act immediately to ease the economic situation, rural people were going to be affected by this psychosis for decades to come. In 1989, Wallace could only guess how this community depression would eventually express itself. Today, he has seen his worst fears realized in the form of the highly organized antigovernment movement. "We knew the antigovernment backlash was just around the corner," says Wallace, "but we didn't know exactly what form it would take. You can't treat human beings in a society the way rural people have been treated without them organizing and fighting back. It was just a matter of time."

Armed with its blame-shifting message ("it's not your fault, it's the government's fault"), the antigovernment movement has become the perfect host to carry this germ of anger and paranoia into almost every economically insecure place in the country, including, most recently, the urban landscape.

The studies of rural sociologists Bill and Judith Heffernan of the University of Missouri support Wallace's view of community depression. The Heffernans found that the rural crisis has caused a severe loss of leadership in towns with low populations. Traditional role models, such as Sunday-school teachers, physicians, baseball coaches, and doctors, have all but disappeared as small towns have been boarded up because of a failing economy. The Heffernans determined that this loss of community leadership, coupled with the loss of community institutions such as churches, schools, hospitals, and mental-health and substance abuse treatment systems—which also fell victim to rural economics or government cutbacks—will ultimately "weaken this nation even more than what happened to the United States in the Great Depression."[4]

On a recent trip to North Dakota, Bill Heffernan attended meetings on the sad state of the northern beef industry. Ranchers claim that monopolies such as Cargill have purchased or caused to be shut down many of the independent feedlots, creating very few buyers to bid on their cattle at sale time. Ranchers believe this lack of competition has kept the prices too low for them to survive. At a meeting held in North Dakota between ranchers, bankers, and the monopolies, Heffernan couldn't believe what he was hearing. Bankers were telling ranchers that their time was up, that they were going to have to start a large-scale effort to foreclose on their cattle operations.

Heffernan told me that it was clear from what the ranchers were saying at these meetings that they were not going to go quietly. According to Heffernan, "The bankers and government officials [at the meetings] just didn't get it. With the level of community depression in North Dakota right now, I'd guess we're maybe a year and a half away from a serious shooting war up there."

A 1990 study conducted in Ohio found that 35 percent of the farmers surveyed showed signs of depression. But perhaps more telling was the fact that over 20 percent of all rural residents, including those who live in towns, also showed signs of depression, regardless of their occupation.[5] One study of depression in rural America reached this conclusion: "Perhaps economic and social events of the magnitude of the rural transformation are too great a match for the psychological palliatives of rural community spirit. It is under these conditions that community-level malaise may become rooted in rural communities and affect psychological distress of residents."[6] These studies demonstrate that what started on the farm is now firmly rooted in the villages and towns that connect the thinnest highways on American road maps.

A more in-depth study by researchers at Iowa State University found that depression among farmers tends to fluctuate up and down depending on the economy. The study also showed that towns with 10,000 or more people had a rate of depression at the level of major cities, and the level showed improvement when the economy improved. Surprisingly, however, the researchers also discovered that in small rural communities with a population of less than 2,500, the rate of depression has remained permanently high since the beginning of the farm crisis—higher than the rates found in inner cities. And the rate of depression shows no improvement, even if there has been an economic recovery in the area.[7] It would seem that Wallace's prediction about entire communities suffering from "delayed stress syndrome" has become a reality.

One explanation for this permanent depression in small towns is that the outmigration—which consists of services, supportive institutions, the young, and those economically able to leave—usually gravitates toward the midsize towns in the region with a population of 10,000 or more. This keeps the larger towns reasonably healthy, while ensuring that the smaller towns remain pockets of poverty wrought with depression.

Another example of the ability of depression to spread is quite interesting. During the 1980s, lenders were showing the same increased levels of depression as other rural residents. According to Wallace, "we had to develop programs for the lenders that were very similar to what we were doing for farmers. The day-in and day-out interaction between the farmers and lenders made it nearly impossible for the lenders to stay healthy." Even though the lenders had nothing to lose personally, being constantly placed on the defensive took its toll. Some lenders paid a price for their own empathy. One banker who killed himself left a suicide note describing how he just couldn't stand the thought of foreclosing on his friends and neighbors.

Just as the farmers have done, the lenders have turned, and continue to turn, their depression-induced anger in one of two directions. They either become aggressive toward the borrowers they blame for their stress or they internalize the anger and suffer physical illness and sometimes suicide.

Wallace points out that even health-care workers who are trained to understand how depression works aren't immune from its effects. "It's really pretty common for counselors, rural psychologists, and hot line operators to begin showing signs of depression; they'll go days without sleep, lose or gain weight, and occasionally, you'll even find counselors who'll begin to blame the government and the banks for the problems their clients are presenting them with. This crisis hurts everyone that comes in contact with it."

No One Is Immune

In her years of answering telephone calls from stressed-out rural residents, counselor Mona Lee Brock says she has had well over a hundred thousand conversations with desperate callers from all across the United States. She spends an average of twelve hours a day trying to give hope to people whose lives have been destroyed. People call her in the middle of the night to read her their suicide notes or just to have someone to visit with who understands their pain. The middle of the night can be a busy time for hot-line counselors because psychosis often makes it impossible for their clients to sleep, for days and weeks at a time.

Brock understands these people. She's been there herself, and callers can sense her sincerity. In 1985, Brock and her husband went through the pain of losing their own farm. Her husband never recovered from the stressful process and collapsed and died of a heart attack a year later. Thus, Brock can say, "When someone calls me with tears in their voice, I know that feeling, to lose everything."

I've met dozens of people from Montana to Texas who can recount talking to Mona Lee Brock, whose telephone ministry to the rural world began in 1986. I can honestly say that I have never heard higher praise for anyone. Literally thousands of people attribute having their life saved to Brock.

Brock's biggest challenge these days is trying to make people in high places realize that the rural crisis isn't over. She says that the rural community's need for services now is greater than at any time since the Great Depression, and she blames Washington for making those needed services almost extinct in the places her clients live. She shudders when she hears someone say that things have gotten better in farm country, pointing out that USDA figures showing improvement in the farm economy in the 1990s are skewed by large farming cooperatives and corporate agribusinesses. Small farms are still facing an impossible battle against the food monopolies and the lenders, and they continue to fail at a disproportionately fast pace. Mona Lee Brock tells anyone who will listen that the rate of suicides in the 1990s is still bad and that she continues to take as many phone calls as ever. "Nothing has changed," she says.

Brock, who spends most of each day, seven days a week, talking on the phone to people in trouble, gets frustrated with bureaucrats who keep telling the public that these people don't really exist or that their numbers are too small to matter. Brock believes that "today's economy is more and more based on the greed of corporate giants that manipulate the market and the government." She says that "the government we have now supports these corporate giants and turns a cold shoulder to rural people who are just trying to seek an income to raise their families."

Brock is also partial to quoting William Jennings Bryan, her favorite quotation being: "Let American cities be destroyed by bombs, the economy or natural disaster and they will reappear, rebuilt almost overnight; but destroy our farms, and grass will grow in the streets of every town and city in America."

For more than a decade, Mona Lee Brock has racked her brain trying to find ways to help desperate people who often rely on her for their very survival. She makes no effort to hide her disdain for the federal government she holds responsible for the devastation of the rural economy.

In 1994, a group calling itself We the People appeared on the rural scene all across the middle of the country. It was an antigovernment group promoting all the usual conspiracy theories, though they were well hidden behind a "how-to-save-your-farm" facade. But We the People was unique in one way. Organizers of the group told desperate listeners—who were vulnerable to any message that might enable them to save their land or somehow recover the property they had lost—that they could each receive a windfall of up to $20 million from the federal government. The group explained to their audiences, which sometimes numbered more than five hundred, that they had won a judgment against the federal government for allowing the country to go off the gold standard. We the People offered its prey a chance to be included in the class-action suit for a mere $300 fee. As is true of many of the "patriots-for-profit" organizations, their promises were false. There was no judgment, and most of the leaders of the group are now in jail.

When Brock heard We the People's fantastic claims, she was excited. Maybe she had found a way to help the desperate men and women who daily turned to her for answers. When the telephone rang, she would be able to do more than empathize. She would tell them about this new group, and maybe, just maybe, they would be able to save their farms. In her effort to save lives, Mona Lee Brock was counseling people to enter the world of the antigovernment movement.

Brock is far from the first rural counselor whose sympathy toward their clients has become tangled with the "anti" faction. In fact, the majority of the rural psychologists, hot-line operators, and rural church leaders I've spoken to have had similar experiences. This is true despite their training and the fact that their backgrounds run the political gamut from far left to far right.

According to psychologist Glen Wallace, it's practically impossible to spend a substantial amount of time in the wreckage of rural America without sharing in the beliefs, at least to some degree, of those who have decided to take matters into their own hands to stop the decline of their communities and the loss of their way of life. Wallace says, "That's the nature of depression. If you're around it long enough, you're going to catch it."

One rural chaplain, who travels around the backcountry warning communities of the dangers posed by hate groups within the antigovernment movement, gave me her honest opinion concerning the folks to whom she lectures: "I consider myself a liberal. But if I had to live like most of the people in the towns where I speak, I'd probably be blowing up buildings, too. Something has to be done."

If the mental-health workers in rural America can, at least to some degree, fall prey to the message of the antigovernment movement, how much more so can it affect the general rural population, which has felt the burden of the changing times firsthand? The antigovernment movement has its best success in recruiting in economically depressed areas, but it's no longer restricted to economic casualties. The movement has become large enough to be, to some degree, self-perpetuating. It has enough people involved in enough places to create new recruits simply through the process of exposing people to its conspiracy theories and "anti" rhetoric over and over again.

An undercover investigator who has been working the antigovernment movement for thirteen years described to me the recruiting process he has observed countless times.

> At first someone will stumble across a flyer or a pamphlet that says something pretty innocuous like "taxes are too high" or "abortion is murder," something like that. There's usually an address for more information or maybe a date for an upcoming meeting.
>
> When people attend their first meeting, they usually seem pretty skeptical about what they're hearing, stuff like Jews have taken over the banks and government and that Americans have to prepare to go to war against the government. But the group treats them really nice and they [the recruits] can tell there's a lot of camaraderie among the people. Most times they'll come back for more meetings. It's a very social thing.
>
> After they've been coming for a while, you can watch 'em change. They start buying into everything that's said, no matter how ludicrous. They start spending all their free time with other members of the group. All they hear is conspiracy talk, and everyone around them believes it, so they do, too.
>
> After a while, a person who was just a little ticked off about taxes is building up an arsenal in his basement. It happens all the time. Once you join that culture, you just go deeper and deeper.

Farmers and laid-off factory workers are now just one part of larger segments of the population that are succumbing to the "anti" rhetoric. At an ever-quickening pace, people of all backgrounds within these pockets of depression are being persuaded to join in the battle against a future that's threatening to put an end to their preferred way of life. More and more, the antigovernment movement—from its conspiracy theories to its automatic weapons—is becoming the protector of nostalgia in the decaying world of rural America.

You Reap What You Sow

America's rural places are in bad shape. A half-century of ever-increasing economic restructuring and corporate consolidation has, according to numerous studies, left 25 million of the 63 million rural inhabitants poor, farmless, underemployed or jobless, inadequately housed, physically ill with little or no access to health care, and, perhaps most important, depressed.

Rural people are a unique subculture, and as such, they have responded and will continue to respond differently from their urban counterparts to the changes in their world. By their very personality types, they will not adjust well to the inevitable destruction of the rural way of life. Their desire to hold on to the old ways has left them vulnerable, willing to embrace any message that promises them that opportunity.

As we plow ahead into the next millennium, a high-tech global marketplace and an increasingly global monetary system are forcing working-class and farming rural peoples to compete on a rapidly leveling playing field with their Third World counterparts. This is a nasty proposition for someone born into the American dream, someone who already finds the standard of living harsh and unacceptable.

In a twisted sort of way, the message of the antigovernment movement is a message of hope. It offers those who feel they've been stripped of their way of life the perception that it's possible to fight back. It allows millions of depressed rural residents to shift the blame for their difficult circumstances from themselves to the government, freeing them from their self-destructive guilt and shame.

The damage has been done, and it cannot be reversed. If anything, the next decade promises to become worse for rural residents. The economic genocide and its subsequent flood of depression have left our rural ground fertile and ready to be planted. The crop that ultimately grows in this disenfranchised soil depends on what seeds are sown. While our leaders in Washington, the media, and health-care professionals concentrate their energies on the problems of our cities, the antigovernment movement is busy sowing row after poisonous row across the fields of rural America.

Part Two

The Seeds of Influence

5

The Religion of Conspiracy

Conspiracy: 1. An agreement to perform together an illegal, treacherous, or evil act. 2. A combining or acting together, as if by evil design. Conspiracy refers to such a plan by a group usually intent on a bold purpose, such as overthrowing the government.

—American Heritage Dictionary

The conspiracy theories being spun by today's antigovernment movement are anything but simple. They are intricate works of fiction designed to explain rural America's ongoing slide toward a "Third World" existence. They've been specifically designed to take advantage of the widespread mental depression that has engulfed much of the rural landscape. These well-crafted theories combine fundamental religion, fear, patriotism, and a grain of truth, and to that brew, they often add racism and hate. The finished products ease the pain of those who place their faith in the theories, allowing people to scapegoat the government for their problems. The antigovernment movement's success at spreading its conspiracy theories throughout the hurting rural population accounts for much of the movement's rapid growth since 1980.

The antigovernment movement has been in existence for decades. Christian Identity–influenced groups such as the Ku Klux Klan first appeared in the 1800s, whereas other such groups are much younger: The John Birch Society came along in the 1950s, followed by the Posse Comitatus in the late 1960s. But until the last few years, these groups existed in relative obscurity, claiming less than a hundred thousand participants (divided among them) at any given time. The radical Right has always turned to rural America's failing farms and pockets of small-town poverty for recruits, but historically, this practice has only garnered enough new believers to hold their numbers steady, at best. All that changed in the 1980s, when millions of people were forced from their land during the farm crisis, making them receptive to the movement's conspiracy-laden message.

The KKK, John Birch Society, and Posse Comitatus had been predicting that the sky would fall for decades. They had created conspiracy theories that explained why it would happen and who would be behind it—Communists, Jews, the Antichrist, and the Illuminati, for example. But not many listened to their wild tales because they were opposed to the blatant racism behind the theories, and the outrageous warnings seemed fictionalized in light of observable reality.

But then came the 1980s, and the sky did fall. The scenario that unfolded for the tortured farm families seemed to fit perfectly with the antigovernment movement's prediction. For lack of a better explanation from a more reliable source, many believed and converted. Some of the rural refugees joined the ranks of the established movement, while others created their own antigovernment offshoots with names like We the People, Freemen, Christian Patriots, Family Farm Preservation, and North American Freedom Council. But regardless of what a new group calls itself, there's a tie that binds it to the past: The conspiracy theories and printed propaganda on which it bases its antigovernment dogma are being created and carefully controlled by the radical leaders of the old guard.

To understand today's antigovernment movement, we must understand its central conspiracy theories and determine why elements in today's rural crisis seem to fit so well with those teachings. We must decipher the complex nature of the one-world-government theory, which is the driving force of the antigovernment movement. This one-world theory originated in the Bible, was then enhanced through racist myths, and has now become the means for reinterpreting the very Bible from which it came—a deadly combination, as we will see. In today's antigovernment movement, religion and conspiracy are inseparable.

We must also look hard at the very real forces, such as banks, corporations, and government, that are playing a role in the tragic saga of rural restructuring. It's too easy to dismiss the movement's wild, racist theories about these real and powerful forces without looking for the proverbial grain of truth. Would the ancient Greeks have attributed the creation of lightning bolts to Zeus if the mysterious electrical charges hadn't actually been striking the ground? Like myths, conspiracy theories are, at their core, a distorted explanation of some sort of real occurrence.

There are only a few basic themes behind today's antigovernment teachings, but they are practically obscured by the conspiracy jargon: religion, the Constitution, the monetary system, gun control, international trade agreements, and monopolies. These are today's lightning bolts, and understanding that they are the true sources of the conspiracy rhetoric is the only chance to bridge the growing chasm that threatens to divide America.

An Acceptable War

A man cannot have two masters. Yahweh Yahshua Messiah, the anointed one of Saxon Israel, is our law giver and our king. We will obey him and no others . . . "A long forgotten wind is starting to blow. Do you hear the approaching thunder? It is that of the awakened Saxon. War is upon the land. The tyrants' blood will flow."

—Vicky Weaver,
1992 Ruby Ridge shoot-out victim[1]

With the help of the antigovernment movement, all the ingredients of the rural crisis—global economics, mental depression, corporate monopolies, and poorly planned government policies—are being passed through a sieve of religion, and this will ultimately determine the direction and intensity of the heartland war. At first glance, religion appears to be the driving force of the people in the antigovernment movement. Listen to their rhetoric or read their literature, and you will find it on or near the surface of almost every statement made. If you attend a movement function and ask people why they are there, most of their answers will pertain to God or patriotism. But if you stick around long enough to shake hands and get below the surface, you'll get another take on the situation: lost homes and farms, trouble with the IRS, inability to feed the family, a recent layoff, and the like. In my seven years' experience with the movement, I have rarely encountered people whose initiation into the "anti" cause couldn't be traced to an economic source. But in that same time period, it's been equally rare to find someone who would admit to their economic troubles right up front.

People in rural America are proud to a fault—to their own detriment. Church and social workers will tell you that it's sometimes hard to figure out which families are hurting because rural people refuse to publicly display their pain or accept anything resembling charity. Ag-Link counselor Mona Lee Brock told me that more often than not, she has to slip into people's kitchens and look in their empty cabinets to get an accurate picture of what's going on with a family. Even then, her clients will tell her that they're doing just fine. Brock has learned that the best strategy is to come back under the shadow of night and deliver groceries to these families, whose appreciation is often shown in tears.

Hard-core evangelists of the antigovernment message realized years ago that the majority of the rural population would never take up arms against the government, simply because these people were hungry and hurting. Such self-serving actions would violate everything that the rural lifestyle stood for: pride, loyalty, self-sufficiency. Ultimately, the movement's success in turning rural Americans against the government hinged on its ability to find a cause more powerful than the personal pain of farmers and their families.

The answer came from an unlikely place: the Bible. The most sacred writ of the heartland has been twisted into a literal call to arms against the federal government, a brilliant ploy that allows a desperate rural population a way of escaping the bounds of its own long-held traditions. Under the movement's guidance, the "economic" war that can't be fought has been transformed into the "holy" war that must be.

The Bible Tells Me So

Men, in the name of our Father, we are called upon to make a decision, a decision that you will make in the quietness of your heart, in the still places of the night. As you lie on your bed and look up at the ceiling tonight, you must answer the question: Will it be liberty or will it be death?

—Louis Beam, speech at Estes Park, Colorado, 1992[2]

Studies have shown that over 80 percent of the rural population claim some sort of affiliation to a church.[3] Just as with the majority of Americans, the religion of choice in the rural world is some form of Christianity. Even those who rarely, if ever, attend a church function consider themselves Christians, if for no other reason than that they were born in America. The foundation for this Christian influence has been laid by our history and supported by such customs as recital of the Pledge of Allegiance and the Lord's Prayer. Because of this orientation, it only makes sense that when the world is crashing down around them, rural people look to someone claiming to have a "Christian" explanation for their particular situation—regardless of how loosely the term is being applied.

Out of all the people I've met in the antigovernment movement, only a few have claimed to be anything other than some sort of Protestant Christian. Of these, some belonged to radical Catholic groups like those in and around St. Mary's, Kansas; others were part of Mormon "anti" factions sprinkled throughout Utah and Idaho. In addition, there are cultlike strongholds that have formed around a dominant personality, such as the Branch Davidians and their leader David Koresh. And occasionally, there are groups that claim that they want to change the government for purely secular, political reasons. All of these groups, with the exception of the secular type, have one commonality—a belief that the Bible justifies or even demands that they rebel against the current American government.

This belief that the Bible demands rebellion compels these rural warriors to see themselves as an army of holy patriots rather than as a mutinous force attempting a coup. They believe that the Bible is to be interpreted literally and that a proper understanding of its prophecies leaves true Christians with little choice but to fight. People are being taught that the founding fathers intended the country to be a Christian nation and that they wrote the Constitution with that in mind. Some groups teach that the Constitution was derived directly from the Bible and is therefore a sacred document. Recruits are told that God added the Second Amendment—the right to keep and bear arms—for an important reason: If the time ever came when the government strayed from its constitutional Christian purpose, the weapons of the people were to be used to force the government back onto its godly course. Many in the movement believe that now is the time for this armed, spiritual redirection. Christians who hold to this theocratic view of government are known as "dominionists."

Most of the people in the antigovernment movement fall into two categories: those claiming to be traditional Christian fundamentalists—composed of the usual denominations—and those who adhere to some or all of the teachings of the Christian Identity sect. Many, though not all, of the fundamentalists in the movement are of the dominionist persuasion. Identity believers are also dominionist, the difference being that they desire to establish a white theocracy in which their unique biblical interpretations would compose the rules.

The religious terminology used by both fundamentalist and Identity believers can, at first hearing, give the outsider the impression that the two groups are very similar. In truth, they are not. Fundamentalists view Identity beliefs as heresy, whereas Identity practitioners see fundamentalists as misled, Jew-loving wimps. The Identity movement relies heavily on its interpretation of the Old Testament to justify its beliefs that white people are the true nation of Israel, that Jews are the offspring of Satan, and that other minorities are soulless subhumans, a sort of creation experiment gone awry.

Fundamentalists, however, believe that Jews are the true nation of Israel—an idea that infuriates Identity believers—and that all people, regardless of race, are equal in God's eyes. Although there is some racism among the various fundamentalist groups, it seems to be tied to certain cultural roots. Fundamentalists make no argument to justify racism biblically, but Identity-influenced groups, such as the Aryan Nations and the Ku Klux Klan, attempt to do so.

In further comparing these two factions, it's safe to say that Identity believers are more prone to violence. Their white supremacist or, in some cases, separatist theology practically demands it. Identity adherents believe that they are God's enforcement arm. They believe that they should punish those of us who have strayed from the Old Testament's laws. Often, the prescribed punishment is death. To get a feel for the Identity movement and its goals, consider these comments made by Louis Beam, as he addressed members of his Texas Emergency Reserve Militia:

> Enough of this backing up and retreating. Enough of this lip service and no action. It's time to begin to train. It is time to begin to reclaim this country for white people. Now I want you to understand that they're not going to give it back to us. If you want it, you're going to have to get it the way the founding fathers got it—Blood! Blood! Blood! The founding fathers shed their blood to give you this country, and if you want to hold on to it, you're gonna have to shed some of yours. Never let any race but the white race rule this country.[4]

The theology of the fundamentalist groups is normally less violent than that of the Identity adherents, but there are exceptions. How dangerous a group becomes depends almost entirely upon how its leaders interpret the prophecies of the Bible. Within fundamentalist groups and throughout Identity factions, there is a subset of people who are operating under the belief that the violence-filled period predicted by the Bible and known as the tribulation is rapidly approaching or has already arrived. It's likely that this smaller group, the one influenced by the tribulation belief, is responsible for the antigovernment movement's most violent episodes such as the Oklahoma City bombing. They believe that they have nothing to lose since the end of the world has arrived. Several of the people I've interviewed have told me that the tribulation has already started and that God has commanded them to start carrying out his judgments. "We're holding courts right now in every part of this land," said an Identity believer from California who identified himself only as Tim. "We're finding people guilty and we're keeping records so we can carry out the sentences." When asked how these death sentences would be carried out, Tim said, "There's a part of the militia that's getting ready to start working on that [death sentences]. I think they're ready to go now. You'll start seeing it soon." Tim was right.

Most Americans are unaware that they are already feeling the impact of this apocalyptic time of judgment. The Oklahoma City and Atlanta bombings; the countless pipe bomb incidents; the illegal liens, such as those filed by the Montana Freemen; the common-law courts; and many of the bank robberies that we read about in the daily papers—all are part of the antigovernment movement's "time of judgment."

Despite their mutual dislike and their extreme differences in biblical interpretation, fundamentalists and Identity adherents have, of late, managed to bury the hatchet in their pursuit of a common goal: a new Christian government. Presumably, they will hash out the theology of their new theocracy once they have toppled the existing democratic regime. In the last two years, while meeting with various antigovernment factions throughout the United States, I have noticed a marked increase in the number of groups that now have both fundamentalist and Identity adherents under one roof.

A Common Enemy

This idea of putting aside differences for a common goal got a big boost in 1992. On August 21, marshals, assisted by FBI agents, scaled Idaho's Ruby Ridge in an attempt to arrest white separatist

Randy Weaver for missing a court date to settle a minor firearms charge. During their surveillance of the Weaver cabin, the family pet, a dog named Striker, wandered toward the marshals and began to bark. Fearing that their position would be given away, one of the marshals shot the dog.

Unfortunately, Randy Weaver's fourteen-year-old son, Sammy, witnessed the incident and reacted as any teenager might under the circumstances. He fired his rifle in the direction of the unknown men who had shot his dog. As he turned to run back toward the cabin, the marshals shot Sammy Weaver in the back. The boy died a few minutes later, and a standoff ensued.

The next day, Randy Weaver and houseguest Kevin Harris went to the small shed next to the cabin where they had placed Sammy's body. As they ran back toward the main house, Randy's wife, forty-three-year-old Vicky Weaver, opened the door for the two men while holding her ten-month-old daughter in one arm. Just as the men reached the cabin, an FBI sniper fired a shot that blew off much of Vicky's head. She bled to death on the floor of her cabin a few minutes later, still holding her baby daughter. Randy Weaver—and what was left of his family—surrendered to authorities nine days later.

The government had badly overreacted, a point that would be proven in 1993 by famed attorney Gerry Spence, who represented Randy Weaver at his trial. Time and again, Spence told the jury that Randy Weaver's Christian Identity beliefs were irrelevant. He pointed out that in America, the government has no right to kill you or your family just because you are a white separatist who was coerced by a government agent into cutting off the barrel of a shotgun. Spence's words helped to convince the nation that the government had been out of control. Many Americans didn't grasp the importance of the Weaver case until after the trial. But there was one group of people who understood its significance even as Vicky Weaver's shattered body was hitting the cabin floor.

In response to the Weaver tragedy, 160 people gathered in Estes Park, Colorado, on October 22, 1992. The meeting later became known as the Rocky Mountain Rendezvous. The assembly was made up of the Who's Who of the radical Right, including John and Randy Trochmann from the Montana militia; Louis Beam; Richard Butler, founder of the Aryan Nations; Identity pastor Pete Peters; tax protester Red Beckman; and scores of Identity believers. But the meeting was more than an Identity revival. Also present were mainstream fundamentalist representatives from Baptists to Mennonites. Larry Pratt, founder of Gun Owners of America, who for a short time served as Pat Buchanan's right-hand man during his 1996 presidential campaign, was also in attendance.

The rendezvous brought together a collection of men who would normally never sit down together. Prior to the Weaver incident, their divergent religious beliefs would have overshadowed any common ground they might have had. But in 1992, all that changed. They now understood that they had a common enemy—the federal government. They knew that their only chance to defeat this common foe was to join forces. In some ways, this meeting may well have been the birth of the modern antigovernment movement. Morris Dees, of the Southern Poverty Law Center—which, among other things, operates Klanwatch, an organization that keeps tabs on right-wing extremist groups—described the rendezvous this way: "Plans were laid for a citizen's militia movement like none this country has ever known. It's a movement that has already led to the most destructive act of terrorism in our nation's history [the Oklahoma City bombing]. Unless checked, it could lead to widespread devastation or ruin."[5]

The "common enemy" theme was summed up best by Rendezvous participant Louis Beam, who said,

> The two murders of the Weaver family have shown us all that our religious, our political, our ideological differences mean nothing to those who wish to make us all slaves. We are viewed by the government as the same—the enemies of the state.
>
> When they come for you, the federals will not ask if you are a Constitutionalist, a Baptist, Church of Christ, Identity Covenant Believer, Klansman, Nazi, homeschooler, Freeman New Testament believer, [or] fundamentalist. . . . Those who wear badges, black boots, and carry automatic weapons and kick in doors already know all they need to know about you. You are enemies of the state.[6]

What's missing from Beam's words are the racial slurs that usually fill his diatribes. In fact, the hard-core racism that drives Identity-influenced groups was nearly invisible during the entire weekend retreat—a development more significant than any other aspect of the Estes Park gathering. This missing ingredient marked the beginning of a new era, a change in strategy for the radical Right. The racism that had long been a barrier to its recruiting efforts in rural America went underground. The Identity movement's long-held concept of a white America would now be given a new, more acceptable, moniker: "Christian America."

Since 1992, fundamentalist and Identity adherents have been fighting the same enemy, using the same words—at least in public—and professing the same goal, a new Christian government. Since the Weaver tragedy, rendezvous participants have formed militia units, common-law courts, and sovereign townships from California to North Carolina. It's as if a temporary antigovernment amnesia now binds these incompatible religions together. And the longer they're bound together, the more their ideologies and behaviors take on a single hate-filled form—an unfortunate end result that was likely the very goal of the Identity factions attending the rendezvous.

The End of the World

For nation will rise against nation, and kingdom against kingdom, and in various places there will be famines and earthquakes.
But things are merely the beginning of birth pangs.
Then they will deliver you to tribulation, and will kill you, and you will be hated by all nations on account of My name.
And at that time many will fall away and will deliver up one another and hate one another.
And many false prophets will arise, and will mislead many.
And because lawlessness is increased, most people's love will grow cold.
—Matthew 24:7–12

Is the tribulation at hand? Perhaps it would be more accurate to ask, Is "a" tribulation at hand? The one thing that's certain is that a holy war is blazing all across the nation in the form of terrorist bombings in places like Oklahoma City, Atlanta, Los Angeles, Spokane, and Dallas. Which holy war it is—whether the one described in the Bible or the one started by people who decided the Bible version was taking too long to get here—doesn't really matter. For the men, women, and children killed by bomb shrapnel or assassinated in front of their homes, for law enforcement officers shot dead trying to arrest antigovernment radicals, or even for the radicals themselves who are killed by authorities, the tribulation is here. The death and destruction are real.

Bible-influenced antigovernment groups believe that Jesus will one day return to earth. They also believe that the closer we get to that day, the more we will experience pestilence, famine, and cultural up-heaval. This is all part of the tribulation—a time Christians believe will be defined by the appearance of new technologies; by the "mark of the Beast" (the symbolic number 666) being put upon our bodies; by the creation of a one-world government headed by the Antichrist; and by the murder and persecution of Christians. It's at the end of this period of tribulation that the Battle of Armageddon—the final battle between Jesus' forces of good and Satan's forces of evil—will be fought, ushering in a one-thousand-year period of peace known as the Millennium. At some point during this tribulation process, the rapture will take place. The rapture is the simultaneous ascension of all Christians. Most fundamentalists believe this will happen in a sin-gle moment without any warning: A Christian driving down the road will suddenly disappear, leaving the car to careen out of control.

Christian teachers have been warning their followers that the tribu-lation is approaching for years. But their doomsday messages have es-calated of late, for a number of reasons. First, we are rapidly ap-proaching the end of a century. Historians have noted that apocalyptic scenarios always escalate before a change of century, and not just among Christians. New Age believers also point to the year 2000 as the beginning of a new era. Many Hopi Indians have inter-preted the appearance of the Hale-Bopp comet in the sky in March 1997 as fulfillment of their "Yellow Star" legend. According to some Hopis, the comet marks the end of the world by the year 2004.[7]

Another reason for the increase in end-times thinking is that the media have made the delivery of apocalyptic information easier, faster, and more profitable. Christian authors like Hal Lindsey and Pat Robertson have created a pseudoscience, not to mention a pretty good living, out of their end-of-the-world interpretations of biblical prophecy. Lindsey, in books beginning with the publication in the 1970s of *The Late Great Planet Earth* and ending with his 1995 *Planet Earth 2000,* has interpreted thousands of today's current events, such as Israel becoming a nation in 1948, as absolute proof that the tribulation is just around the corner. Lindsey's work is im-portant because it offers a clue to how many people hold his apoca-lyptic worldview and, therefore, may be more susceptible to antigov-ernment end-times conspiracy theories. In that context, it's not a good sign that Lindsey's books have sold over thirty million copies.

The biggest problem for pop prophets like Lindsey and Robertson seems to be keeping up to speed with the unraveling of the world.

Robertson's 1991 release, *The New World Order*, starts out with a description of the August 1991 coup attempt in the Soviet Union. Robertson tells his readers that the book was "on the presses" when this significant piece of the prophetic puzzle transpired. He had to stop the presses to get it in. Robertson goes on to explain how the coup was staged to make Mikhail Gorbachev, president of the Soviet Union at the time, look more democratic. Robertson says that the coup was a KGB ploy orchestrated by eight of Gorbachev's buddies, including Boris Yeltsin, designed with the ultimate goal of getting the West to cut back its military capabilities, thus making it possible for the new world order to usher in the reign of the Antichrist. Although Robertson didn't mention it, I'm sure that peculiar birthmark on Gorbachev's head figured into the scenario somehow.

It doesn't disturb me that Pat Robertson is trying to keep his flock prepared for what he claims to be the inevitable and immediate end of the world. However, the absolute authority with which he makes his predictions concerning every political nuance that occurs on the planet works people into a paranoid frenzy—a dangerous and paranoid frenzy. It's too bad Robertson couldn't have stopped the presses again and told his followers something like this: "Cancel that last dogmatic, prophetic prediction. It seems that the Soviet Union really is falling apart and its people are near starvation. The wall is coming down and Yeltsin wasn't Gorbachev's buddy after all and this is a legitimate opportunity to help the Soviets develop a market economy and a democratic government."

If Robertson, Lindsey, and the other seers would write an equal number of books describing the times their "absolute proof of the world's end" has been completely wrong, we would, no doubt, have thousands fewer people in rural places storing food and weapons for their impending war with the government of the Antichrist. In many antigovernment circles—and that includes the survivalists (those who remove themselves from society in an effort to survive the end-times violence)—books by Lindsey and Robertson have become required reading, the first step in movement initiation. Randy and Vicky Weaver are said to have been heavily influenced by *The Late Great Planet Earth* before moving from Iowa to their isolated cabin atop Ruby Ridge.

Whereas Lindsey tends to stick to prophecy, Robertson has been very vocal in his antigovernment rhetoric. Between his Christian Coalition and his *700 Club* television show, Robertson has exerted a powerful influence over millions of people, a fact that lends his words great importance and makes them deserving of careful scrutiny.

In early 1997, I found myself watching Pat Robertson interview William Bennett, the former drug czar and secretary of education under Ronald Reagan, on the *700 Club*. They were expressing their usual disdain for the government and bemoaning the decline of morality in the American culture. All the while, they were hawking Bennett's new book about virtues, which had already sold some 2.5 million copies—"and don't forget the new video version."

The conversation contained such quips as "It's not about the enemy out there, it's about good and evil right here." "The governing elites have turned against their own society." "They [the governing elites] have been attacking the American people." Then, Bennett made an interesting observation while discussing a particularly foul-mouthed bunch of rock 'n rollers about whom Robertson had been complaining. He pointed out that the information being transmitted by television and radio is more powerful than anything happening in Washington, D.C.

I couldn't have agreed more. I wondered if TV preachers like Robertson, whose *700 Club* reaches five million people almost daily, realize that their message of an evil government is being interpreted as a literal call to arms by countless people across the country? I wondered if these men ever consider the impact they have on the lives of a stressed-out rural population that is already being bombarded by toxic antigovernment conspiracy theories, which are just souped-up versions of Robertson's message. What are rural people to do when they hear their trusted TV preacher telling them nearly the same thing as movement radicals who are calling them to arms? Bennett was right. Television is more powerful than Washington. Knowingly or not, media prophets have become directly involved in the growth of the antigovernment movement in numerous ways— through their "anti" rhetoric, their prophecies for the world's end, or through their silence when they fail to discourage paranoid antigovernment behavior.

For years, traveling messengers of impending doom made their way along our back roads, creating small groups of converts to their apocalyptic doctrines. But these days, with the rural landscape in worse shape than ever and with the power of television as a vehicle, the end of the world has never seemed so real to so many. A 1994 survey conducted by Market Facts Telenation found that 59 percent of American adults fear that the world will come to an end. Twelve percent of the population believe it will happen in the next few years. That means there are approximately 25 million people whose lives are being influenced by their belief that the end has arrived.[8]

Pretribulation, Post-tribulation

There are literally millions of Christian fundamentalists who, like Robertson, oppose the current federal government as a part of their basic dogma. These believers are often referred to as the "New Right," and they are basically Christian dominionists. That is, they believe that America should follow the precept "One Nation Under God" and be more a theocracy than a democracy and that it is their job to return the nation to biblical rule. These dominionists believe that the current government is being influenced by the supernatural forces of the Antichrist, forces that are leading the people away from this Christian rule.

For now, the majority of dominionists are interested in the idea of antigovernment politics only in order to use their votes to push the nation toward this perceived original Christian intent. They're more interested in a democratic Contract-with-America approach to forcing change than a violent one. But there is a more radical minority of dominionists, including Identity believers, who see pipe bombs as the means to their end. How radical this theocentric population eventually becomes is, to a large degree, contingent upon its members' different theologies, particularly their personal interpretations of biblical prophecy.

There's no better illustration of how a seemingly subtle theological nuance can have a major impact on an antigovernment believer's actions than the differing interpretations regarding the tribulation. The vast majority of fundamentalists fall into one of two categories: pretribulation or post-tribulation.

On the one hand, "pretrib" Christians, including Lindsey and Robertson, believe that they will be called up to heaven by the rapture before the tribulation begins. Consequently, they're not likely to become convinced that now is the time for a holy war. The fact that they're still earthbound is proof to them that the tribulation has not yet started. Hal Lindsey has made a point to tell his followers that they shouldn't take radical action and need not go beyond prayer and repentance because they'll be carried away by the rapture before the tribulation arrives.

On the other hand, "post-trib" Christians believe that they will have to live through the tribulation before they're raptured. They are therefore left to use their own faculties to determine at what point they've entered that terrible time. For these believers, the stress of poverty, the loss of a farm, or any other devastating circumstance can be interpreted as a sign that the tribulation has started and, consequently, that now is the time for an all-out holy war. The words of the TV prophets can push these believers over the edge.

In my experience, those of the pretrib, antigovernment persuasion are just as strongly opposed to the government as their post-trib brethren, but they are more likely to exhibit that opposition by participating in some form of peaceful defiance such as common-law courts, refusing to pay their taxes, or home schooling their children. As a group, they are less likely to become terrorists.

On the other hand, the Christian dominionists and Identity believers with a post-tribulation theology compose the ranks of the movement's more violent underbelly. For them, there is no theological roadblock to declaring war on the government and establishing a theocracy. In fact, once they become convinced that the time has arrived, they believe it's a sin not to fight. Much of the energy of the movement's most radical elements—particularly among Identity believers—is being directed at convincing people that the war has begun. In Identity circles, people have already declared war on the Zionist Occupied Government. ZOG describes the current federal government, which Identity followers believe is already under control of the demon Jews. And in their view, this is not some intellectual, political, or spiritual war designed to intimidate enemies. It's a real war of guns, assassinations, bombs, and death.

Anti–Uncle Sam Wants You

The one-world conspiracy theory, which has given birth to creations like ZOG, has allowed the movement to convert religious rural Americans into antigovernment soldiers. It's the great conspiracy theory, along with the smaller conspiracy offshoots, that gives the movement the appearance of being able to explain what's going on in the world. And these supposed explanations enable the movement to target specific segments of the population for recruiting.

Today's antigovernment groups have become particularly astute at salvaging economic refugees for their greater purpose. They work the crowds at foreclosure sales, telling people that the sale is part of the Antichrist's plan to control the food supply of Christians. They tell people that the Constitution says they don't have to pay income tax. They promise farmers that they can recover their farm even after it has been sold at auction. They describe how the government took the United States off the gold standard as part of a plot to rob us of our wealth. They even take out ads in local newspapers and offer spiritual guidance to people who are losing their property. The movement has had great success with this economic targeting, but it also reaches out with strategies designed to entangle those involved in other religious-political debates such as those over abortion, gay rights, home schooling, and doctor-assisted suicide.

The movement carefully constructs its message to convince people—who have already become politically charged over these other issues—that these religious and political issues of the day are all part of a bigger plot by an evil government to desensitize them to perversion and murder, steps necessary to eventually enthrone the Antichrist. As is the case with converts pulled into the movement through poverty, many of those won over on these other issues are already in a mental frenzy, just looking for a direction to vent their anger.

One of the movement's most successful recruiting grounds over the last decade has proven to be the pro-life movement, which has become very much a part of the antigovernment phenomenon. Militant groups that oppose the government are overflowing with people who started in the pro-life movement but became frustrated with what they perceived to be pro-life's often less than radical approach to stopping the murder of children.

Most people thought episodes like Operation Rescue, in which thousands of pro-life activists shut down the abortion clinics in several cities by orchestrating massive sit-ins, were radical. But hardliners viewed such strategies as merely another form of protest that only accomplished its goal for a few hours, at best. The antigovernment movement offers these hard-liners a chance to actually stop abortion by blowing up clinics or even killing those who perform the abortions. The bombing of an Atlanta clinic in late January 1997 is a perfect illustration of the two movements' merging. Two bombs were exploded: The first was positioned to destroy the clinic; the second was hidden near a dumpster and was set to explode one hour later. In

THE RELIGION OF CONSPIRACY 91

all likelihood, this second explosion was designed to kill Bureau of Alcohol, Tobacco, and Firearms (ATF), FBI, and media personnel (those said to be a part of the one-world conspiracy), who the bombers knew would rush to the scene after the first explosion. In the most radical levels of the antigovernment movement, it was the best of both worlds. Fortunately, two parked cars shielded most of the intended victims of the second blast from the deadly shrapnel, and there were only a few injuries.

The fact that pro-life groups are largely composed of fundamentalist Christians makes them a perfect recruiting ground for the dominionist antigovernment movement. Converts from the pro-life factions enter the movement already possessing a required ingredient: the understanding that there's no room for compromise.

Both the antiabortion and antigovernment movements are the very real manifestations of dominionist theology carried to its logical end. If the Bible, including its many Old Testament laws, is the inerrant word of God that must be adhered to, then both of these factions have no choice but to exist and to pursue their ultimate goal of establishing a fundamentalist Christian government that will treat abortion as murder and strike down any statutes that contradict their interpretation of the biblical laws.

The Funnel

Understanding that Christian fundamentalism is the backbone of the antigovernment movement is important because this illustrates the ultimate potential for the movement's growth. In *A Force upon the Plain* by Kenneth S. Stern, Kenneth Toole of the Montana Human Rights Network describes the antigovernment movement as being analogous to a funnel. How many people are eventually forced down into the deepest, most violent levels of the movement is limited only by the breadth of the funnel's larger end. In other words, if the millions of people who practice fundamental Christianity and believe we should have a biblically based government represent the big end of the funnel, then it stands to reason that a large number of very radical people will eventually be forced through the funnel's smaller, more violent end.

Atlanta felt the results of this funnel effect in February 1997. A few weeks after the clinic blast, an additional attack targeted an Atlanta gay bar. Authorities found the second bomb before it exploded. A group calling itself the Army of God took credit for both the clinic and the bar bombings. Authorities have speculated that the same bombers may be responsible for the 1996 Olympic bombing in Atlanta's Centennial Park. This target also fits with the conspiracists' one-world theory. In radical factions of the movement, the Olympics are seen as an attempt to foster cooperation among the world's governments and break down desirable cultural barriers—hastening the arrival of the evil, one-world government. The targets chosen indicate that the bombers could be Identity believers, fundamental-dominionists, or a combination of the two. Whatever the group's makeup, these Atlanta bombings have ushered in the new era of religion-based terrorist attacks in the United States. Targets will no longer be limited to those tied to the government. They will now include any and all that this holy "anti" force perceives to be its enemies, the breakers of the holy laws. Transgressors will include gays, blacks, Jews, and other minorities; doctors who perform abortions; people in mixed marriages; proponents of other religions such as Islam, Buddhism, Hinduism, and New Age believers; manufacturers of products deemed to be offensive; and media personnel whose reports are found to be blasphemous.

Increasing the Flow

Most people aren't joiners, but millions of white Americans who five years ago felt so cowed by the government and [the Jewish-] controlled media that they were afraid to agree with us are becoming fed up, and their exasperation is giving them courage.

—William Pierce, author of *The Turner Diaries*, 1994[9]

The flow toward radicalism within the antigovernment "funnel" is being enhanced through a subplot that is now taking shape in the movement's recruiting efforts. The more violent Identity believers are attempting to attract fundamental-dominionists to their own violent, racist message.

I knew a man with tax problems who was active in a small fundamentalist church. As soon as the IRS filed its tax liens against him, he started to receive a subscription to *Media Bypass*, a magazine that bills itself as the "uncensored national news." The magazine is sympathetic to the movement and the Identity message. The man had no idea who had sent him the magazine or for what purpose, yet within weeks of receiving the publication, he was sharing conspiracy theories about "the illegal income tax" with the other members of his congregation. A few months later, antigovernment and Identity talk had become commonplace among the one hundred or so members of the small church.

Susan DeCamp of the Montana Association of Churches told me about another technique she has seen used by evangelical Identity believers. Several Identity families will move into a rural area and start attending the same church, usually a small fundamentalist congregation. Over time, they slowly begin to insert their Identity doctrines into the meetings, sooner or later getting a hold on the group. By the time the pastors of the infected congregations figure out what's going on, it's too late. Even if church leaders ask the Identity people to take their conspiracy-laden white supremacist beliefs elsewhere, most often the Identity infiltrators have already made converts that leave with them. Occasionally, the entire church, including its leadership, will begin to incorporate the radical Identity message into its doctrine.

The Identity movement also spreads its influence by using a top-down strategy. Several rural pastors have told me about being invited to meetings billed as rural chaplain seminars. The events were supposed to be an opportunity to share ideas on how best to deal with rural issues in the church. But the real purpose was to infuse the visitors with the Identity gospel. Some pastors left when they realized what the agenda was, but presumably, those who stayed took the new teachings back to their unsuspecting congregations.

The Identity movement's techniques for spreading its message are working surprisingly well. A great deal of its success can, no doubt, be attributed to its new and less blatantly racist style of recruitment, as the speech at the Estes Park gathering quoted earlier in the chapter demonstrates. Under the guise of the "common enemy" theme, Identity adherents can now interact with non-Identity dominionists for long periods of time. And Identity believers are slowly infusing fundamentalist groups with their ultimate purpose: creating a white dominionist nation where the Bible is the law. The success of this approach is more understandable when you consider that the Identity game plan has been tailored to fit a stressed-out rural population that perceives that its way of life is being destroyed by such modern agendas as affirmative action, the environmental movement, global economics, gay rights, abortion, gun control, and pretty much any cause taken up by the ACLU. This recruiting subplot is important because as Identity spreads, so does the promotion of violence by the antigovernment movement. For that reason, it is imperative to examine the beliefs of Identity adherents.

Identity 101

Identity is not racist. Jews and blacks are what they are. God chose to make Jews the offspring of Satan and he chose to make blacks with the animals, we didn't. I have to believe God, and he spelled it out clear in the Bible. I'd give the shirt off my back to a black man if he came to my door. But I can't make him the same as me.

—Tim Houser, Identity believer, 1996

Racism is a sin in the humanist religion, not the true Christian faith based on the Bible.
—Pete Peters, Identity preacher[10]

We intend to establish God's law as our government.
—Gary Yarbrough (currently in prison),
Identity believer and member of Aryan Nations, 1985[11]

Christian Identity, which is also known as British Israelism, Israel Identity, and Kingdom Message, got its start in Great Britain in the mid-1800s. The best estimate for the number of Identity believers is approximately three million worldwide, a number that can hardly be classified as insignificant.

The Identity doctrine holds that white Christians are the true Israelites of the Old Testament and therefore are God's chosen people. For that reason, Identity proponents in the United States believe that America is the true promised land (Israel) spoken of in the Bible. They teach that the ten lost tribes of Israel migrated from the Middle East to Europe, Great Britain, and, eventually, the United States and that an accurate accounting of history proves that these lost tribes were Saxon (white). This belief has created two strands within Identity: the white separatists and the white supremacists. The separatists believe that the races should not mingle, but they stop short of saying that the white race is superior. The supremacist views are those espoused by the KKK, Aryan Nations, and other radical dominionist groups.

The supremacists' hatred of Jews and other minorities is founded in their belief in a Jewish new-world-order conspiracy, which they claim is revealed in the Bible. The idea that there is a conspiracy by Jews to take over the world is not new. In fact, this conspiracy theory predates the appearance of the Identity movement. Some scholars believe that it was actually this preexisting anti-Semitic idea that influenced Christian Identity's founders to adopt their controversial interpretations of the Bible. The account of the creation and other teachings in the Identity doctrine are assembled in such a way as to transform the new-world-order conspiracy theory into a religious theology.

Perhaps the most controversial of the Identity teachings is the two-seed theory. The idea is that nonwhites were created along with the other soulless animals—before Adam and Eve—and lived outside the Garden of Eden. They were, as the teaching claims, a sort of subhuman species that had more in common with beasts than men. Identity doctrine further instructs that when Eve sinned by eating the apple, she was impregnated with two seeds: one from Adam, which produced Abel, and one from Satan (the serpent), which produced Cain. Then Cain killed Abel and ran away to live with the subhuman nonwhites. Consequently, Jews, blacks, and other minorities are descendants of the seed of Satan through Cain.

After observing the Identity interpretation of biblical creationism, it is easy to see why some of the movement's adherents have a hard time believing that they are racists. After all, can you be racist over goats or chickens? Can you be called a racist for despising Satan? How can you be a racist if the group you are accused of subjugating is not even human? However, taking these beliefs to their logical end opens the door to far more heinous transgressions than mere racism.

In his book *Gathering Storm*, Morris Dees of the Southern Poverty Law Center reached this conclusion:

> It is through these and other interpretations of the Bible that Identity gives its followers a sense of divine guidance and approval to engage in racial hatred, bigotry, and murder. When Identity councils "lawful" ways and means, it does not mean local, state, and federal statutes. It means God's law. Literally. Therefore, if one accepts the Identity's teaching that Jews are the children of Satan and people of color are subhuman, one can kill with a clear conscience. It is neither a sin, nor is it against the law, to murder a race-mixer when a person is simply following God's commandments. Instead, it is virtuous. It is righteous.[12]

Dees's observation that Identity teachings lead to violence has been confirmed by the new trend in movement terrorism, as exhibited in the Atlanta and Oklahoma City bombings. Identity adherents believe that they should judge the rest of us by the standards of the Old Testament laws, as set out in the Bible's Book of Ecclesiastes. At the

Rocky Mountain Rendezvous, Identity pastor Pete Peters elaborated on his goal for the new movement. "There is a host of Christian soldiers . . . that are willing and able to do something but they don't know what to do. If given a direction, a powerful force could be tapped, harnessed, and used for the establishment of a Christian civil body politic for carrying out the judgments of God."[13]

Unfortunately, Identity teachings only allow for a single punishment: death. That's the sentence for being a homosexual or a murderer. An Identity farmer in Oklahoma explained it to me this way: "We believe in God's law and justice, not prisons."

It goes without saying that the Identity doctrine adamantly encourages segregation at all costs. Any sort of mixing of races is a sin. To drive home this point, Identity-influenced groups have gone so far as to create a map showing what a fully segregated United States will look like. A copy of the map, titled "The National Premise" and subtitled "A Proposed Geographical Relocation and Regrouping of America's Unassimilable Minorities," ran in the December 1984 issue of David Duke's *NAAWP News* (National Association for the Advancement of White People). The map shows small colored areas of land where minorities would be forced to live. The areas have names like Navahona (for Indians) and New Africa (for blacks). According to the map, the minorities get about 10 percent of the United States; white Americans retain the rest.

As pointed out by Louis Beam to his militia, Identity believers are aware that nonwhites will never assume their assigned stations voluntarily. Consequently, the map would not come into play until after Christian Identity's "day of judgment"—the day when godly justice (Identity-style) is doled out all across America to those who have transgressed the law. In his book of Identity wishful-fiction, titled *The Turner Diaries*, William Pierce paints a vivid and horrible picture of this day of judgment if Identity has its way. It's one thing to think of Identity as an esoteric belief system, but it's quite another to think of it in real-life terms. Pierce's description of Identity's concept of practical application is nothing less than shocking. Timothy McVeigh was in possession of photocopied portions of *The Turner Diaries* at the time of his arrest in the Oklahoma City bomb case. The following is an excerpt from that book.

> Today has been the day of the rope—a grim and bloody day, but an unavoidable one. Tonight, for the first time in weeks, it is quiet and totally

peaceful throughout all of southern California. But the night is filled with silent horrors; from tens of thousands of lampposts, power poles, and trees throughout this vast metropolitan area the grisly forms hang.

In the lighted areas one sees them everywhere. Even the street signs at intersections have been pressed into service, and at practically every street corner I passed this evening on my way to HQ there was a dangling corpse, four at every intersection. Hanging at a single overpass only about a mile from here is a group of about 30, each with an identical placard around its neck bearing the printed legend, "I betrayed my race." Two or three in that group had been decked out in academic robes before they were strung up, and the whole batch are apparently faculty members from the nearby UCLA campus.

In the areas to which we have not restored electrical power the corpses are less visible, but the feeling of horror in the air there is even worse than in the lighted area. I had to walk through a two-block-long, unlighted residential section between HQ and my living quarters after our unit meeting tonight. In the middle of one of the unlighted blocks I saw what appeared to be a person standing on the sidewalk directly in front of me. As I approached the silent figure, whose features were hidden in the shadow of a large tree overhanging the sidewalk, it remained motionless, blocking my way.

Feeling some apprehension, I slipped my pistol out of its holster. Then, when I was within a dozen feet of the figure, which had been facing away from me, it began turning slowly toward me. There was something indescribably eerie about the movement, and I stopped in my tracks as the figure continued to turn. A slight breeze rustled the foliage overhead, and suddenly a beam of moonlight broke through the leaves and fell directly on the slightly turning shape before me.

The first thing I saw in the moonlight was the placard with its legend in large, block letters: "I defiled my race." Above the placard leered the horribly bloated, purplish face of a young woman, her eyes wide open and bulging, her mouth agape. Finally I could make out the thin, vertical line of rope disappearing into the branches above. Apparently the rope had slipped a bit or the branch to which it was tied had sagged, until the woman's feet were resting on the pavement, giving the uncanny appearance of a corpse standing upright of its own volition.

I shuddered and quickly went on my way. There are many thousands of hanging female corpses like that in this city tonight, all wearing identical placards around their necks. They are the white women who were married to or living with Blacks, with Jews, or with other non-white males.[14]

If we keep in mind that Pierce's words are used as a guide by Identity believers, we can better imagine the thoughts that lurk in the dark corners of Timothy McVeigh's mind, and we can better assess the horrible potential for violence that exists within certain radical elements of the movement, such as in Atlanta's Army of God. It's clear that their thirst for righteousness gained through other people's blood is limitless—and I'm not talking about Jesus Christ. We cannot take these groups lightly or pretend that they are a disorganized bunch of ragtag fringe dwellers who will soon go away. The terrible truth is that the radical Identity adherents are substantial in number, and they are becoming more influential throughout the antigovernment movement every day. They are well organized and heavily armed—and they are fully committed to a holy war that has already been declared. They will continue to be a deadly force in America for many years to come.

Who's the Enemy?

*It is strongly suggested that ALL Christian Americans purchase at least nine months of food for Everyone in the family, munitions, guns, and other supplies.
. . .*

   The Posse is growing in ranks . . . The middle-class workers are striding with us, having found out why they are unemployed. The corrupt Jewish money and banking system that has bankrupted this Christian republic is the cause for the illegal foreclosures of their property.

   The "Cashless Society" [bank computers] is now interlocked from East to West Coast. Each business can be connected with their electric cash register through a telephone hookup to their local bank computer . . . Isn't it nice how Rockefeller and his Jewish cohorts have made it so easy. Only one thing wrong—many people are waking up to the scheme and also to the constitutionality of LAWFUL MONEY versus PHONEY MONEY and the LAWS and RIGHTS of "We the People." . . .

   The Federal Reserve System is a private Banking system that manipulates the international gold and silver standard in the world. It is run by the Rockefellers and can create the recessions and depressions at will.

Please bear in mind that the Jews controlling our government on the local, state, and federal level, are selling the American people down the river.

Matt. 12:34–37, John 8:41–47, Luke 19:27

   Arm every American, there are criminals on the loose in Washington.

—James P. Wickstrom,
national director of counterinsurgency,
Posse Comitatus, *Posse Noose Report,* May 1981

Since the antigovernment movement has declared war, it would be helpful to know who the enemy is. It is in this arena of "creating the foe" that conspiracy becomes the all-powerful force, overshadowing every other element of thought, including religion.

Today's antigovernment teachings are the result of three factors: fundamentalist interpretations of the Bible, fundamentalist interpretations of the Constitution, and the belief in a one-world conspiracy. When these three are mixed together, they paint a terrifying picture of what's going on in the world. The Bible describes the horrific events of the end-times in somewhat vague and symbolic terms, whereas conspiracy theories conveniently flesh out all the details omitted by the scriptures. The man-made details that drape the biblical framework are designed to explain American culture's most unacceptable events: loss of property, wealth, and individual freedoms—the very losses that most rural people believe they are experiencing as a result of the global restructuring.

Most of the antigovernment movement's conspiracy theories—and there are hundreds, if not thousands, of them—are used to explain specific parts of its larger one-world government, aka the new world order theory. In today's version of this conspiracy, the major players are as follows: the banks, the Federal Reserve, the IMF (International Monetary Fund), the World Bank, the federal government, communism (despite its collapse), the United Nations, the Trilateral Commission, the IRS, the multinational corporations, the media, and the world's Jewish population, which acts through various secret organizations such as the Illuminati and Freemasons (more on which later).

Within the movement, there are many subtle variations on the one-world conspiracy. For Christian Identity believers, it's a Jewish conspiracy. For others, such as traditional fundamentalists, it's a conspiracy composed of the evil forces of the Antichrist, not necessarily Jews. But for the most part, the story is the same, and it goes something like this: A one-world government is being formed under the auspices of the United Nations, the Trilateral Commission, or some other mysterious quasi-governmental agency that's really controlled by the Illuminati or Freemasons, or both. Conspiracists see the United Nations as usurping the historic independence of the United States and other countries. They believe that it is solidifying its position of power by using the World Bank and the IMF to make huge loans of worthless paper money—too big to ever be repaid—to countries throughout the world. Once a country falls under the power of this unrepayable debt, it is forced to dance to the tune of the international bankers, who, according to the rhetoric, are composed of the world's richest Jewish families. The idea is that once all the governments of the world are under the control of the United Nations, the Antichrist will step in and assume all power.

Antigovernment proponents believe that the United States is now one of these "controlled" countries. They believe that when the United States went off the gold standard as the basis of its monetary system and adopted the current Federal Reserve system, political leaders were really just fulfilling the biblical prophecies by giving the forces of the Antichrist the reins of government and instituting a means to take away the property and freedom of the people, actions that will ultimately result in the control of all Christians. And to make sure that this grand plan goes unopposed, the infiltrated government is now attempting to take away our guns—the very firepower that we could use to thwart this enemy within. Those in the movement are quick to point out that this sinister scenario could not have transpired had America adhered to the original intent of the Constitution.

A Two-Thousand-Year-Old Idea

That same year, 1782, the headquarters of the Illuminated Freemasonry moved to Frankfurt, a center controlled by the Rothschild family. It is reported that in Frankfurt, Jews for the first time were admitted to the order of Freemasons. If indeed members of the Rothschild family or their close associates were polluted by the occultism of Weishaupts Illuminated Freemasonry, we may have discovered the link between the occult and the world of high finance. Remember the Rothschilds financed Cecil Rhodes in Africa; Lord Rothschild was a member of Rhodes' English Round Tables; and Paul Warburg, architect of the Federal Reserve System, was a Rothschild agent.

—Pat Robertson, *The New World Order*

The roots of this one-world government conspiracy theory can be traced directly to the Bible. Both the Old and New Testaments contain plenty of prophecies that have historically been interpreted as predicting that the end of the world will be the result of political maneuvering on the part of the Antichrist.

For centuries, Christians have tried to interpret the events of their day to fit the Bible's end-times scenario, whether they lived in 62

A.D., the 1100s, or 1929. But the Good Book's prophecies proved to be difficult to pin down, as they lack the necessary details to fit the actions of specific individuals or specific natural disasters. In response, frustrated people started developing stories to fill in the blanks. It's clear that this one-world government idea has its roots in the Bible, and its detailed fleshing out via conspiracy theories can be traced back to the 1300s. As evidenced in his book *The New World Order*, Pat Robertson has embraced these conspiracy theories and is presenting them to his millions of followers as fact.

Village Voice political correspondent James Ridgeway provides an excellent history of the origin of this one-world government conspiracy theory in his book *Blood in the Face*. Ridgeway's analysis draws heavily on *Warrant for Genocide* by Norman Cohn.

Ridgeway explains that as originally conceived, the conspiracy group was thought to be composed of Christians, not Jews, and took the form of the Order of the Templars, a group founded during the Crusades for the purpose of protecting religious pilgrims. As a result of their high-profile duties, the Templars became wealthy landholders all across Europe. This fact eventually led the rulers at that time to perceive the Templars as a threat, that is, until the leaders of the group were burned at the stake in 1314.

But the story didn't end there. In the late 1700s, a French cleric named Abbé Barruel claimed that the Templars hadn't really been destroyed but instead had begun a secret quest to overthrow the European monarchies and, eventually, the pope as well. According to Barruel, the now underground Templars hatched a scheme to take over another secret organization, the Order of the Freemasons, which had been formed by the stonemasons who built the cathedrals in the Middle Ages. With the help of the Freemasons, the Templars were once again plotting their path to ultimate control.

Barruel also claimed that at about the same time, yet another secret group called the Illuminati was also infiltrating the Freemasons. Exactly who was a Templar and who was an Illuminati is not completely clear. The Illuminati was formed in 1776 by Adam Weishaupt, a Bavarian law professor. It was a secret group devoted to rationalistic philosophy, the humanities, and occult practices, which made it very unpopular with the church. Barruel attributed a number of significant events to the subversive Illuminati, including the creation of a conspiracy that ultimately led to the French Revolution. The Illuminati spread all across France and Germany before finally being condemned by the Roman Catholic Church and ordered to dissolve in 1786. But the secret organization survived. The group resurfaced in Germany at the end of the nineteenth century and remained there until it was again ordered to dissolve by Hitler, along with all other secret societies. The first evidence of a world conspiracy is also found in the writings of Barruel: He warned that unless the Illuminati was stopped, its power would continue to grow until it ruled the world.

Cohn notes that Jews didn't play much of a role in the French Revolution and hence did not figure into Barruel's initial one-world theory. Jews first appeared in this great conspiracy around 1806, after Barruel apparently received a letter from a man named J. B. Simonini, a retired army officer from Florence. Simonini told Barruel that he was pleased that Barruel had exposed the secret organizations that were preparing the way for the Antichrist. Simonini went on to tell Barruel how he had infiltrated a sect of Jews from northern Italy by pretending to be Jewish himself. Simonini claimed he had overheard the Jews discussing their plans for world domination. He told Barruel that the Jews explained that they had actually been the masterminds behind the creation of the Illuminati and Freemasons and that they had even posed as Christians, with the ultimate goal of having a Jew selected as pope. According to Simonini, the Jews were buying up land and houses at such a rate that Christians were becoming dispossessed. He claimed that Christians were going to be reduced to slaves and that their churches would be turned into synagogues.

Cohn points out that the Jewish conspiracy received further acclaim some seventy-five years after Simonini's letter, when a novel by Sir John Retcliff entitled *Biarritz* became popular in Europe. The novel describes how the leaders of the twelve tribes of Israel gather around the grave of the most senior rabbi once every hundred years and report on how their goal of world conquest is going.

The part of the book that describes the meeting at the cemetery was reprinted as a pamphlet and circulated throughout Russia and France. In its pamphlet form, the story was widely accepted as a true account. These pamphlets would eventually provide the plotline for the final version of the great conspiracy book titled the *Protocols of the Elders of Zion*. This twelve-hundred-page book (the version of the *Protocols* being circulated today is approximately one hundred pages long) is supposedly the report issued following a meeting of a Jewish world congress that gathered in Cracow, Poland, in 1840. The book consists of several lectures that lay out the final plan for Jewish world domination, including how to create industrial and food monopolies to be controlled by Jews, how to create wars in which Jews would turn a profit but non-Jews would die, how to take over the monetary systems of existing countries, and how to create large centralized governments that would one day be run by Jews. Ultimately, these large governments were to be fused into a single worldwide government under Jewish control.

Heil Henry

In the United States, the *Protocols* received its biggest boost by none other than automotive tycoon Henry Ford. The looser morals of the Roaring Twenties had once again sent fundamentalist Christians into a "Book of Revelation" frenzy to figure out the end-times scenario that they felt was surely about to transpire because of the marked increase in alcohol consumption and bare skin.

This modern search for an end-times answer ended as earlier ones had, with the Jewish conspiracy. Ford was a big believer in the *Protocols*. He was also a Nazi sympathizer, but that's another story. Ford was the owner of a Michigan newspaper called the *Dearborn Independent*, which, under Ford's direction, ran a series of articles titled *The International Jew*. The articles were based on the *Protocols*, and they assured the reader that the Jewish plot to control the world had been well researched by the editorial department and found to be absolutely true.

The International Jew blamed everything on the great conspiracy: the decay of morality, the loss of family values, too many immigrants, an intrusive central government, monopolies, corrupt banks. In short, Ford's series of articles, which are widely circulated in rural America today, point a condemning finger at the very thing that still threatens the traditional way of life: a modernizing world.

In many ways, the 1920s were like the 1990s—a time when a world filled with technological wonders is again threatening to change the way of life to which many long to cling. In the 1920s, it was cars and factory mechanization that sparked fear in the hearts of citizens. Today, it's television, microchips, satellites, and the Internet. In this context, where technology=fear=end of the world, it only makes sense that we would once again find ourselves searching for heavenly answers and, in so doing, that we would rediscover the *Protocols of the Elders of Zion,* converted now into Christian Identity and dominionist conspiracy theories. They are simple explanations for all that is wrong in a complicated, scary, and often unjust world.

Another Open Door

The antigovernment movement's success in pulling rural Americans into its "funnel" and away from the traditional religious structure is, to some degree, attributable to the fact that the existing structure is flawed. The study of farm families conducted by the Heffernans of the University of Missouri found that 92 percent of the men and women participating in the study were members of a church, two-thirds attended church at least once a month, and over one-half attended once a week. The most significant finding was the fact that 55 percent of the families who attended church felt that their church had failed to support them during the rural crisis.[15]

A discussion of the study's findings was printed in a report created by the Cooperative Extension Service of the University of Missouri–Columbia: "Many of the families we talked to said we didn't really want to know what they felt about the church," says Bill Heffernan. "When we assured them that we did, we heard some surprising things. I heard on more than one occasion, 'People came to see us time and again before we joined the church. Now that we're in trouble, nobody comes.'"[16]

Judy Heffernan comments, "These people have been actively involved in their churches and actually feel as though they have been abandoned." The Heffernans believe they may understand to some degree why this is happening. The more formalized denominations tend to start their pastors in small rural churches. In other words, the myth that rural America is somehow less in need than urban places even spills over into the religious realm. At the time when rural places are in crisis, most churches are providing the people that live there with their least qualified personnel to counsel them.

Sister Stephanie Mertens, rural life director, Catholic Diocese, Jefferson City, Missouri, has an additional explanation. "Many times our pastors are simply misinformed. Some may be influenced by state policy aimed at reducing the number of farmers and may have been told that the farmer is to blame for his situation. When a farmer comes to them for help, some may react poorly."

Judy Heffernan points out still another problem with the current religious structure:

Very often, decisions come from urban areas because of the way the system works. It's difficult for these people to see the urban blight in their cities and believe that it could be anywhere nearly as bad in the rural areas. And frankly, there's a certain lack of openness on the part of some of the pastors [who make the decisions] to listen to that.

Besides, many people around the country have been trying to convince others that people going out of farming were bad managers. Now, if you don't know much about the situation to begin with, and a lot of our rural pastors don't, you're not likely to get real concerned about people in your congregation. After all, we've been blaming the victim at the national level for quite a while. Many people still believe that the church should deal only with spiritual issues. They have been reluctant to get involved on a social and political level.

Obviously, those in the antigovernment movement have no such reluctance. If they find even the slightest crack of opportunity—like the one being created by the current rural religious structure—they fill it. And like water when it freezes, the movement can make a tiny crack expand until it threatens the integrity of the entire structure.

Once again, as with rural health care, the door has been left wide open for the antigovernment movement and, in particular, for the teachings of Christian Identity and other dominionists. If the system can't provide an explanation for what's happening, then the movement will.

The State of the "Urban" Union

As if to underscore rural America's second-class status and Washington's lack of understanding of the people who live there, President Clinton—during his 1997 State of the Union address—used the word "urban" no fewer than a dozen times. The word "rural" came up only once and only then as a symbolic gesture. The president proposed idea after idea on how to fight the problems of urban America. Not once did he even acknowledge that problems exist in rural places, let alone offer a suggestion on how to fix them.

Clinton's constant effort to be a visionary played well to his urban TV audience. But without a doubt, it scared the hell out of a lot of rural citizens. During his speech, the president described how we have become one world and must, therefore, continue to knock down all cultural barriers that stand in the way of universal free trade and global prosperity. He pronounced that to accomplish this goal, we must have a computer hooked up to the Internet in every child's bedroom.

Clinton might as well have declared himself the Antichrist. A lot of rural people, particularly those who fear that this new technology is hastening the end-times by way of the one-world conspiracy, don't share the president's enthusiasm for a computer in every child's bedroom. For many, his words would seem more like a threat or the fulfillment of prophecy than a vision of hope.

Religion laced with conspiracy is outperforming its traditional counterpart—mainstream religion—in rural America. This is so for the simple reason that it offers explanations that seem to make sense—explanations for the problems that the rest of the system, both religious and political, has failed to address. In lieu of any alternative explanations for its increasingly rapid decay, rural America will continue to embrace the antigovernment gospel with growing enthusiasm.

6

A Grain of Truth

There's a fine line between progressive and right-wing organizations. We often want the same thing; we just go about it in different ways. There is no doubt that a lot of groups dropped the ball in rural America. They didn't offer a plan for action and the right-wing groups, like the Posse, did. But it's not too late. We now work with these [antigovernment] people every day in an effort to fight consolidation.
—**Rhonda Perry, Missouri Rural Crisis Center, 1997**

The power of conspiracy rests in faith: in the ability to believe in things unseen, to be sure of something that cannot be proven by our senses or by documentation. Faith has always been a stronger force in the world than mere reason, and because of that, debunking conspiracy theories is almost impossible. I asked an antigovernment farmer what he thought of Norman Cohn's history of the one-world Jewish conspiracy. He said: "Cohn, what kind of name is Cohn? Those people are just covering their tracks."

If a problem arises that seems to contradict a particular conspiracy theory, a new theory is created to explain why the inconsistency doesn't really exist. This is a never-ending cycle, designed to prevent rational argument from assaulting the movement or its goals. This seems absurd unless we remember the real purpose of conspiracy thinking: to offer a more culturally acceptable excuse for rebellion than the real reason, which is largely economic. In that context, it occurs to me that the movement's myriad of endless and irrational theories may well be an outgrowth of a mental process that functions to protect the mind from the truth. Using fictional conspiracies to block out a painful and difficult-to-accept reality seems no more bizarre than when people create selective amnesia to block out very real episodes in their lives such as witnessing a murder.

There is apparently no reality that a good conspiracy theory can't overcome. Consider the Oklahoma City bombing. When it exploded, its deadly concussion threatened to discourage the faint of heart from continuing to support the "anti" cause. But within hours of the blast, right-wing radio hosts like Mark Koernke of Michigan were assuring their listeners that the federal government had blown up the building and murdered innocent people in order to ensure passage of the Anti-Terrorism Bill, a piece of legislation designed, among other things, to make infiltration into the antigovernment movement easier and faster.

Militia leaders told their stunned followers that it was out of fear of the growing movement and its higher calling that godless Washington had ordered those innocent people killed. That the government would blow people up is a far-fetched idea to the average Joe, but to a hard-core antigovernment adherent who already believes that Satan is now in control of government leaders, it's only a small step of faith to accept the idea. What should have been a severe blow to the ranks of the movement was transformed—nearly overnight—by the power of conspiracy. Today, the Oklahoma City bombing has become a re-cruiting tool.

Immediately following the Oklahoma City blast, the movement's numbers declined slightly. But as Ron Cole, the leader of what's left of the Waco Branch Davidians, told me, "It [the Oklahoma City bomb] created a weeding-out process. Before the bomb you had a bunch of 'James Bond wanna-bes' in the militias. You couldn't be sure if you could trust them in a crisis. You knew you could count on the people who didn't run away after Oklahoma City. It made the militias stronger." A few months after the deadly bombing, with the help of the "government-did-it" conspiracy theory, the movement's numbers, once again, began to grow.

In light of this example, it seems clear that attempting to debunk conspiracy theories is the wrong path to take to persuade antigovern-ment adherents to rejoin the democratic process. Redirecting them into reality may prove a better and more successful course for two reasons. First, people in the movement may find that they have a po-litical reality to act upon. And second, those outside of the movement may realize that the people inside are not crazy. How so? Assume that Cohn's history of the Jewish conspiracy is accurate. That still doesn't explain the reason for its existence. Would people in the 1800s have latched onto a belief that Jews were trying to take over the world and control their lives if some problem hadn't actually existed? Simonini noted that Jews were trying to buy up all the houses, leaving Christians on the street. Maybe the issue was something as simple as a neighborhood housing dispute. How many times in recent history have we heard similar arguments from people in neighborhoods that were once predominantly white, black, Irish, or just plain wealthy as they began to shift toward a diversity of culture? Any anomaly could have sparked Simonini's angry and paranoid claims. It is important to realize that, as a rule, it's only after our lives have been affected by something real that we set out to explain it with a conspiracy theory.

Something Stinks

The Zionist Jew is pure evil, and they have designs on my farm.
—Dan Hawkins, Nebraska farmer, *20-20* interview, 1985

We can look, for example, at today's theory that claims that international Jewish bankers are trying to steal the land from American farmers so they can control the food supply of Christians. The claim sounds silly to most of us, but it's really just an oversimplified explanation for the very real and complicated problem of agricultural consolidation.

Farmers know something is up because there is no competition for their products. They either sell to the one or two companies in their area that make ridiculously low offers for their goods, or they let their crops rot in the fields. They may falsely interpret their predicament as an evil Jewish plot, but if something didn't stink in farm country, the conspiracy theory wouldn't exist.

Consider that for decades only five to eight multinational companies have, for all intents and purposes, been the sole purchasers and transporters of not only the American grain supply but that of the entire world. It sounds like another tall tale, but it's a fact. The entire grain supply of the world is basically controlled by a handful of privately held companies: Cargill, Continental, ConAgra, Louis Dreyfus, Bunge, Carnac, Mitsui/Cook, and newcomer Archer Daniels Midland. Some of these companies have been owned by the same families for centuries, making them among the oldest commercial enterprises in the world. And some of the families are Jewish. The point I am trying to make here is that there is usually a smidgen of truth buried inside these fictional theories.

In 1982, at the beginning of the farm crisis, these companies controlled 96 percent of U.S. wheat exports, 95 percent of U.S. corn exports, 90 percent of U.S. oat exports, and 80 percent of all the sorghum leaving the United States.[1] As an example of the government turning a blind eye to antitrust problems, consider that in 1921, the Federal Trade Commission reported that the grain trade business had become dangerously concentrated. So what has happened since then? Today's supercompanies now account for a higher percentage of grain exports than the largest 36 companies did in the 1920s. It has gotten worse—much worse.

Consider this fictional story of "farmer Jones," a family farmer trying to make ends meet by growing wheat and raising a few head of cattle and some chickens. This is how his year went. Jones bought his wheat seed and his cattle and chicken feed from Nutrena Corporation. His old tractor bit the dust last year, so he had to go to the Bank of Ellsworth and get a loan for a new tractor that he bought from Waycrosse, Inc. Jones had another bit of bad luck—his irrigation system fell apart. He called his insurance company, the Horizon Agency, but the agent said it wasn't covered. He had no choice but to buy a new system from Venture Sprinkler, Inc. Jones then bought his fertilizer from Cargill, and his wheat was under way. At harvesttime, the prices were low, so Jones decided to hold his crop in storage. He shipped his wheat by rail to the Heinhold Elevator Company. Eventually, Jones sold half of his crop to a Panamanian company called Tradax and the other half to a domestic milling operation owned by the Burrus Company. The Tradax half was shipped on a barge owned by Cargo Carriers, Inc., to a giant port elevator owned by Producer Marketing. A few days later, it was loaded on a ship owned by Rogers Shipping and transported to Europe.

Meanwhile, Jones's animals were ready for market. He sold the cattle to a feedlot owned by Caprock Industries, which later sold them to Cargill's meatpacking plant. He sold the chickens to Dean Farms. Unfortunately for farmer Jones, the prices he received were disappointing. By the time he subtracted out the cost of the seed, feed, chemical fertilizer, tractor, sprinkler system, elevator storage, rail transportation, and insurance, he'd lost money and couldn't pay the bank, which, therefore, repossessed his land.

Jones was depressed. He couldn't figure out why the companies wouldn't pay him enough for his products to keep him in business. He thought about suicide, but then he heard about the one-world conspiracy and joined the antigovernment movement instead.

If we looked at this situation as outsiders, we would probably reach the conclusion that farmer Jones had some bad luck and probably was a poor businessman. We would think Jones latched onto a conspiracy theory in his effort to scapegoat someone to alleviate his guilt. What we probably wouldn't consider is that farmer Jones did some investigating on his own and made a startling discovery. The fifteen different companies in the fifteen different industries to which Jones had paid out money during the year were all owned by one company—Cargill. And that is the same company that paid him such a low price for his products and eventually repossessed his land.

The very real companies named in the farmer Jones illustration are just a few of those in Cargill's vertical integration. The company owns many more subsidiaries in still more industries, and Cargill is not unique. The other grain giants are equally integrated.

In his book *Merchants of Grain*, former *Washington Post* reporter Dan Morgan describes the giant companies that own practically all of the regional grain elevators farmers depend on to store their surplus crops. They own or lease all of the world's port elevators from the Mississippi and the Great Lakes to the mouth of the Amazon and the Black Sea. They own the grain cars and barges needed to provide rail and water transportation from farm to elevator. Farmers today must turn to these giant companies to buy their seed, their fertilizer, and their machinery. The companies own banks, investment firms, insurance companies, steel companies, chemical companies, and lumber companies. They are the buyers of the farmers' products as well as the processors of those products. In many cases, they even own the companies whose familiar names appear on our supermarket shelves.

Consider the cereals we buy at the local store. Only four cereal companies now control over 80 percent of that market.[2] Several of the giant cereal companies are merely subsidiaries of the multinational grain companies. For all the hard work and risk farmers take, they only receive about one thin dime's worth of the price of a box of cornflakes. The multinationals get the rest. And control of the grain trade is only one of the tentacles stretched out by these lords of the food supply.

Take It or Leave It

In the beef-packing industry, Cargill, ConAgra, and Iowa Beef Packers (IBP) control over 80 percent of the total market. The independent feedlots that once made up their competition are quickly becoming extinct, for two reasons. First, the big three can use their own grain supplies to feed their beef at prices lower than those available to their non–grain company competitors. And second, the big three—who are the eventual buyers after the feedlot, anyway—can simply refuse to purchase their competitors' cattle or can offer them substandard prices. With no guarantee that they'll be able to sell their cattle for a profit, the independent feedlots have been forced to close their doors. In the 1970s, a rancher would take his cattle to a sale barn, where a group of buyers would bid against each other, driving up the price. Today, the idea of competitive bidding is just a memory. Cattle are often sold to a lone buyer, who, for all intents and purposes, dictates what price the rancher will be receiving for his product. The North American Free Trade Agreement (NAFTA) has also improved the big three's ability to control the market. To ensure that prices don't get too high, captive supplies of Canadian beef are kept on hand so that they can periodically be used to flood the U.S. market and depress prices.

Occasionally, ranchers will try to bypass the companies by selling directly to stores—an option that is clearly theirs in a free market—but, apparently, not in the current American market. In Montana, rancher Jeannie Charter found consumer demand high for the aged beef she was processing and selling directly to a Super Valu store. But when the sales representative for one of the big three found out about her enterprise, he made certain that the practice stopped. Charter commented: "He basically made it clear that he could do anything we could do for 30 cents a pound cheaper no matter what we charged. The Packers and Stockyards Act was written to make that kind of pricing illegal. But it doesn't seem like anybody enforces it." However, as bad as the beef industry is getting, it's still in good shape compared to the hog and poultry industries, in which consolidation has relegated the growers to the status of corporate serfs.

The Company Store

These days, it's all but impossible for a farmer to raise hogs or poultry without first getting a contract with one of the monopolies that guar-

antees his animals will be purchased when the time comes. That's because, as in the beef industry, in most regions of the country there's
only one buyer. Independent hog farmer Ron Perry of Chillicothe,
Missouri, put it this way: "It used to be within 10 miles, you could go
to five or six places every week to sell your hogs. Now you have to
take them 50 miles to one place, one day of the month and take
whatever the one corporate buyer will give you."[3]

In order to get a contract with Continental, Tyson, or ConAgra,
the corporations that now control the industry, farmers must agree to
the companies' terms. And those terms are the equivalent of the
farmer becoming a hired hand on his own land. In the poultry and
hog industries, the companies tell the farmers what type of chicken
houses or hog buildings they must build, forcing them into more and
more bank debt as they struggle to keep up with the technological
advances demanded by the company. The hog industry is particularly
expensive. Modern operations consist of giant buildings, where hogs
live in small high-tech crates from birth to slaughter. The animals live
out their entire existence without ever having been outdoors or having breathed fresh air. High-tech systems feed the animals and remove their excrement. The hog simply stands in one place and grows
until it is killed.

Because the animals have no way to build up their immune systems,
a simple disease could quickly spread throughout the indoor hog
population. Farmers are therefore forced to constantly administer an-
tibiotics to the animals. How these drugs ultimately affect the consumer is still being debated. The hog giants have assured the public
that their process doesn't pose a health risk, as have tobacco companies concerning cigarette risks. I have yet to interview a family farmer
who wants to raise his animals in this fashion. But farmers have little
choice if they want a buyer for their product. And in fact, many farmers are not raising "their" animals this way.

Many hog and poultry farmers no longer own any animals. The
farmers get the chicks and hogs from the multinationals. Even the
grain the animals are fed is provided by the company. At the end of
the season, the full-grown animals are trucked to the company's processing plants where they're weighed. After rating each farmer's per-
formance in pounds, the company deducts its charges for the chicks
or hogs, feed, transportation, and any other services or products it
supplied, such as propane to heat the buildings. If there's anything
left over, the farmer is compensated. The only thing that the com-

pany allows the farmer to own are the heavily indebted buildings and land where the company raises "its" animals. And those buildings never get paid off. Farmers say that nearly every year, the company requires new innovations in exchange for the all-powerful contract it knows the farmer must have to avoid bankruptcy. Once in the system, there's no way out except foreclosure—a sad reality that the companies exploit to the fullest.

If a natural disaster strikes—such as the ice storm that hit eastern Oklahoma in the late 1980s, leveling many of the area's chicken houses—the company has no responsibility to support the farmers. In the Oklahoma incident, many area poultry growers were unable to get the federal disaster funds they needed to rebuild in time for the next contract period. With no contract, they were forced into foreclosure.

As bad as the system is, the giant companies get few complaints. If a farmer gripes about the injustices, he runs the risk of not being given a contract and subsequently losing his farm. It's like the old company-store routine in coal-mining towns. The miners risked their lives to pull the rock from the sides of unstable shafts. In return, the mine's owner paid them in otherwise worthless company scrip that could only be redeemed for products in the company-owned store, where prices were way too high. With no actual money in their pockets, the miners couldn't leave the area to search for better job opportunities. They, like many of today's farmers, had become prisoners of the corporation.

One Step Away

From their farmhouse on a butte above the small town of Burly, Idaho, Sarah Thompson, her husband, Roy, and their two daughters can look down upon the grandeur of the Snake River. Sarah says, "When you come here, you can understand why we'd do anything to stay." In the evenings, the Thompsons like to watch the sunset over Idaho's fabled City of Rocks—a surreal combination of granite and yucca that erupts out of the high desert and looks as if Hades had driven rock spikes through the outer wall of his underworld kingdom.

Nearby, the wagon ruts of the Oregon Trail are still devoid of grass, testimony to the tens of thousands of heavy wagons that carried the dreams of a rugged people to this spectacular land more than a hundred years ago. The names of those early settlers can still be seen on what locals like to call "signature rock." Even now, a century later, the oddly shaped fifty-foot-high stone resembles a giant autographed baseball, due to the hundreds of names and dates carved into its overhanging sides. There are no plaques or other signs to commemorate the rock's historical value. Such markers are only needed in places where the last remnants of the old are being engulfed by the new. In south-central Idaho, the new never came—until now.

The Thompsons' potato farm is a family farm in the truest sense. The one-thousand-acre spread was handed down to Roy by his father, who got the farm straight from the government, back when it still gave land away to people willing to be farmers. In the early days, people weren't sure what would grow in this high desert. But they soon found that with the aid of irrigation, Idaho could produce the best potatoes in the world. People wanted and needed the big spuds, so life on the Thompson place was good.

But things have changed. Nineteen ninety-seven may well be the last year of farming for the Thompsons and for a good number of their Cashia County neighbors. It's not that people don't want their tasty potatoes—demand has never been greater. The problem for the Thompsons and other growers is that they only have one company willing to buy their crop, and that company is offering them less for their product than it costs to produce it.

In the past, according to the Thompsons, there were always several buyers in the area who bid up the price. But for the last couple of years, the reality has been that either you sell to ConAgra—in the form of its subsidiary Lamb/Weston—or you let your potatoes rot in the cellars. The two smaller buyers in the region, Ore-Ida and Simplot, quickly hit their capacity each year, leaving the majority of the area farms with no other option but to sell to the multinational.

As of February 1997, the Thompsons had yet to sell one potato from their 1996 harvest. They refuse to accept that they must sell their crop for less than it cost them to raise it. Sarah describes their dilemma this way:

> No business in the world is like this; it doesn't make sense. Even hookers know what they're going to get paid up front. But we work hard and raise a crop and then have to go to some big company to find out if we lost money or not. If we lose money this year, that's it. We'll be gone. All we can do is store the potatoes and hope that we can get a better price from them later on. They're holding up pretty well in the

cellars for now, but that's not true for everyone around here. Once they start to go, you can only get a dollar per hundred [pounds] for them as cattle feed. That's three dollars a hundred less than it cost to grow them.

The Thompsons thought this might be a good year. But that was before the late blight hit—late blight is the same plant disease responsible for the Irish Potato Famine. The Thompsons lost about 30 percent of their crop, but they were lucky compared to some others. "Normally a big crop loss will push up prices and you can still break even. But not with ConAgra," says Sarah. "We thought we had a contract at $5.18. That would have let us make about a dollar profit per hundred pounds. But they broke us and there's nothing we can do about it."

In the past, farmers like the Thompsons have banded together with other area growers to make sure they got a fair price. They would sign contracts with a co-op program such as that offered by the Idaho Potato Growers Association (IPG), which would in turn sell the contracts to a processor. By controlling the crop production of many area farms, IPG, in theory, had a certain amount of bargaining clout. In 1996, IPG signed what seemed like a modest $5.18-per-hundred-pound contract with the Thompsons. But their clout theory was about to be disproved. Bargaining power only exists when there is more than one player in the game, a fact well known to the food giants. When it came time for the association to sell to ConAgra, the company turned it down flat. Instead of paying $5.18, ConAgra offered families like the Thompsons a $3.50 contract, 50 cents per hundred less than it cost the family to raise their crop.

The Thompsons and their neighbors had no option left but to turn to the banks for loans against their stored potatoes. Sarah and Roy were lucky. They're still eating because they were one of the few families that managed to get such a loan. Sarah says there are a lot of banks in the area, but they've cut the farmers off in light of the contract problems. "The banks don't think that ConAgra is going to budge, and they don't want to get stuck with millions in bad loans with rotten potatoes as collateral." Even Sarah's brother-in law was turned down by the banks. Her family is trying to help him hang on, but there's little they can do under the circumstances.

At first glance, it would seem to be a short-sighted approach for the giant company to put the farmers who grow the product it needs out of business. In fact, that wouldn't make sense at all—but apparently, that's not the plan. Sarah claims that as farms like hers fail, the company is bankrolling two area farmers who have been instructed to take over the foreclosed-on land. "They're creating these company-owned farms that will eventually be hundreds of thousands of acres in size."

Perhaps Idaho is offering us a glimpse into the future of agriculture. In another decade, million-acre farms owned and operated by the food monopolies may well be the norm. Would anyone like to guess how much potatoes will cost when potato farms are all owned by one company? Even now the price is around $30 per hundred pounds at grocery stores, and that's for potatoes thrown into a bin, without any processing. The company makes ten to twenty times the profit of the farmers they're running out of business.

There's only one reason the multinationals can get away with this kind of behavior. They know that Americans will not drive to the country to buy their potatoes directly from the grower, and they can make sure the stores don't buy directly either. As long as there's no competition in buying from the farmers, they can pay them as little as they want and charge consumers whatever they want. By the time we decide prices are too high and become willing to make that drive, companies like ConAgra will be the only growers. It will be too late. America is literally betting its future on the idea that once these megacorporations have achieved total consolidation, they will suddenly become good neighbors and not gouge the public on prices. This is the same mentality we exercise when we believe our representative won't give special treatment to a corporation that donates $50,000 to a political campaign. The truth is that the Thompsons' battle should be our battle. But the reality is that potatoes are still too cheap at the store for anyone to care.

Life in the Thompson home is hard these days. Sarah says the hardest part is seeing her husband unable to sleep night after night, as he racks his brain trying to think of a way to save the farm. She sums it all up, saying:

All we want to do is farm and have a good life. My husband is such a good man. He's the most honest person I've ever known. Even in times like these, if someone gives him too much change, he gives it back. And that's how all the people here are. They're the kindest and most caring people in the world. This whole thing is wrong. ConAgra treats us like we're a dime a dozen. I guess as far as they're concerned that's about right.

For now, all the Thompsons can do is wait. Each passing day, the deadline to repay the bank gets nearer. Each day, their potatoes are closer to rotting. Their lives are dangling by a thread that is tied to a ConAgra boardroom, and Sarah and Roy are powerless to influence their own destiny. They suspect that their farm has already been colored in as part of the ConAgra holdings on a giant wall map somewhere. As Sarah says, they are trying not to give up:

> It seems like I've been battling something ever since I married a farmer. . . . We want this life so badly. I just have to remain optimistic, or I'll slip to the brink like so many who have joined a militia. If farmers would just stick together, we could stop these people. But someone always gets scared that they're going to lose their place, and they sell at a loss. That just kills the rest of us, and they'll still be gone in a year or two. Maybe this is the end of the world. Maybe that's better.

Antitrust, Antigovernment

When people hear about folks like the Thompsons, they usually react by saying that there should be laws against such corporate behavior. But that's not the problem. The laws already exist in the form of the Clayton and Sherman Antitrust Acts, the Packers and Stockyards Act, and the Robinson-Patman Act. The problem is a lack of fortitude on the part of elected officials when it comes to enforcing the statutes against the companies that fill their political campaign coffers. It is this lack of action on the part of government that transforms an economic problem into a conspiracy theory.

Farmers know what's happening to them. They're well-read on the subject. A friend of mine, journalist William K. Burke, was the first one to tell me about the book *Merchants of Grain*. In the early 1980s, Burke had been sent into farm country to research a story about a father and son who had murdered their banker after losing their farm to foreclosure. He recalled that everywhere he went, another farmer handed him a copy of the book that exposes the giant grain companies. The farmers understood what was happening. They just couldn't understand why it was being allowed to happen. If you want evidence about the conclusion they ultimately reached, check out a copy of *Merchants of Grain* at the local library and flip through its pages. I've done this in a number of different libraries and have always found the same thing. Every Jewish name in the book has been underlined. The margins are full of scribbled notes about the Rockefellers and the Trilateral Commission. The entire book has been reinterpreted as proof of the great conspiracy. It's easy to see how that conclusion could be reached. After all, what other explanation could there be? If the government wasn't in on the deal, it would enforce the laws and stop the monopolies. The conspiracy idea is more believable than the truth. Trying to tell a farmer that his life has been destroyed because serious campaign finance reform has not been enacted is just asking for a good gut laugh.

For years, Congress has listened intently to the lobbyists hired by multinationals like Cargill, Continental, ConAgra, Archer Daniels Midland, and the rest, as they have presented their less than objective opinions about the proper course for American agriculture. As early as 1964, congressmen were being told by industry giants like Pillsbury, Swift, General Foods, and Campbell Soup that the biggest problem in agriculture was too many farmers.

The companies' idea was that technology had made a major consolidation possible and that the result would be cheap food and, consequently, a more robust overall economy. That 1964 report was first handed to me by a farmer as proof that there is a conspiracy to get rid of people like him. I must admit that the report, titled *An Adaptive Program for Agriculture* and prepared by the Committee for Economic Development, would prove a chilling read to most rural residents.

In 1962, the Committee for Economic Development comprised approximately seventy-five of the nation's most powerful corporate executives. They represented not only the food industry but also the oil and gas, insurance, investment, and retail industries. Almost all groups that stood to gain from consolidation were represented on that committee. Their report outlined a plan to eliminate farmers and farms. It was detailed and well thought out.

The committee had observed that a large percentage of farm children who attended college never returned to farming. It therefore recommended that scholarships should be made available to all farm kids, in an effort to break the generational chain on family farms. The committee encouraged Congress to provide large sums of money to retrain farmers and even suggested that the government should pay to move any farm family willing to relocate. All these suggestions were made under the guise of helping the struggling farm families. Unfortunately, no one bothered to ask the farmers if they minded being socially engineered out of their way of life. Of course, this report of heartfelt recommendations by industry leaders never mentioned the fact that their plan would result in unfathomable profits for the corporate food industry, which, out of the goodness of its heart, would step in to fill the void left by the displaced farmers. Reports like this have become fuel for the conspiracy fire in the 1990s.

Because it sounded like a good idea—or because the companies' campaign contributions had their desired effect—Congress turned a blind eye to antitrust laws and let the giants seize control. In recent years, it has even allowed representatives from the food monopolies to help write much of the content of federal farm bills. Apparently, these elected government officials never asked themselves whether this plan for consolidation was really beneficial. Had they asked, they might have heard another side of the story, albeit one that offered no campaign contributions to enhance its believability. For fifty years, evidence has existed that challenges the concept that consolidation is a good thing.

In his book *Broken Heartland: The Rise of America's Rural Ghetto,* Osha Grey Davidson points out an early study that demonstrates that consolidation does more harm than good.[4] In the 1940s, Walter Goldschmidt compared two similar rural communities in California: Dinuba and Arvin. The major difference between the towns was their agricultural structure. Arvin was surrounded by large "industrialized" farms. Dinuba, by contrast, was still located in the midst of family farms.

Goldschmidt found that this difference in agricultural structure expressed itself in startling ways. Dinuba supported no less than twice as many businesses as the corporate-farming Arvin. Not only did Dinuba have twice the businesses, it had a 61 percent greater retail volume. Arvin citizens were found to have an overall lower standard of living, despite their commitment to technological advances in agriculture. And the differences didn't stop there.

Dinuba residents enjoyed more civic organizations, newspapers, public recreation centers, parks, schools, and even churches. Even the style of government in the two towns had evolved differently. Dinuba commonly made town decisions through popular vote; Arvin had most of its decisions dictated to its residents by county officials. Arvin had become a town of haves and have-nots, whereas Dinuba had maintained economic and social homogeneity throughout its entire population.

There is other evidence of the destructive nature of consolidation. The towns that once fought to be the location for one of the monopolies' big plants in hopes of creating jobs are having second thoughts. They've seen their towns and way of life destroyed. Mark Anderson, an employee and union representative at a meatpacking plant in Sioux Falls, South Dakota, presented the worker's perspective on monopoly impact to the Western Organization of Resource Councils in April 1990.

Let us not kid ourselves. This concentration of power is not good for livestock producers, workers, the communities they live in or the consumers. The destruction resulting from the monopoly in the meat packing industry is devastating and continues to take a heavy toll, especially throughout the mid-west.

It is widely recognized that the big three packers are anti-union, low wage operators who force their employees to work under brutal working conditions. A workforce turnover of over 100 percent a year at their plants tells us they are not a good place to work at.

As the big three packers have run competition out of business, they have driven workers' wages to their lowest level. During the past year, front page stories have appeared in numerous newspapers, not union publications, concerning how workers at the big three working full time are unable to afford low income housing.

Noted publications such as the *Wall Street Journal* have written in-depth stories of how the big three wreck communities with low wages, high workforce turnover and staggering injury rates. Where the big three have plants located, those communities have become a tragic human dumping ground for poverty wages and workers who are transported across several states to be put to work only to be dumped after they arrive in the area. *The Wall Street Journal* ran this headline on April 3, 1990. "A town in Iowa finds big new packing plant destroys its old calm. Housing and crime become big headache as IBP hires jobless from far away."

The big three packers of 1990 have returned the workers and the communities they live in back to the "Days of the Jungle" that Upton Sinclair wrote about in 1906. This whole question of monopolization of the industry and the destruction that results has gone well beyond legal issues and has now become a moral issue, simply because it is immoral for these large packers to treat human beings like they do. One would certainly like to believe that our government, the watchdogs and enforcers of the laws in this land, would not let a group of employers return to the barbaric society where human beings are worth less than the meat that they work on, where the communities they live in would be ravaged by poverty, crime, inadequate housing, but this is exactly what they have permitted to happen. Every decent thinking compassionate human being must condemn what exists in the meat packing industry and condemn those packers who created those conditions. The laws of this land must be vigorously enforced, but there must be a higher law also enforced. Our business is also to have a civilized society and to prevent this type of corporate violence against those people who live in that society.[5]

When the cost of social problems stemming from rural consolidation and restructuring, such as stress-induced illness, crime, job-related injuries, loss of retail business revenue, and welfare are thrown into the equation, the multinationals' prediction of a more robust overall economy is likely dead wrong. But, as long as the government opens its doors only to those with cash in hand, the chances that it will provide the funds for the research necessary to determine the truth about consolidation is somewhere between nil and zero. And for millions of people, it's already too late.

It's easy to understand why devastated rural citizens would view their situation as the result of a conspiracy of biblical proportions. But in fact, the reality is that the rural crisis is the result of politics as usual in the corporate system of government that has taken over our democracy. Global restructuring and its resulting trade agreements have forced the government to look at the entire world market before deciding whether a monopoly exists. For that reason, 1996 was the biggest year in history for corporate mergers. There were 1,471 corporate name changes in that twelve-month period that resulted from consolidation.[6] In the new world market, the philosophy has become "merge or die." But it appears that even on a global scale, Washington is unwilling to enforce its own domestic laws. Consider that aviation giant Boeing bought its only U.S. competitor, McDonnell Douglas. Government regulators in charge of enforcing antitrust laws decided that the Boeing deal was not against the law because there was still one other company in the entire world—Europe's Airbus—that made passenger planes. By the government's own guidelines, this particular aviation merger is nearly five times as consolidated as American antitrust laws allow. The merger created a total monopoly. The Boeing deal has made the government's position perfectly clear. Washington has suspended all antitrust laws. We have once again entered the world of J. P. Morgan, a world of great gains for the rich and powerful and of great suffering for the working classes.

Conspiracy theories are irrational explanations for what's going on. But the scary part is, they're less laughable than we'd like to admit. Consolidation in the food industry and in most other industries as well is just one of the components propelling the antigovernment movement toward violence. There are more.

7

The Root of All Evil

Yap Islanders kept huge stones in their front yards. The size of your stone indicated how rich you were. Nobody could move these stones, but nobody cared, because they knew you had the money "in the bank." We've used wampum, beads, silver, and gold, and now we use paper and call it money. The next transition will be to smartcards.

—Walter Wriston, former chair and CEO of
Citicorp/Citibank, *Wired* magazine interview, 1996[1]

Strangely enough, it's almost impossible to understand one of the central teachings in today's antigovernment movement without at least some knowledge of monetary theory. That's because there is no greater rallying cry for the "anti" groups than their belief that there's a conspiracy to take control of the world's monetary system and, in particular, our own central bank, the Federal Reserve. Potential recruits are made dizzy by the endless piles of paper that the movement uses to explain its concept of real money that is backed by gold and silver, versus conspiracy money that they claim is backed by no more than the paper it's printed on. Many of the movement's dispensers of information will only sell their printed material in exchange for silver or gold, making it clear that they believe what they preach.

It's no wonder that the movement's arguments are so persuasive. How many people do you know who can explain why our current money has value or why we abandoned the gold standard some sixty years ago? When it comes to understanding the concept of money, we behave much the way the Cowardly Lion did when confronted with the mighty Wizard of Oz. We're afraid to pull back the curtain that protects our economists and other so-called experts from public scrutiny, choosing instead to believe that only they can grasp the complicated details that make our monetary system work. We never bother to ask ourselves, "Why is this green paper worth anything at all?" It's as though we're afraid to hear the answer.

But in rural America, one calamity after another has made people brave and curious. They feel the need to understand the forces that are reshaping their world, and they've started asking questions. They're on a quest to find someone who can make sense of all this financial hocus-pocus. And as has become its specialty, the antigovernment movement is there with a short and simple explanation.

The movement tells them that the banking system is part of the great conspiracy. First, they explain that the evil-infiltrated government stole all of our gold and now wants the rest of our wealth, and it has a scheme to get it. When a farmer needs money to keep his operation going, he goes to his local banker and mortgages his land and equipment. In return, he gets paper money—or even less. In exchange for his life's work, the bank gives him a piece of paper showing a long account number on one side and another number next to it that represents how many dollars are credited to that account, say, for instance, $30,000.

Then, according to the conspiracists, the local bank notifies the Federal Reserve that it needs $30,000. In response, the Federal Reserve calls the World Bank—composed of twelve international banks that are run by people like the Rockefellers and their European counterpart, the Rothschilds, the people said to be at the center of the great conspiracy. At this point, the international bankers turn on a printing press and out pops a fresh batch of $30,000 in paper money. The money is created out of thin air and is backed by nothing more than the paper and ink that constitute it. Conspiracists estimate that the real cost to the World Bank is about $20 for paper, ink, and handling. But if the farmer should find himself unable to repay the loan, the bankers take his farm. Not bad for a $20 investment.

The funny part is that this wild idea of how the monetary system works isn't all that far from wrong. Money has been turned into paper. And even the paper is going out of style. The holy coins that were once minted in ancient temples to provide a sense of divine authority, which, in turn, assured the acceptance of the currency among the population, are being transformed into bits and bytes that fly through computer terminals and satellites at the speed of light. Now they can save their $20 with the stroke of a key—they can steal farms for free.

The idea of "money" has always been controversial, shrouded in mystery and somewhat tied to the spiritual realm. Few acts require as much faith as a person accepting paper dollar bills in exchange for their property, which has actual value. Yet we exercise this faith millions of times every day. I asked a friend of mine—who happens to be a tax attorney—why my paper money has value. I expected some long, detailed explanation befitting a member of the bar. Instead, she said: "It doesn't. The only reason I accept it from you as payment for something is because I have faith that someone else will accept it from me later on." That was my answer? The key to the whole monetary system of the world is blind optimism. Although this is, of course, an oversimplified explanation, it's also accurate. It basically describes the real concept behind the use of money that has existed since its inception.

Over the centuries, we have used cows, seashells, stones, food, grain, and, of course, gold as a method of exchange—as money, if you will. It's not easy to carry around or even to figure out how many cows it takes to buy a Lexus or how many words a journalist has to write to equal a house. For this reason, we created money. It allows us to buy and sell by converting a product we have into something small and easy to transport that can then be redeemed for other products owned by someone else.

Seashells worked fine for New Mexico's Native American population because there weren't very many of them lying around in its mountainous deserts. But then trade routes opened up to the West Coast and seashells became too abundant. With sack loads of shells arriving regularly, corn that once cost two shells suddenly cost a thousand. The convenience factor had been lost.

Over time, we figured out that whatever we use for money has to be something with a limited supply—something scarce, like gold. For centuries, the shiny metal was the perfect money. It was beautiful, hard to get, and could be made into almost any shape. But if you were wealthy, you had more gold than you could carry. You were forced to keep it at your house, which left you vulnerable to theft. So we created banks, places with secure vaults to store our gold.

We gave our gold to banks, and in return, banks gave us paper certificates that we could redeem for our gold when the time came to buy something. We quickly figured out that it didn't make sense to go to the bank, get our gold, and then carry it across town to a merchant who was only going to take it back to the same bank for safe-keeping. It was a waste of time. So we started giving the merchants our gold certificates, which allowed them to redeem our gold. This was the birth of paper money, born out of convenience.

It is here that the antigovernment movement has drawn its line, asserting that only gold and silver, or paper money based on gold and silver, is real money. Everything else is part of the conspiracy. The idea behind the movement's teachings is that gold and silver were created by God in limited supply and are therefore ordained to be the only true form of money.

As a matter of observation, it's a little unclear why "anti" proponents find God-made gold more acceptable than God-made cows or God-made seashells when it comes to the idea of ordained money. But it's easy to understand why they would have a hard time accepting the concept of today's paper and computer-generated money. After all, its value is based on paper, or so it seems, and if that's the case, whoever controls the presses must therefore control the world. Once again, there's a certain amount of truth behind the paranoia.

Where's the Gold?

We thus see the title to the people's gold was seized and passed into government hands. We also see that it was contemplated that the gold would be redistributed through some future agreement of the nations of the world. This came in 1945 in the form of the Bretton Woods Agreement.

Taking the gold was a seizure of war.

—Dr. Eugene Schroder,
Constitution: Fact or Fiction

The antigovernment movement teaches that a major step in the great conspiracy occurred in 1933 when President Franklin D. Roosevelt declared war on the Great Depression. In order to accomplish his economic goals, Roosevelt greatly enhanced his personal power by assuming the emergency war powers that the Constitution makes available to presidents in times of war or rebellion. Roosevelt's actions were controversial then, and thanks to the antigovernment movement, are so again. In his book *Constitution: Fact or Fiction*, which has become the Bible of the movement when it comes to monetary conspiracy, Dr. Eugene Schroder tells his readers that Roosevelt tossed the Constitution out the window and became a dictator who stole the nation's gold reserves and replaced them with worthless paper.

What Roosevelt did to the monetary system under his newly ac-
quired war powers was unquestionably radical. Although most
"anti" proponents view his actions as a trick to steal the wealth of the
nation, most economists view it as a natural and well-thought-out
step in monetary evolution. Roosevelt believed that the gold standard had created a system that would never provide enough currency
to fill the needs of our growing population. He believed, to some
degree, that America could only escape the bounds of the Great Depression by spending and investing its way out of the mess. He
needed more money in the pockets of the people, but he knew that if
he simply ordered more money to be printed, based upon our limited gold reserves, the result would be hyperinflation. It would create something similar to the disastrous situation in Germany in the
postwar 1920s, when people literally had to carry trunks full of their
worthless cash with them just to buy a loaf of bread.

To resolve the problem, Roosevelt planned to change the resource
that backed our money from gold and silver to all the assets controlled by the banking system. In other words, the new Federal Reserve notes would be backed by the mortgages and loans controlled
by the nation's banking system. In order to accomplish this task with
some appearance of legality, the president had to do some pretty in-
ventive tinkering with the existing laws—something he could only accomplish with his new emergency powers.

Schroder claims that during Roosevelt's first one hundred days in
office,

> he seized all gold and silver, took the country off the gold standard and
> established a banking system based on the debts of the people, ex-
> panded the Trading With the Enemy Act to redefine "enemy" as to in-
> clude all American people . . . and bailed out the banks. Roosevelt's acts
> abrogated the gold clause in all public and private contracts, thus usurp-
> ing the legality of private contracts. At the same time he established
> control over financing and the price of homes, and inserted into the
> Agricultural Adjustment Act a clause which shifted the power to coin
> money and regulate its value (granted by the constitution to congress)
> from congress to the president.
>
> In addition, the government decreed that ownership of all property is
> in the state, that individual ownership is only by virtue of the govern-
> ment, amounting to mere user, and that use must be in accordance with
> the law and subordinate to the necessities of the state.[2]

Schroder's observation that Roosevelt radically changed the banking system and the concept of money is accurate. The question is, was it sinister? In the end, it allowed for the printing of billions of dollars in new paper money. There are those who argue that Roosevelt's paper money is what allowed the Great Depression to enter the history books.

But who got the gold? In the overall scheme of things, it really doesn't matter. It becomes important only because of the significance placed upon it by today's antigovernment movement. In 1934, Roosevelt answered the question.

> Such legislation places the right, title and ownership to our gold reserves in the government itself; it makes clear the government ownership of any added dollar value of the country's stock of gold which would result from any decrease in the gold content of the dollar which may be made in the public interest.
>
> The title of all gold being in the government, the total stock will serve as a permanent and fixed metallic reserve which will change in amount only so far as is necessary for the settlement of international balances or as may be required by a future agreement among nations of the world for a redistribution of the world stock of monetary gold.[3]

A "redistribution" as may be "required" by a future agreement among nations of the world: The great conspiracy got a big boost right from the mouth of the president.

The government got the gold, and that's fine with people who believe that the transfer was the result of democracy in action, in that our supreme leader made a decision that was for the good of the people. However, for those who believe that Roosevelt suspended the Constitution as part of the one-world conspiracy, all the explanation reveals is an admission of theft and a future plan to give the nation's gold to the secret force of Jews who are taking over the world's governments. It would be funny—if it were not deadly serious. In reality, Roosevelt trampled on our constitutional liberties sixty-four years ago because he thought it was the right thing to do. Today, people are willing to commit murder because, in retrospect, they disagree with his decision.

But that's how conspiracy theory works: You can always find a sinister side to every action. Had Roosevelt failed to act and allowed the depression to continue, there's no doubt that the conspiracists would interpret his lack of action as a plot to sink the economy, making us vulnerable to the international bankers. Conspiracies exist because people are unhappy with the powers-that-be, whom they blame for their problems. When times are tough, as they are now in rural places, conspiracy reigns supreme.

In his excellent book *Secrets of the Temple: How the Federal Reserve Runs the Country*, William Greider, former managing editor for the *Washington Post*, describes this transition from gold to paper.

> Finally, the last prop of the money illusion was kicked away in this century: the gold standard was abandoned. Demand deposits had been backed by the same promise that applied to currency—any private citizen could, in theory, go to the bank and redeem his money in a quantity of gold. That promise was extinguished by government edict, starting with the warring nations of Europe during World War I, joined belatedly by the United States in 1933. Without the gold guarantee, money was only money—"Legal tender for all debts, public and private," as it says on every Federal Reserve Note. A citizen can still go to the bank and redeem it, but his money will be redeemed only in new, identical Federal Reserve Notes.
>
> In the long sweep of human history, the abandonment of gold was a fairly recent event, cheered by most mainstream economists as a progressive development but still deeply traumatic to many ordinary citizens. Without gold, what is money really worth? The question still troubles a fervent minority sometimes called "goldbugs," people who yearn for a return to the old guarantee—"a dollar as good as gold" instead of the government-issued currency they speak of contemptuously as "fiat money." John Maynard Keynes, on the contrary, described the transition from gold as a historic liberation for the world's economies—an enlightened step beyond the fetishistic values attached to shiny minerals. "Commodity money" was replaced by "representative money."[4]

Keynes may have felt he had achieved enlightenment, but the "goldbugs" have pipe bombs and machine guns, and in their minds, the argument isn't quite over. They've yet to accept the reality that money is merely an idea.

The Mark of the Beast

At the center of the money controversy is a simple question that not even the "anti" folks can explain away: Why is gold worth more than quartz or seashells or lead, if all of them are made by God? In reality, it isn't. This is a societal illusion, a matter of cultural perspective and choice. Money changes as cultures change. It always has, and it always will.

Today, we operate in a global economy that is pushing us closer to a global culture, and once again, money is changing its shape. Electronic cash in the form of smart cards is coming into use all over the world. The United States experimented with them at the Atlanta Olympics and pronounced them a smashing success. Bar codes know no nationality or language, and consequently, they are replacing paper money as the push for global commerce intensifies.

But to the conspiracists, electronic money is the last step in the Bible's prophecy of the mark of the Beast (666), a move to place all commerce in the hands of the Antichrist. Most fundamentalists believe that in the near future, even smart cards will be deemed inconvenient. Banks will turn to a system that will require us to have these codes placed directly on our hands. They believe that this evolution in money will be masked under the guise that smart cards can be stolen, but permanent (invisible to the naked eye) marks on our hands cannot be.

In *The New World Order*, Pat Robertson tells his readers that the technology of the Antichrist is now in place.

> Super high speed mainframe computers coupled with modular file-servers hooked together in wide-area networks can hold and process trillions of bits of information with lightning speed and accuracy. There is absolutely no doubt that a world government, for the first time in history, would have the ability to build and recall, in microseconds, the complete vital statistics and life record of every citizen in the world.
>
> If we went to a world currency, then a so-called checkless, cashless society, it would be possible to monitor and control all wealth, other than primitive barter transactions. At some time it would be possible to tax the wealth stored in computers under law, or given a dictatorial environment to freeze the accumulated wealth of any individual or any class of individuals just by simple instructions to a computer.
>
> Never before has our world known a time when the words of the Book of Revelation could be literally fulfilled "that no man could buy or sell without the mark of the Beast." The supercomputer in Brussels handling worldwide bank clearings at the Society for Worldwide Interbank Financial Telecommunications (SWIFT) has already been nicknamed the "Beast."[5]

It would seem that the money controversy is only going to escalate over the next few years. The bombings of ATMs in California in early 1997 are likely just the beginning of the movement's war on the Antichrist's electronic money. Barter societies have already become a mainstay of the antigovernment movement. Gold and silver are once again becoming the official exchange for tens of thousands of Americans who are flying under the radar of the Satan-controlled Internal Revenue Service. Regardless of whether you see electronic money as progress or prophecy, one truth is undeniable: Whoever controls the computers that send out the bits and bytes, controls the world.

The Fed

The only requirement necessary to assure that a culture's chosen form of money will, indeed, have value is that there must be a way to ensure its scarcity. Someone must decide how much money (bits and bytes) is needed in a country or in the world at any given time. Too much, and uncontrolled inflation results—just like the seashell fiasco of New Mexico. Too little, and interest rates—which are simply the cost of money—go too high and threaten the citizen's ability to spend, ultimately creating a recession or depression. It was for this reason that the Federal Reserve was created. The Fed's job is to maintain the correct amount of money in the system. It puts in or pulls out dollars, depending on how it wants the economy to react. For the most part, the plan works. Other factors, such as consumer confidence, are beyond the Fed's control. But on the whole, the bankers and economists appointed to the Federal Reserve Board, known as governors, run the show.

It makes sense that this whole "money" thing is hard to swallow for people who are losing their property and therefore their way of life. They had to risk everything, and the bankers seem to have risked nothing. They wonder, "Why can't the bank just accept a few dollars to cover their costs and let me keep my farm? The banks haven't been harmed." Sadly, I watched Oklahoma farmer Sam Conners make this very argument, as he stared at his foreclosure notice with tears running down his face. If only it were that simple. In order for people to maintain their perception of the value of money, there must be penalties attached to its misuse. In the Federal Reserve system, the economy reacts to forgiven debt exactly the same way it does to money being added into circulation. Forgiving the debts of all those in financial trouble, even though it would be as easy as the stroke of a key, would result in hyperinflation.

"A Pretty Queer Duck"

It's easy to lay blame on a system that we don't understand. But that lack of understanding doesn't diminish the very real control that the Federal Reserve has over the lives of Americans. The awesome power that has been bestowed on the Federal Reserve becomes terrifying when you realize that it isn't accountable to a democratic process but rather answers only to its political constituents—banks, bondholders, and financial markets—hardly a healthy cross-section of society. The Federal Reserve is autonomous. It's not under the authority of the Treasury Department, the president, or even Congress. The chairman and other governors are appointed to long terms by the president to assure that they don't have to answer to anyone elected by the voters. This and other peculiarities of the Fed's structure led Representative Wright Patman of Texas to state, "A slight acquaintance with American constitutional theory and practice demonstrates that, constitutionally, the Federal Reserve is a pretty queer duck." Patman's statement is anything but an exaggeration.

Greider points out just how bizarre the structure of the Fed truly is.

> The Federal Reserve system was an odd arrangement, a unique marriage of public supervision and private interests, deliberately set apart from the elected government, though still a part of it. The Fed enjoyed privileges extended to no other agency in Washington—it raised its own revenue, drafted its own operating budget and submitted neither to Congress for approval. At the top were the seven governors of the Federal Reserve Board, appointed by the President to fourteen-year terms and confirmed by the Senate. But the seven governors shared power with the presidents of the twelve Reserve Banks, each serving the private banks in its region.[6]

In other words, the Fed is a hybrid between government and private interest, an ambiguity that the Fed exploits to the fullest. Federal Reserve Governor Phillip E. Coldwell noted, "To some extent, the Federal Reserve considers itself government. Other times, when it serves, it considers itself not government."[7] This split personality has expressed itself in strange incidents that have greatly fueled the conspiracy theories. In 1935, the Federal Reserve Board purchased the land it's now housed on from the federal government for $750,000. The Treasury Department signed the deed, giving up all the "right, title and interest of the United States of America."

Antigovernment conspiracists wonder why, if the Fed is really a part of government, it had to buy its building from itself. That's exactly what populist Wright Patman wanted to know in 1939. After Patman raised the question, the District of Columbia tax collector sent the Fed a bill for back taxes, declaring that it was not a part of the federal government. The Fed refused to pay. In 1941, the District of Columbia scheduled a public auction of the Federal Reserve's building for back taxes. Four days later, Pearl Harbor was bombed, and the auction was postponed. This land discrepancy is often referred to by today's antigovernment adherents as proof that the Fed is part of a conspiracy. Eventually, the twelve reserve banks issued quitclaim deeds attesting that the government owned the building. What this episode really illustrates is that the Fed is dangerously far removed from normal government oversight and, consequently, from the voters.

Greider points out that the world's other central banks have no such free reign.

> The American arrangement was quite different from those of the central banks in most other industrial nations, where the appendage of the regional reserve banks did not exist. The crucial difference, however, was that the other central banks, even the prototypical Bank of England, were democratized in a way the Fed was not. They all operate on the same basic principles of finance, but other central bankers took their orders directly from elected politicians. When the Bank of England wished to raise interest rates, it could not move without approval from the Prime Minister's Cabinet. The same subservient relationship applied in Japan, France and Italy.[8]

This lack of democratic oversight with regard to the central bank in the United States has monumental implications. A great deal of the anger in rural America exists because its residents have been told by the movement that the Federal Reserve caused the farm crisis and, subsequently, the rural crisis and that it has the power to single-handedly start economic depressions and recessions at will. It's here that, once again, we find the "grain of truth" in the movement's beliefs— that part of the antigovernment rhetoric that is partially true but slightly askew. There may well be a conspiracy underfoot. But it's not a conspiracy of Jewish bankers against Christians; it's a conspiracy of wealth holders versus the rest of us.

The Fed has the ultimate power to steer the economy in any direction it chooses. It therefore has the power to decide who wins and who loses—and to what degree—in the game of economics. The United States, like all places, is divided between its lenders and its borrowers, the haves and the have-nots. It's impossible for both sides to be winners in a system based on interest-bearing money. Without any fear of democratic reprisal from the people it was designed to manipulate, the Fed is basically free to serve only those it views as its constituents. And the Fed has always been perfectly clear about where its loyalties lie. To put it bluntly, powerful bankers will always decide in favor of other powerful bankers and their wealthy friends.

This is to say that rural Americans who perceive the Federal Reserve as an evil force with ultimate power over their lives do have some grounds for believing this. A central bank is a good idea; in fact, that is the only workable plan in an economy the size of the United States. But the fact that the Fed has been removed from the oversight of our democratic process has created some serious drawbacks in the current system. These drawbacks were never more clearly demonstrated than by the recession that rocked the country in the early 1980s, an economic downturn that gave birth to today's rural crisis and, subsequently, to today's antigovernment movement.

Winners and Losers

When our Lord and Master defied them by upsetting the tables and casting the money changers from His temple with a whip, He knew full well within a week He would be nailed to a cross on Calvary . . . Abraham Lincoln, whose rash defiance [of bankers] cost him his life, saved this country billions in interest, because the money was not issued against debt as is that issued by the Federal Reserve System. . . . Since the Babylonian Captivity, there has existed a behind-the-scenes, under-the-table, atheistic, satanic, anti-Christian force—worshippers of Mammon—whose underlying purpose is World Control through the control of money.

—**Wickliffe B. Vennard, Sr.,** *The Federal Reserve Hoax*

"Plant fence row to fence row" was the proclamation of Secretary of Agriculture Earl Butz. The 1970s had arrived, and just like the rest of America's industries, agriculture had entered author John P. Kotter's new global marketplace. The giant grain companies were moving American food to Russia, Europe, and the Third World in unprecedented quantities. In the 1970s, approximately 40 percent of the grain raised in the United States was destined for the international market. The world's people were hungry, and prices were going up. As a result, farmers were experiencing their most profitable years in history. By 1980, North Dakota had the second-highest number of millionaires per capita in the nation. It seemed the good times were here to stay.

But Secretary Butz wasn't finished with his pronouncements. He offered one more piece of advice to the farmers he was appointed by the president to direct: "Get big or get out." Butz had been right before, so there was no reason to doubt him now. Farmers began to buy every piece of available farmland they could find. To pay for this new land—which was doubling in price every few years—farmers mortgaged their existing farms and machinery as heavily as possible. And why not? Everyone from the secretary of agriculture to the banks and university extension offices was assuring them it was a wise move. The inflation rate—which had reached 14 percent—was driving up land values faster than the interest rates were rising. The wisdom of the experts was that those who didn't leverage themselves completely to enlarge their operation were fools.

Unfortunately for the farmers, they were unaware of the real motivations of many of the government's loan officers. The advice they were being given was designed more to increase the salaries of the federal employees than to enhance farming operations. In 1988, Frank Naylor, the top regulator of the Farm Credit System, described the atmosphere at the government lending institutions during the boom of the 1970s. Naylor said it was a time of bizarre banking practices when xsome loan officers' salaries were based entirely on how much money they lent, thereby encouraging them to push enormous loans. He recalled competitions among those lending officers to see who could "put the most business on the books" in a given day or week. Government loan officers were calling farmers and asking them to take more money for no more reason than that the loan officers could win a trip to Hawaii if they could create the most farm debt that month. Times were so good in the 1970s that no one remembered that what goes up must come down. Farmers trusted the experts; and they trusted the government—so they did as they were told.

But not everyone in the 1970s was happy. The nation's wealth holders were losing out. America's rich, who make sizable fortunes every day just by virtue of having their money draw interest in the banking system, were going downhill financially. Inflation was chipping away at their holdings.

Every night on the news, Americans heard in no uncertain terms that high inflation is bad and low inflation is good. But that's just one perspective. Inflation and interest rates are the great distributors of wealth in our capitalist system. They are the fast-forward and rewind buttons on the economic tape player. The only difference between them is which way they make the economy spin. When the rate of inflation is running higher than interest rates, people in debt can actually gain wealth. If a person has a home or farm mortgage at 10 percent and the inflation rate is 14 percent, that person is making a 4 percent return on debt. On the other side, if a wealthy person is making 10 percent interest on investments—such as an interest-bearing savings account—and the inflation rate is 14 percent, that individual is losing 4 percent on his or her money. This is a simplistic illustration, but it makes the point. Inflation is a threat to the wealthy, and in the 1970s, they were threatened.

Meanwhile, the heat was on at the Federal Reserve: It was being blamed for a decade of double-digit inflation. The logic was this: If the Fed hadn't flooded the economy in money, inflation wouldn't be running out of control. Unfortunately, the Fed's only recourse was to throw on the economic brakes by pulling money out of the system, a strategy that would drive up interest rates and push the economy into a deep recession or possibly even a depression. The Fed held the fate of millions of people in its hands.

The Most Powerful Man in America

It was 1979, Jimmy Carter was president, and he was coming up for reelection. Sending the economy into a tailspin just before an election year would be political suicide. Carter lobbied hard at the Fed to postpone the inevitable until after the election. But he had forgotten that the Fed is an autonomous institution, beholden to none but itself and its wealthy constituents. And he underestimated the resolve of Paul Volcker, his newly appointed chairman of the Federal Reserve.

In *Secrets of the Temple*, Greider gives a vivid account of this tumultuous time period at the Fed.

Paul Adolph Volcker was fifty-one years old, a graduate in economics from Princeton and public administration from Harvard, a familiar figure in Washington policy circles and Wall Street finance but largely unknown to the general public. At the moment, few in the White House appreciated what would become obvious in the next few years, that this was the most important appointment of Jimmy Carter's Presidency.

What the President also did not grasp was that he was inadvertently launching a new era and ceding his own political power. The choice had occurred by accident, driven by political panic and financial distress. In time it would profoundly alter the landscape of American life, transforming the terms for virtually every transaction in the national economy and the world's, creating a new order.

In subsequent months and years, Paul Volcker would effectively seize control of events and force them in a direction of his own choosing. In the course of challenging the inflationary spiral, Volcker and the Federal Reserve would prove to be more powerful, more effective than any element of the elected government in Washington, but the democratic anomaly remained unexamined. Millions of Americans would lose jobs, homes, farms and family savings in the tidal shift that followed. For others, the transformation would create new opportunity and fortune. Virtually every American, indeed the entire world, would share directly in the consequences. Only a few understood what was happening to them or why.[9]

What was happening was this: Volcker had decided to pull the plug. He had listened to those around him and made the decision to combat inflation at any cost. He had decided to give the bankers and the financial markets what they wanted: a dramatic recession that would send interest rates through the roof, eventually driving down inflation. The bankers and the nation's wealthy were to be the winners. The nation's middle and lower classes—particularly those in rural America—were destined to lose.

On October 8, 1979, Volcker made the historic announcement of his plan to purposely contract the U.S. economy deeper and longer than at any time since the Great Depression. As always, the message was cloaked in enough financial gibberish to ensure that average people would have no clue as to their impending doom. It's clear that Volcker knew he was going to inflict a deadly recession on the American people. It was a price he was willing to pay. But in 1979, he had no idea that his decision would ultimately give birth to the nation's greatest internal threat since the Civil War—the antigovernment movement.

Federal Reserve Governor Phillip Coldwell knew what the October 8 announcement meant: "Others would say to me, 'Well, you know this will likely cause a recession.' I told them, 'Yes, I know that. But that's the penalty you have to pay for going out too far on the inflation side.' There wasn't any question that the Board knew that recession would follow."[10]

On October 7, 1979, farmers were better off than they had ever been. On October 8, their lives, their history, their farms, and their way of life had been deemed expendable by the Federal Reserve in its war to protect the riches of the nation's upper class.

Senator William Proxmire of Wisconsin, then chairman of the Senate Banking Committee, also understood the decision the Fed had made. He commented:

> This policy is going to cause pain. Anybody who says we can do it without more unemployment or more recession is just deceiving you or is deceiving himself, because there is no way you can do it without more unemployment, without some business failures you would not otherwise have, without serious farm losses.
>
> As I say, this is a bad policy from the standpoint of sacrifice and it hurts many, many Americans, hundreds of thousands, millions of them. But we ought to either come up with an alternative or say that we are not interested, really, sincerely in fighting inflation.[11]

Volcker decided not to seek an alternative.

Volcker's election-year recession sealed the fate of Jimmy Carter, and Ronald Reagan was elected. As if the Fed chairman's decision to force interest rates to new heights wasn't bad enough, Reagan decided to deregulate the banks based on his "supply-side" economic policy—the same basic philosophy that led to the Great Depression. Interest rates could now rise to whatever level the markets could bear, and desperate people can bear a lot.

What's That Sucking Sound?

Greider describes the case of Pearl S. Merriwether, a sixty-two-year-old disabled woman in Washington, D.C., who was unable to pay her gas and telephone bill. The desperate Merriwether turned to the First American Mortgage Company for help. What she got was a $25,000 mortgage with an effective interest rate of 142 percent; under the new rules, that was perfectly legal. In all, First American reported that over a two-year period, it lent more than $2 million at interest rates ranging from 100 to 150 percent.[12] Clearly, the excessive interest rates on the First American loans were not the norm. Most Americans could still borrow money at 16 to 25 percent interest. But it was obvious that usury was once again alive and well. All across the country, those with the least were being made to pay the most. After a decade of losing money to inflation, the rich had decided to recoup their losses—thanks to Volcker and Reagan—with no regard for the human cost.

The high interest rates created by the actions of the Federal Reserve redistributed the wealth of the country. It was as if someone had turned on a giant vacuum cleaner. The money in the pockets of America's middle and lower classes was being sucked into the bank accounts of the wealthy at an astronomical rate. In rural America, two hundred years of history and culture were being sucked away as well. And the vacuum's still on.

The heavily leveraged farmers were the hardest hit of Volcker's sacrificial lambs. Land deflation and higher interest rates did more to forward the idea of agricultural consolidation than all the technological advances and lobbying combined. The value of farmland fell drastically almost overnight. At the same time, interest rates on farm loans—which were often variable—were skyrocketing. Banks and corporate agriculture seized the opportunity.

Even farmers who had never missed a payment had their loans called in. The diminished value of their land had left their giant mortgages undercollateralized, making them subject to demand for immediate repayment. After a while, the banks found themselves awash in farmland, but most were still unwilling to restructure the farmers' debts. They disposed of the land in ways that made no sense. Experienced farmers who owed $500,000 against land now worth $200,000 pleaded with the banks to write down the difference so they could stay in business, but they only saw their farms foreclosed on and resold to less capable people for the same $200,000. Congressional testimony confirms that farm families that were pushed into foreclosure by interest rates as high as 13–15 percent on their notes had been denied refinancing by banks that turned around and resold the same farm, financed by new 10 percent loans—loans at the very interest rate they had told the families was out of the question. The difference between 13 percent and 10 percent to an average cow-calf operation is about $26,000 a year, and that's the difference between making it and not making it.[13] Instead of working with the people who had held the land for generations, the banks chose to hold a fire sale on the properties.

Even the government lenders like FmHA, which had the means to reduce debt under the 1987 Farm Bill, did little restructuring. Farm activists in a few places had lobbied hard for the debt language that was eventually added to the 1987 bill. But the write-down provision became one of the government's best-kept secrets. The vast majority of struggling farmers were never made aware of this debt restructuring opportunity by their county agents. Most farmers found out about the government's secret attempt to help them out only after the time limit for the restructuring had expired. However, the final chapter on the 1987 Farm Bill's write-down has yet to be played out.

The farmers who took advantage of the bill may have only delayed their extinction. The write-down allowed a family to reduce its debt based upon the prevailing land values for a period of ten years, at which time 50 percent of the new land value would be added back on. Translation: Say a farmer borrowed $1 million against his land back in 1979 when it was appraised for that amount. In 1989, the land was appraised at $200,000. The farmer was able to reduce his debt by $800,000 for a period of ten years. In 1999, the farmer must have the property reappraised. If it is appraised for $1 million at that time, the government will issue a $400,000 note against the farmer.

Rhonda Perry at the Missouri Rural Crisis Center told me that people are very concerned about this: "Most people restructured in 1989, so in about two years they're looking at getting hit with a big debt. Around here, property that appraised for $200 an acre in 1989 is now going for $700. That means a lot of people, who are still just barely hanging on, are going to get a $250 an acre lien put against them in a couple of years. We could be looking at a whole new farm crisis in 1999."

The FmHA wasn't the only government lender that created confusion. The federal land banks (supposedly created to help farmers) made a bizarre decision concerning their loan portfolios. The land banks' interest rates were high, higher than their local competition. The big farmers who still had financially viable operations had begun to pay off their land bank loans with cheaper money borrowed from their local banks. This process was leaving the land banks with nothing on their books but the troubled loans given to farmers whose operations were considered a bad risk by the other lending institutions.

To combat this outmigration of their preferred customers, the land banks decided to lower their interest rates to the preferred farming operations. But they were unwilling or unable to afford the loss in interest rates on their books. So they decided to simultaneously raise their rates for the struggling farmers. On paper, the deal showed that the land banks' profit margin had remained the same. In reality, the land banks had sealed the fate of the marginal operators. The new higher rates that demanded new higher payments pushed thousands of struggling farmers over the edge.

Just when it seemed things couldn't get worse, another disaster struck. Reagan decided to try his economic ideas on rural America at the most inopportune time in history. The 1985 Farm Bill decreased government subsidy payments in an experiment to make agriculture more market-driven. According to the League of Rural Voters, the result of Reagan's experiment was devastating. Prices for crops such as corn fell by as much as 46 percent almost overnight.[14] For the grain processors and the international grain exporters, this created a financial boom beyond their wildest dreams. The money taken out of the farmers' pockets at their greatest time of need was put into the hands of the multinationals.

To make sure that the gravy train wouldn't stop, the companies lobbied hard for Reagan to write the changes into the General Agreement on Tariffs and Trade (GATT) agreement assuring the permanence of the policies. Never one to say no to a multinational using words like "free trade," Reagan implemented their GATT plan. With bank payments based on double-digit interest rates demanding more and more money from farmers, the decreased prices were the final nail in the farmers' coffins. Six hundred thousand family farms failed before the end of the decade. As their farms failed, farmers began to blame the government, the lenders, the monopolies, and the Federal Reserve. In many ways, their anger was well directed. And the end results were tragic. Lenders and government workers were shot down in cold blood in small towns across the plains. Rural America had snapped. It was just what the antigovernment movement had been waiting for.

Conflict of Interest

Despite the desperate plight of millions of rural people, America never missed a beat in its food production. The family farms had been resold and absorbed by large corporate operations at dirt-cheap prices. The food industry's long-held dream of massive consolidation was at last being realized.

The farm crisis made newspaper headlines for several years. The public was concerned on a humanistic level, but the fact that food was still readily available at affordable prices made the situation less than critical for the majority of Americans who lived in urban locations. But for the 25 percent of the population that lived in rural areas, the crisis was just beginning. Reagan's "trickle-down" economic theory finally proved to be legitimate, albeit in a reversed fashion. The chain reaction started by the failing farmers cascaded through every home and business in rural America.

Around the world, the Federal Reserve was praised by bankers, market analysts, and political leaders for its fortitude in combating inflation. The Fed had made its decision on who would win and who would lose, and it had stuck to its guns. But as rural psychologist Glen Wallace pointed out so well, "You can't treat people the way rural Americans have been treated without them eventually organizing and fighting back."

The rural crisis is not the result of a Jewish plan for world domination as described in the *Protocols of the Elders of Zion*. The truth is that the rural crisis was created in large part by the Federal Reserve and the Washington politicians who continue to refuse to make the Fed accountable to our democratic form of government and continue to base their policy decisions on the recommendations of whoever is holding the biggest check with their name on it. A slower, gentler monetary retraction could have curbed inflation over the long haul, with fewer human tragedies.

At least one Federal Reserve governor understood that a slower monetary retraction was an option to curbing inflation. Governor Nancy Teeters argued with Volcker that the same results could have been achieved with lower interest rates over a longer period of time. She believed that such a policy would have allowed more small businesses and farmers to survive. Unfortunately, Teeters's opinion did not prevail. If it had, perhaps today's antigovernment movement would be considerably less substantial. A "democratic" Federal Reserve could have been forced to do the bidding of the middle- and lower-class majority, forced to follow Teeters's gradual plan instead of listening only to its wealthy constituents.

There are reasons Congress refuses to democratize the central bank, which it has the power to do. Politicians believe that by keeping the Federal Reserve independent and beyond the control of democracy, they provide themselves with someone to blame when the economy goes in the tank. They can deflect political fallout by blaming the Federal Reserve.

Greider points out another reason for the apparent cooperation between our elected officials and the Fed.

> Many members of Congress were themselves involved in finance. More than one-fourth of the congress owned a direct stake in financial enterprises. In 1980, 129 House members and 38 senators reported that they earned part of their income from stock shares in commercial banks, S&Ls and other financial institutions. As a private interest of congressmen and senators, ownership of financial institutions far exceeded their holdings in manufacturing, law firms, or oil and gas. Even some elected representatives were engaged in finance beyond the passive ownership of bank stocks. Forty House members and four senators were active as directors, officers or partners of commercial banks, S&Ls and investment companies. Finance was, therefore, in the front rank of political influence.[15]

Rural America, alongside small business and the working class, was destroyed because it was considered less important than other sectors of society. The Federal Reserve determined its policies based on the oldest of formulas: The winners would be its friends and associates, its peers. The losers would be the faceless masses that lived in faraway places, places far enough away so their destruction wouldn't have to be witnessed by those who had wrought it. Perhaps it wasn't a conspiracy as such—but rural America has a damn good reason to be mad.

8

Original Intent

Have any of us been told that the secretaries of state, the secretaries of the treasury, the heads of the CIA, the heads of the National Security Council, the heads of the Federal Reserve Board and countless others are in agreement that American Sovereignty is to be "eroded piece by piece"? When has there ever been a referendum for all of the people to decide whether they want to discard our Constitution in favor of a one-world government? The clear answer is "never."

—Pat Robertson, *The New World Order*

They have kept us in submission because they have talked about separation of church and state. There is no such thing in the Constitution. It's a lie of the left, and we're not going to take it anymore.

—Pat Robertson, address to a
Christian Coalition gathering, 1993

As Pat Robertson's statements illustrate, the fundamental-dominionist view of the Constitution is somewhat schizophrenic. On the one hand, they are willing to spill blood to preserve the document, yet on the other, they seem all too willing to throw it out the window in their effort to establish a Christian theocracy. I suspect that the idea of a one-world government is only displeasing if it's not *their* one-world government. This is not to say that fundamentalist Christians shouldn't participate in the democratic process to their fullest ability. The view that such Christian participation is somehow wrong is a paranoid idea put forward by cliché progressives and makes no more sense than excluding Jews or Buddhists from the democratic process. But Robertson has made his dominionist quest well known. He is in-

terested in a Christian government, not a democracy, and therein lies
the difference.

Second to the Bible, there is no greater influence on the antigovernment movement than the Constitution of the United States. In
fact, many within the movement refer to themselves simply as consti-
tutionalist, although constitutional-dominionist would be more accurate in most cases. Go into any public place in rural America these
days—a barber shop, bar, or grocery store—and you're likely to find
someone with a small red-white-and-blue booklet peeking out of a
shirt pocket. It's a copy of the Constitution, and 99 times out of 100,
the person in possession is participating at some level in the antigovernment movement. But what does that really say about the current
state of affairs? That citizens who carry around the foundational document of America must therefore be attempting to overthrow the
government? Could there possibly be a more ironic indication that
something in this political system is seriously wrong?

I must make a confession. When I scribbled out my original outline
for my book, under the heading for this chapter I wrote the words:
"Dispel the constitutional arguments of the movement with real interpretation." In all my years as a journalist, I've never written a more
naive statement. I knew how the antigovernment movement interpreted our most famous document: simply. I even thought I knew
where the movement seemed to be off-base. What I didn't know was
that trying to dispel a wrong interpretation of the Constitution by
defining a correct one is like trying to describe the Invisible Man to a
police-sketch artist. The more you describe, the less accurate the
drawing gets.

I read volumes. I'm pretty sure I found a whole floor at the University of Colorado library filled with books dedicated to the interpretation of the Constitution. They all had differing opinions—and almost
all of them had merit. I would read one book describing the Supreme
Court revolution of 1937, followed by a book explaining why there
was no 1937 revolution. After weeks of research, I realized—if nothing else—why the movement is so strongly drawn to constitutional issues like the right to bear arms, money backed by gold, and freedom
of religion. It's because those issues are presented in a straightforward
fashion in the Constitution. Not that they haven't become complex
over the centuries, particularly lately. However, figuring out what the
Constitution says about those things seems easy enough compared to
its more vague sections such as the general welfare clause. The only

thing that prevented me from becoming completely and utterly humiliated by my dearth of knowledge was the fact that my research revealed that not even the justices on the Supreme Court can figure out how to interpret the Constitution, or more accurately, each of them has figured it out differently than the others. This raises an interesting question. Why are the greatest legal minds in the United States embroiled in an interpretive battle over a document that so many rural Americans claim is simple to understand? This paradox seems to stem from differing presuppositions. The rural citizen reads the Constitution with the goal of trying to understand what powers government "can" have, whereas legal experts seem to look to the document to discern what powers were not specifically denied the government. This is no small difference.

The antigovernment movement, with its rural roots, believes that the Constitution should be interpreted based upon its "original intent." They see no reason that the same rules that applied two hundred years ago shouldn't be sufficient for today. Contrary to this belief, the government thinks of the Constitution as an "evolving document," meant to be interpreted to fit the challenges of an ever-changing world. There is a reason for these differing views.

When our country was founded, it was a low-tech agrarian society. The simplicity of the Constitution reflects that. Not that the founding fathers weren't visionary, but even their far-sighted vision could not have anticipated today's world, or more specifically, today's urban world. For most of us, the place we live in has undergone a radical transformation since the Constitution was written, but just how much has rural America really changed in that time? It's true that rural places have cars, television, and computers, but people there still farm, spend their lives in near isolation, and remain somewhat self-sufficient, compared to their urban counterparts. For most rural Americans, a simple interpretation of the Constitution would still provide an adequate degree of government for their culture.

But that's not true of urban areas, where technology has created an entirely different world than the one that existed two hundred years ago. In an urban society with millions of people, millions of transactions, and, generally, millions of ways to oppress and abuse each other, a broader and more updated approach to the Constitution is a necessity. And the interpretation of the document is changing yet again, as we move toward a global society. The Constitution must be interpreted to provide the utmost freedom for every citizen under the present circumstances of the world in which we live. But with such a cultural chasm between rural and urban places, it has become impossible to govern both types of places in a manner that both would find appropriate. For the most part, the best a democracy can hope for is to act upon the needs of the majority. In light of that reality, things are not likely to improve for the minority in rural America.

The "Funnel" Gets Bigger

Poland has precisely the firearms laws that the NRA has been opposing in the United States. . . . The courageous Polish people are willing to . . . fight against . . . a tyrannical government. . . . but "the authorities have all the guns." Fortunately for us, the founding fathers had great foresight. And so long as the Second Amendment is not infringed, what is happening in Poland can never happen in the United States.

—NRA newspaper ad, Jack Anderson, *Inside the NRA*

The more globally minded and urban-conscious Washington becomes, the more out of step it gets with rural places. As with other split personalities, America is hearing voices. For years, rural America played out its frustrations through the agency of the National Rifle Association (NRA). But as things have gotten worse, a new, more volatile persona has developed, one that is very similar to the NRA personality, only more dangerous. It's known as the militia movement.

When it comes to pouring people into the broad end of the antigovernment "funnel," the NRA has made almost as large a contribution as fundamental Christianity. The NRA, which is largely composed of rural citizens, sees itself as the defender of the Constitution. Its message of holding the line against an out-of-control government was, for years, a low-volume version of the antigovernment theme. But lately, the difference between the NRA rhetoric and the antigovernment ideology has become almost indistinguishable. This similarity of doctrine means that the NRA is providing the movement with several million potential recruits who, like the movement's religious quarry, are predisposed to the antigovernment cause.

For the NRA's 3.5 million members, gun control is the main issue. The modern-day version of the organization was born out of the desire of a frustrated minority to protect its western way of life from a federal government increasingly dedicated to the urban agenda.

The NRA's membership reflects this western mentality. It's made up of hunting enthusiasts, people who feel the need to keep a gun on hand to protect their families, and, increasingly, people who fear or distrust the federal government. It's clear from the NRA's language over the last decade that this latter category of member has become the organization's driving force. In an effort to capitalize on the fear that now grips the rural landscape, the NRA has developed its own brand of conspiracy theories. In the current sales pitch, gun control has become just the first step in a government plan to strip Americans of all their constitutional rights. Here are a few examples of the organization's correspondence to its membership:

> The gun banners simply don't like you. They don't trust you. They don't want you to own a gun. And they'll stop at nothing until they've forced you to turn over your guns to the government. . . . if the NRA fails to restore our Second Amendment freedoms, the attacks will begin on freedom of religion, freedom of speech, freedom from unreasonable search and seizure. . . .
>
> Congress must be forced to restore the Constitution, repeal the gun bans, investigate abuses by government agents and focus the public debate on criminal control, not gun control. . . . Or what we're seeing now will be only a momentary patch of sunshine on the road to doom for the Second Amendment and our Constitution.
>
> THE FINAL WAR HAS BEGUN.
>
> A DOCUMENT SECRETLY DELIVERED TO ME reveals frightening evidence that the full-scale war to crush your gun rights has not only begun, but is well under way . . . What's more, dozens of federal gun ban bills suggest this final assault has begun—not just to ban all handguns or semi-automatics but to ELIMINATE private firearm ownership completely and forever.[1]

I needn't elaborate on how words such as these affect a person already mired in the conspiracy-riddled, psychological wasteland of the antigovernment movement, but it's safe to say that such messages exacerbate an already dangerous situation. The harder Washington pushes the urban gun-control agenda, the harder rural people push back. Until a few years ago, it was a battle of words, but that's changing. Antigovernment militia units, which are nothing less than small private armies, are popping up all over the country. This is happening in response to the federal government's recent gun control legislation activity: passing the Brady Bill and the ban on assault weapons and attempting to pass the Anti-Terrorism Bill.

The Southern Poverty Law Center now estimates that there are over four hundred militias located throughout all fifty states.[2] And they admit that there are likely many more. This militia phenomenon should not be taken lightly. America's history is full of examples of bloodshed in response to the public perception of lost constitutional rights. It would be dangerous to assume that today's constitutional debate is somehow different or less volatile.

A Lesson from the Prophet

Washington's persistence in the area of gun control—nearly two hundred pieces of gun control legislation were proposed in the first session of the Ninety-fourth Congress alone—may well be having the opposite effect to that desired. The result of the government's actions has been to throw open the valve on the antigovernment funnel, greatly increasing the flow between NRA gun enthusiasts and the movement's most violent factions.

The line that separates these armed private armies from the NRA has become increasingly blurred. Although not officially sanctioning the militias, the NRA has condoned them. In 1994, it stated, "Although the NRA has not been involved in the formation of any citizen militia units, neither has the NRA discouraged, nor would the NRA contemplate discouraging, the exercise of a constitutional right."[3] In many respects, the NRA and the militias are simply different branches of the same tree.

Think of rural America as a separate nation. The NRA is its political voice. The militias are its military force. This "separate nation" idea is not as far-fetched as it seems when you consider that in 1996–1997, several antigovernment meetings billed as the "Third Continental Congress" were held near Kansas City. One of the goals of these meetings—which I will describe in more detail later—was to bring the various militia groups under the control of a newly created provisional government.

Once again, those who govern have forgotten that rural people are a unique subset of society and, as such, will react differently to certain situations than their city counterparts. Most urbanites view the issue of gun control as a semantics debate over the language of the Second Amendment. Rural citizens see gun control as a declaration of war against everything they hold dear.

When it comes to understanding the rural mentality, you have to give credit to the shapers of the antigovernment movement. Years ago, men like William Pierce understood the incredible power that issues like gun control would have on the rural population. Pierce's grasp of the rural mentality—and his understanding of where rural-federal conflicts were most likely to arise—has allowed him to take on the role of prophet to the movement. For that reason, we should pay special attention to his prophecies regarding gun control.

In his book *The Turner Diaries*, Pierce describes a race war that ends with the government being overthrown. Pierce's book is more than fiction. The most radical elements in the movement view it as a vision or a blueprint for action. In the book, the Aryan forces used armored car robberies to finance their revolution. In real life, the radical white supremacist group called "the Order" used Pierce's book as a guide to their armored car robberies in the Northwest. In the book, the revolutionaries blow up a federal building as a part of their antigovernment war. In real life, the bombing of Oklahoma City's Alfred P. Murrah Building was almost a carbon copy of the incident in Pierce's book. As I mentioned earlier, Timothy McVeigh had photocopies of a portion of *The Turner Diaries* with him when he was arrested. McVeigh also sold copies of the book at gun shows around the country.

What does all this have to do with gun control, then? The revolution that takes place in Pierce's increasingly nonfiction novel comes about due to the enactment of federally legislated gun control. Pierce knows rural America well. He understands the awesome power of this single issue. We would do well to learn from him. If Pierce believes that the key ingredient to the bloodbath—which he and other radical antigovernment leaders predict—is gun control, then we should probably assume that he's correct. So far, the radical Right has been much more adept at predicting which political and religious flash points will expand their movement than the government has been in attempting to bring about the movement's demise.

Extremism for Sale

NRA and militia members universally point to the Second Amendment of the Constitution as their reason to exist. This amendment is one of those constitutional areas where the "legal minds" trying to justify gun control have to work a lot harder than their pro-gun counterparts when it comes to proving their point.

Anti-gun advocates such as Morris Dees of the Southern Poverty Law Center treat the issue of gun control as if it were simple. Dees writes:

> The second amendment provides that "[a] well regulated Militia, being necessary to the security of a free state, the right of the people to keep and bear Arms, shall not be infringed." Courts have always held that the amendment protects only state-sponsored "well regulated militias" from undue federal interference. It does not provide a constitutional right of individual gun ownership. Although some legal commentators maintain that the past judicial decisions interpreting the Second Amendment in this manner are wrong, most scholars agree with the courts that the Constitution's "right to bear arms" applies only to members of official state militias acting in their official capacity, not to unregulated individual citizens.[4]

Even if you agree with Dees's position, his claim that the courts and legal minds of the United States are essentially of one opinion on this matter should be viewed with considerable skepticism.

In *American Militias: Rebellion, Racism, and Religion*, Richard Abanes offers a radically different perspective to that of Dees.

> Most constitutional scholars side with the individual-ownership view of the Second Amendment. An article in the Encyclopedia of the American Constitution summarizes the Second Amendment literature produced in 1986: "[O]f the 36 review articles published, only four support the anti-gun position, while thirty-two articles support the individual right position."
>
> Political historian Joyce Malcolm—a professor whose work has been underwritten by the American Bar Foundation, Harvard Law School, and the National Endowment for the Humanities—writes that the Second Amendment "was meant to guarantee the individual's right to have arms for self-defense and self-preservation."[5]

I offer these differing opinions not as an attempt to argue "for" or "against" gun control but rather to point out that the issue is very controversial. Legal scholars make well-reasoned arguments on both sides of the debate. This lack of clarity regarding the meaning of the Second Amendment points to an even larger arena of debate: What should our goal be when we interpret the gray areas of the Constitution?

Most people I've talked to have expressed the belief that the courts should try to adhere to the intent of those who created the document. But clearly, that's not the court's intention or the Second Amendment debate would be over. The founding fathers weren't vague about their intention to secure the constitutional right of individuals to keep guns. Thomas Jefferson put it this way: No free man "shall be debarred the use of arms within his own land." Patrick Henry's version stated, "The great object is that every man be armed." James Madison described how America's right to bear arms gave it an advantage "over the people of almost every other nation . . . [where] governments are afraid to trust people with arms." And finally, Sam Adams made the intent perfectly clear. He wrote that the Constitution should "be never construed to authorize Congress to . . . prevent the people of the United States, who are peaceable citizens, from keeping their own arms."[6]

Other people I've spoken with have told me that the "will of the majority" should be brought to the forefront in the court's attempt to interpret the Constitution. Again, if this were the case, the Second Amendment debate would be over, at least for now. A 1995 *U.S. News and World Report* survey found that 75 percent of all Americans believe that the Constitution gives them the right to keep guns. But there's a catch. The majority of those gun-loving Americans also want some form of gun control.[7]

Why is it, then, that if the people want guns and gun control, Americans find themselves at the brink of a bloody showdown over the Second Amendment? It's because the political debate on this issue is being framed by special interest groups with extremist positions that don't reflect the opinion of the majority of Americans. The waiting period created by the Brady Bill makes good sense to almost everyone. I've even found that many within the antigovernment movement would have supported it had they not feared it was the first step toward the total suspension of private gun ownership—a fear created by the rhetoric of both the Left and the Right. When you read comments like those of Morris Dees or the legal opinions of the ACLU, it's clear that their position on the Second Amendment would allow the complete eradication of individual gun ownership, an often-heard position with little public support.

But the other side of the argument is just as out of balance with the desires of the general population. To listen to the NRA, you would think that kids carrying bazookas are just exercising their God-given constitutional rights. The vast majority of Americans, both rural and urban, fall between these two extremes.

If our democracy were firing on all cylinders, elected government officials would also be somewhere in the middle. The gun control debates in Congress would be calm, well-reasoned discussions, free from the extremist language that now defines them. But the system needs a major tune-up. Today's government is fueled by its quest for campaign funds, and this is causing the whole system to choke and sputter. In exchange for NRA money, politicians are forced to spout a gun-toting position that would seem more fitting to a John Wayne character. And the opposite is also true. To secure access to the funds from the Left, elected officials must make the illogical argument that we wouldn't have crime if guns were outlawed.

Lack of radical campaign finance reform has left no room for representing the moderate voice of the people. Our politicians have become the elected representatives of the special interest groups that fund their campaigns, and this store-bought political extremism at the national level is doing more than its share to push us toward an era of antigovernment terrorism.

A Line in the Sand

America has reached an impasse. Members of the antigovernment movement, including their cousins in the NRA, refuse to accept any form of gun control because they believe that would be the first step toward the abandonment of the Constitution. They perceive legislation such as the Anti-Terrorism Bill, which would allow the government to suspend a number of constitutional rights in its effort to protect us, as proof of the government's evil intention. Consequently, they are buying more weapons all the time.

The government, by contrast, is turning up the heat on the movement with legislation like its proposed Anti-Terrorism Bill and its outlawing of assault weapons. It claims that it needs such laws because it has noticed that the antigovernment movement is buying more weapons all the time.

Both the government and the antigovernment movement are escalating their behavior in response to each other's actions—slowly but surely inching toward a showdown that neither side wants, in a scenario that's like a domestic version of the Cuban Missile Crisis. Neither side seems to realize that it is fulfilling its own prophecies and, in doing so, is fulfilling the prophecies and desires of radicals like William Pierce—who must be salivating over how well the plan to start a war is working.

A Sinister Plot?

One might better think of ours as a dual political system. First, there is the symbolic political system centered around electoral and representative activities including party conflicts, voter turnout, political personalities, public pronouncements, official role-playing and certain ambiguous presentations of some of the public issues which bestir Presidents, governors, mayors and their respective legislatures. Then there is the substantive political system, involving multi-billion dollar contracts, tax write-offs, protections, rebates, grants, loss compensations, subsidies, leases, giveaways and the whole vast process of budgeting, legislating, advising, regulating, protecting and servicing major producer interest, now bending or ignoring the law on behalf of the powerful, now applying it with full punitive vigor against heretics and "troublemakers." The symbolic system is highly visible, taught in schools, dissected by academicians, gossiped about by newsmen. The substantive system is seldom heard of or accounted for.

—Michael Parenti,
"The Constitution as an Elitist Document,"
in *How Democratic Is the Constitution?*

As with religion, poverty, and the other ingredients of the rural crisis, the movement has escalated the constitutional debate by way of conspiracy theories. There are a number of these theories being spun around the Constitution, all of which point to the movement's claim that the federal government has departed, due to a sinister plan, from the rules set out in the Constitution. In some theories, Abraham Lincoln is the bad guy; in others, it's Bill Clinton. However, the most common focus of the constitutional conspiracy theories by far is Franklin D. Roosevelt, which makes sense when you consider that Roosevelt did more to change the American way of governing than any president in modern history. It was Roosevelt's creation of a powerful central government that has given birth to the dual (symbolic/substantive) system described by Parenti. And it's this two-faced system that is leading us toward revolt. But it needn't be that way.

The hard-core conspiracy-driven circles teach that Roosevelt was placed into power by international bankers and the Illuminati for the purposes of stealing the people's gold and removing the government from the restraints of the Constitution so that the Antichrist could one day waltz in and take over. In the soft-core antigovernment factions—those made up of fundamentalist Republicans in $400 suits—Roosevelt is likewise painted as the beginning of the end.

In his book *America's Dates with Destiny*, Pat Robertson pronounces Roosevelt's policies unconstitutional and declares him the father of today's out-of-control big government. "He [Roosevelt] was building an army, but he forgot that the Constitution had already determined the divisions of that army."[8] Robertson's views are important in the sense that—as with his biblical prophecy teachings—they tend to fan the flames of the hard-core conspiracists.

Eugene Schroder, in his book *Constitution: Fact or Fiction*, puts forward his argument—which has become the antigovernment movement's argument—that we, as a nation, have descended from a constitutional republic into an unconstitutional dictatorship.

> The U.S. Constitution was basically the shackles placed on the federal government by a sovereign people. The people possessed God-given rights. These rights were only "secured" by the Constitution. All rights not specifically granted to the government were reserved for the people.
>
> This country started as a constitutional republic, that is, a union of sovereign nation states. The federal government was to be an agent of the states.
>
> As a safeguard, the Constitution provides that during times of rebellion or invasion, the president may assume all powers. These emergency powers should end after the crisis. President Lincoln assumed all powers during the Civil War. Since he was dealing with a rebellion, we may say that he established a constitutional dictatorship.
>
> Since then, however, the definition of "emergencies" requiring total control has been stretched to include economic problems, social imbalances, and perceived threats to the U.S. by a foreign country's actions on another continent. When authoritarian control is exerted during times other than rebellion or invasion, it is an unconstitutional dictatorship. The federal government has overstepped the bounds placed on it by the Constitution.
>
> Through the insidious, yet steady encroachment of "emergency powers," the government has now achieved the ability to rule the people by statute or decree, without the vote or consent of the ruled. Through a maze of political maneuvers, the emergency powers granted to Franklin

D. Roosevelt in 1933 to deal with economic depression have become part of the U.S. Code as permanent everyday powers. America has continued under the "unconstitutional dictatorship" of war and emergency powers to this day, more than 60 years later.[9]

Schroder makes quite a claim: Unbeknownst to the American people, the Constitution has been abandoned by the government through political trickery. In the movement's thinking, if indeed this claim is true, then every red-blooded American has a duty to do whatever it takes to restore the land to constitutional rule. That's why we fought the Revolutionary War and that's why we must fight this one. But are Schroder's claims accurate?

The trouble all seems to have started with President Franklin D. Roosevelt's handling of the Great Depression. Roosevelt felt that the economic calamity facing the country was as serious a threat to its survival as any invasion. In 1933, he therefore decided to invoke the war and emergency powers that the Constitution stated were only to be used in times of rebellion or enemy invasion.

History bears out Schroder's version of the story. As has been noted, Roosevelt did indeed seize all gold and silver, took the country off the gold standard, and established a new banking system with paper money. He tinkered with many constitutional divisions of power, redefining the president's role, including taking the power to coin money from Congress and giving it to himself, despite the specific instructions of the Constitution.

Never before had a president taken such action in peacetime. But never before had we faced a Great Depression. To those in the movement, Roosevelt's actions in 1933 were nothing short of the creation of a dictatorship. Many writers of the day stated clearly their belief that Roosevelt had become a dictator. Schroder's claim that Roosevelt greatly expanded the powers of the presidency beyond the bounds set forth by the "original intent" of the Constitution is, quite simply, true. But some questions remain: Why did he do it? Was it illegal? Was it part of a sinister conspiracy?

Because the Great Depression was threatening not only the nation's economic status but also the very future of the nation, Roosevelt determined that it was better to sacrifice certain aspects of strict constitutional adherence rather than have the whole country crumble into chaos. No less than one-third of America's population was going hungry. Nonetheless, this was not a victimless process. As a result of

Roosevelt's actions, the democratic freedoms previously enjoyed by people under the pre-Roosevelt interpretation of the Constitution had to diminish. There are only so many "God-given" rights in the world: If Roosevelt claimed more of them, then somebody else had to give them up.

In order to quickly accomplish the radical changes he felt were needed, Roosevelt began to magnify his power by all means possible, regardless of what rules he had to bend or break. He knew it was a controversial step to take and that there would be a public outcry. To reassure a nervous citizenry, Roosevelt stated—though later we would find out his statement was somewhat disingenuous—that it was his intention that the powers would revert to their preemergency constitutional divisions once the emergency had passed. At one point, Roosevelt told the American people that he would return the powers he had grabbed under the state of emergency "to the people to whom they belonged."[10] But he died during his fourth term, having never relinquished those powers.

In all likelihood, Roosevelt never intended to give up his new power. This wasn't because he was a puppet of a great Jewish conspiracy but rather because he felt it was in the best interest of the people for the president to keep them. He believed that society had changed to such a degree that there was no choice about the need for the interpretation of the Constitution to change with it. Roosevelt didn't believe that the founding fathers had ever intended for future generations to be bound by a literal interpretation of the document. He believed that they had understood that the Constitution was a starting point for the federal government and that, as such, its rules would be allowed to evolve over the centuries to fit the nation's needs. Eventually, Roosevelt tried to push his beliefs into law.

Shortly after the president's historic first one hundred days, lawsuits challenging his controversial New Deal policies were filed by a number of powerful corporations. In 1935, the suits were thrown before the Supreme Court. First, the National Industrial Recovery Act was struck down as unconstitutional. Then, the Railroad Retirement Act, followed by the Agricultural Adjustment Act, were rendered in violation of the founding document. Emergency or not, the New Deal was going down in unconstitutional flames. Antigovernment adherents see this as proof that they're correct.

But Roosevelt was sure his vision for America was the right one. After all, he'd been elected by a landslide by people who wanted his

New Deal. In Roosevelt's mind, the Supreme Court was the villain, subverting the will of the people. Roosevelt hatched a scheme to push his reforms through the high court: He would increase the number of Supreme Court justices to twelve from the previous nine. By selecting his appointees carefully, the bullheaded president guaranteed himself a majority on the court.

In 1937, at the height of this Supreme Court debate, Merlo J. Pusey wrote his book *The Supreme Court Crisis.* Pusey put into words what many were thinking: Roosevelt had gone too far.

> No President is so wise or progressive or humanitarian that he can be trusted to remodel to his own liking the agency which interprets the Constitution. Even if there could be a full assurance that the President would not take undue advantage of that vast power, merely to grant it would be a dangerous precedent. There are some disadvantages, as the President [Roosevelt] has suggested, in a system which permits judges to say what the Constitution is. But there would be infinitely greater dangers in a devise which, in effect, might permit the President to say what the Constitution is.[11]

The move to stack the court turned out to be Roosevelt's biggest blunder. Even his staunchest supporters began to realize that the president wanted to implement his programs so badly that he was willing to break all the rules, including those in the Constitution. Congress refused to allow the Supreme Court ploy. In the long run, however, it didn't matter. Several seats on the court opened up on their own and Roosevelt pushed through his like-minded appointees. In 1937–1938, the Supreme Court reversed its decisions on the New Deal reforms and forever changed the face of the federal government by throwing out the "original intent" doctrine and replacing it with the new interpretation that the Constitution is an "evolutionary document." Roosevelt won, but the argument still isn't over.

The antigovernment movement's claim that we have been operating in an illegal governmental condition for the last sixty years is an interesting argument, but it's wrong. Things did change significantly in 1933 at the direction of a power-hungry president with good intentions, but ultimately, they did so with the support of all three branches of government and the people—meaning that the changes were made in accordance with the Constitution, a view that is supported by a strange and circular argument.

The Constitution was written to be the rules for government. It created three separate branches of government to ensure that no single branch could get out of line with its rules. The Constitution could only be changed if the three parts agreed that the changes were within the parameters of the founding document's intent. It's likely that the founding fathers never anticipated that the three branches of government would one day decide that the original intent of the Constitution was that its original intent could be discarded in favor of creating a government that was totally different from the one described in the document. This argument is enough to make your head spin, but that's essentially what happened.

Think of it this way. Imagine the Constitution as a genie with one unbreakable rule: You only get three wishes. Roosevelt was the guy whose third wish was that he could have all the wishes he wanted. On one level, it seems to work within the genie's system, but on another level, we assume that it wasn't what the genie had in mind. Roosevelt's treatment of the Constitution wasn't illegal. It was just incredibly contrived.

Although the movement's claim that the government has been illegal for sixty years is wrong, its belief that we have been operating under emergency powers during this time is accurate. In 1973, the Senate began study on a plan to terminate the emergency powers. A Senate report noted: "Since 1933, the United States has been in a declared state of emergency."[12]

The Senate was actually trying to determine whether there were still any governmental functions started under the war powers that had not yet been written into the U.S. Code. The government wanted to terminate the emergency, without losing any of the changes that had been orchestrated under its power.

In 1976, Congress passed the National Emergency Termination Act. Roosevelt's emergency powers would no longer be considered as such. Instead, they had been written into permanency, forever changing the status of the Constitution. But again, I must point out that this action was done with the blessing of all three branches of government. Like it or not, it's legal.

The Tables Have Turned

The movement claims that the power of today's federal government has increased radically because of Roosevelt's actions. And again, the view is correct; it's a simple fact of history. Based on the movement's hyper original-intent doctrine, it makes sense that the movement would interpret this fact as some sort of subversive treason against the people or, as it often does, as an evil conspiracy. But if that's so, why didn't the people revolt against Roosevelt in 1933? Why was he elected to four terms? Why is his name still revered in homes all across the nation?

The answer is this: He wasn't a part of some sinister conspiracy. He was a determined man who was willing to do anything to get his policies enacted, including bending or breaking the Constitution's intent while staying within its legal requirements. And the reason no one revolted is that they agreed with his goal, which was to create better lives for working people who were living in horrible poverty and being exploited by business interests. They wanted him to do whatever was necessary to help them.

Unfortunately, in their time of hurt, the people forgot the warnings of Daniel Webster, who said, "It is hardly too strong to say that the Constitution was made to guard the people against the dangers of good intentions, real or pretended . . . There are men in all ages who mean to exercise power usefully—but who mean to exercise it. They mean to govern well; but they mean to govern; they promise to be kind masters, but they mean to be masters."[13] In the short term, Roosevelt's circular interpretation of the Constitution rescued the working classes of the nation. In the long term, his tinkering with the Constitution has led us to the edge of revolt. But why is today so different from 1933?

Roosevelt would have done well to heed the words of Merlo J. Pusey: "It would be a dangerous precedent." Roosevelt's primary interest was in bettering the lives of our country's downtrodden. But he should have considered that he was establishing a powerful central government and that one day, that power would be passed on to future presidents who might not share his convictions. In Roosevelt's era, it was the corporations that complained about his meddling giant government, but times have changed.

Today, the politicians who tend the rudder of Roosevelt's creation are a different breed. In order to be elected, they must raise billions of dollars. In order to raise those funds, they must be beholden to the powerful corporations that fill their campaign coffers. The tables have turned.

It's no longer the corporations that are complaining. The farmers and factory workers are no longer the ones singing the government's praises. The power of today's giant government has become a corporate tool. The working men and women are now under the heavy weight of the system Roosevelt created for their liberation. In rural America, the people are being crushed by monopolies, international trade agreements, and their second-class citizenship—all creations of today's version of Roosevelt's government.

The movement's conspiracy theories about the Constitution being abandoned by the evil leaders in Washington are wrong. The truth is that elected officials interpret the document broadly, sometimes ridiculously so, because that's the only way in which a two-hundred-year-old document can adjust to the complexities of today's modern world. The answer isn't to turn back the clock. The answer is to elect people who will not abuse their power. I suspect that if we currently had a Roosevelt in the White House, only multinational corporations would be accusing the government of behaving illegally.

It's unlikely that any argument will dissuade the antigovernment hard-core in its attempt to return to days gone by. In many cases, their constitutional position is tied to their position on the Bible. Many fundamentalist Christians in the movement believe that both the Bible and the constitution are to be interpreted literally. In fact, I have met a number of antigovernment proponents who have told me that the Constitution was given to America by God and that violating its literal interpretation is a sin that will allow the country to be infiltrated by the forces of evil and eventually overthrown. They believe that Roosevelt opened a Pandora's box. Unfortunately, they also believe that armed revolution will be required to force it closed again.

Mainstream Support

It's in the arena of constitutional debate that the movement has drawn its most significant mainstream support. From conservative columnists like Thomas Sowell and George Will to politicians on the state and national level like Newt Gingrich, a cry is going out for a return to the Constitution. The arguments of these people are usually framed in such terminology as "state's rights, good" or "big government, bad." To some degree, the Republican revolution, as they like to call it, can be attributed to this constitutional argument.

As an example of the growing popularity of the "return to the Constitution" idea, consider that in 1996 in the California State Assembly, Assemblyman Keith Ogberg was able to push through a new law that now makes *The Federalist Papers* required reading in all high schools. In one of his syndicated columns, Thomas Sowell, commenting on the California legislation, noted

> that this is not something you might expect from the liberal Democrats who control the California legislature. But few dared to vote against it for fear of public reaction. . . . The concerns of those who wrote these essays [*The Federalist Papers*] are also relevant to the current trend in the United States for government to keep expanding its powers by promising us goodies or claiming to protect us from all sorts of exaggerated hazards in the environment, in the workplace or in the home. Whether freedom is lost by degrees or by a coup d'état, once it is gone, it is gone. These signs of determination to take back this country from the counter-culture left may turn out to be historic in their own way.[14]

The people in California who pushed for the bill have promised to make their crusade national. In Colorado in 1997, Senator Charles Duke—who was selected as a mediator in the eighty-one-day Freemen standoff in Montana due to his militia ties—tried unsuccessfully to push through a similar law that would have required *The Federalist Papers* and other early documents to be taught in schools. It's clear that the constitutional arguments being put forward by those who fancy themselves to be antigovernment are finding a growing mainstream audience.

But it would be dangerous to forget the hard-core elements that are pushing this new conservatism. It would do good for Thomas Sowell, who is black, to remember that a fair number of the people he is whipping into a frenzy consider him to be subhuman. Within the more radical elements of the antigovernment movement, the goal is to return to the "organic" Constitution—the original version, in which blacks, immigrants, and women were relegated to second-class citizenship with no right to vote.

Just like the TV evangelists, these columnists and politicians are unwittingly fanning the flames of revolt. They spout rhetoric about Americans losing their God-given constitutional rights, apparently without thinking about how their hyperbole will be interpreted by a stressed-out rural populace that is storing up arms. Newt Gingrich goes on tirades about giving the government back to the people. But his ideas of reform are laughable in the antigovernment circle, where people aren't interested in politically tweaking a de facto government that's part of the great conspiracy. The movement wants to establish a new government, and it's attempting to do just that. In 1996 and early 1997, various elements of the movement held several national meetings near Kansas City that were dubbed the "Third Continental Congress." These meetings were an attempt to set up a provisional government whose role is to begin operating now in accordance with the Constitution, as interpreted through the movement's "original intent" doctrine. The provisional government is to remain in place until the illegal impostor government is toppled or collapses on its own, at which time elections can be held. That's a slightly more radical concept than the one Newt Gingrich has in mind.

In *Inside the NRA,* Washington columnist Jack Anderson writes these words regarding the militias: "On the whole people who join militias tend to be small town or rural citizens. They also tend to be poorly educated. It has always been common for people to loathe and fear what they cannot understand. The statements of militia members betray how little many of them understand."[15]

The sad truth of the matter is that this passage by Anderson demonstrates how little people like himself understand about today's movement. This kind of clichéd generalizing is the product of people who apparently do their reporting from the confines of their urban office. Their opinions on the antigovernment movement seem to have been formed by no more research than looking out of an airplane window at thirty thousand feet as they fly over those big square states in the middle of the country on their way to the other coast. The cartoonish "Bubba" character that media have chosen to use in their effort to personify the antigovernment movement is misrepresenting the truth and creating a grave situation. People aren't likely to remedy the economically and culturally induced causes of the antigovernment movement if they perceive its only members to be beer-guzzling Neanderthals. The "Bubbas" do exist, but they are only a small feature on the real face of the movement.

Doctors, lawyers, insurance agents, and college professors were all in attendance at the meeting of the Third Continental Congress in 1997. They are revolutionaries, perhaps, but they are not ignorant rednecks. They were all there because they believe that the Constitution has been abandoned illegally and that, most likely, only armed confrontation can restore it to its rightful role in the political system. The real makeup of the antigovernment movement of the 1990s demonstrates just how widespread and serious this internal threat has become.

Germination

The idea that naturally suggests itself to our minds, when we speak of representatives, is that they resemble those they represent. They should be a true picture of the people.

—Jonathan Elliott,
*The Debates in the Several State Conventions
on the Adoption of the Federal Constitution*

I am afraid that Jonathan Elliott, whose essay was published in 1788, would not be impressed with today's version of the American political system. To say that government representatives don't resemble those they represent is an understatement of monstrous proportion. I will say, once again, that the single most powerful force destroying rural America and subsequently creating the existence of a violent antigovernment movement is the lack of radical campaign finance reform.

This lack of reform has handed the reigns of democracy to powerful corporations—"the new king," as attorney Gerry Spence so poetically describes them in his book *From Freedom to Slavery*. The only hope for peacefully addressing rural America's steadily decaying situation is a properly functioning democracy. If government remains in its current form—where only those willing to raise millions of dollars from the corporate manipulators have a chance to be elected—then there is no hope for a peaceful resolution of the problem.

The Federal Reserve must be democratized or the gap between rich and poor will become a deadly chasm. The food monopolies that buy the people's representatives and destroy the rural way of life must be dismantled. The international trade agreements that mean no less than massive rural poverty must be rewritten to protect the lives of the millions of people they are adversely affecting. But first, in order to accomplish any of these goals, the representatives of the people must be made to understand that their loyalty is to their voter constituents, not their corporate constituents. The alternative is that we do nothing—and continue to pay the price in blood.

These goals will be hard to achieve. It's difficult to influence the political system when you are a member of a minority—in this case, the rural minority. As we have democratized the country, we have taken this lack of political clout into consideration for the protection of minorities made up of various ethnic groups and even for women. But no such protection has been contemplated for the rural minority, whose values and traditions are now being voted into oblivion by the larger, urban population.

Laws that now govern the rural culture—which covers 90 percent of the nation's landmass—are, in effect, being dictated by an urban majority that lives in the other 10 percent of the United States, a majority that is often ignorant of the ways of the people whose lives they are controlling. Rural people feel powerless and disenfranchised because they *are* powerless and disenfranchised. If that single fact doesn't change, then the seeds of influence that have been planted in rural America's despair will come to fruition in a harvest of rage like none the country has ever known.

Part Three

The Harvest

9

America on Trial

*There is something very very wrong in this country, and people are realizing it.
. . . Bloodshed is inevitable. No government has ever given up power without some
kind of force being applied.*
—Jessie Enloe, common-law court activist, 1996[1]

In late February 1996, 170 people from seventeen states gathered at
the Howard Johnson Conference Center in Albuquerque to find out
how they could do battle with the government without firing a single
shot. The gathering was billed as the United Sovereigns' "Common
Law and You Seminar and School." The goal of this seminar and of
others like it is to teach the participants how to establish common-law
courts in their respective areas. Considering the rapid growth of the
common-law arm of the antigovernment movement, the seminars are
proving effective.

At the Albuquerque seminar, common-law advocate Darrell Frech
stood before the enthusiastic crowd and exclaimed, "If every person
in America knows what we know and can prove, there would not be a
politician, a judge, or a lawyer that wouldn't be hanging from the
lamppost on every street corner in this nation."[2] Frech had already
shown the crowd several examples of his "proof." Using an overhead
projector, he illustrated his claim that the birds on the gold seals that
hang in federal court rooms aren't really American bald eagles but
rather Egyptian vultures. He also traced the outline of the Beltway
that surrounds Washington, D.C., stunning the crowd when his
drawing formed what he described as an outline of Satan's skull.

The limited media coverage of the Albuquerque event painted its
participants as potentially violent antigovernment extremists. But

there was no attempt by reporters to unearth the root causes that led these people to New Mexico. Darrell Frech didn't always lead common-law seminars. He, like most of the others in the room, arrived in Albuquerque by way of the rural crisis.

The first time I saw Darrell Frech's name was in 1989, attached to the following letter that was part of the Oklahoma Task Force investigation into rural stress and suicide:

Dear Sir:

No one can ever begin to imagine the stress, strain, frustrations, and total helplessness that the American farmer has had and felt the last few years in trying to stay afloat and fight the farm credit system. You get so desperate you do not know what to do or even where your next meal for your kids will come from.

We personally have been fighting Federal Land Bank of Enid and Wichita for the last seven years. FLB lied, cheated, and frauded us. One farmer by themselves can not fight them through the courts. So where do you turn to for help?

We wanted to give up so many times and walk away. You take your frustrations out on each other and on your family. You are always under tension. You can't afford insurance, doctors, or anything. This stress and strain causes arguments, divorces, and extra problems with children. This desperation often causes murder and suicides. They can not face failure and losing the family farm.

Our Plea is this, make the Farm Credit System, especially FLB accountable to someone! No entity should be allowed to do these things to anyone and not be punished. If a borrower was free to sue the Farm Credit System and for punitive damages, they would straighten up their act. A federal grand jury investigation needs to be called to investigate their dealings, contracts, and why their illegal charges, debits and credits appear and disappear at the touch of a button. Please make the Farm Credit System accountable to someone!

—Darrell and Sally Frech, 1989[3]

When I pulled this eight-year-old letter out of my files, I was shocked to see the note I had written across its top margin nearly a decade ago. It said, "good candidate for justice movement." Long before Frech's involvement with common-law courts, his cry for economic justice had fallen on deaf ears. Frech, like many in rural America, didn't have the money it takes to seek justice through our legal system, so he joined the thousands of other suffering rural people who had set out to create their own judicial system known as common-law courts. Rural psychologists saw the birth pangs of this renegade judicial system a decade before most of us started reading about it in our newspapers.

The rural frustrations that would eventually give rise to the common-law courts were described in a 1988 article published in *Farm and Ranch Guide*. In the article, psychologist Val Farmer wrote about the perceived lack of justice in rural America.

> "Where is justice?" That is a common expression by those affected by the farm crisis. It is being said by people on all sides of the devastating downturn of agriculture during the 80s.
>
> It is being said by the farmers who feel betrayed by the use of power, intimidation and questionable tactics of lenders who rapidly became self-protective of their interests.
>
> It is being said by farmers who feel so tied up by lending institutions and the courts that they are "made to feel and act like crooks" in order for their family to survive. . . . It is being said by farmers who deal with the humiliation and the expense of going to court. They face heavy demands on their time, emotions and reputation.[4]

America is on trial in the movement's common-law courts. After decades of watching people with money get preferential treatment, while those with little or no means have been carted off to our overflowing prisons or have lost their property to foreclosure, rural America is fighting back. The common-law courts that now exist in over forty states are spreading like wildfire for one reason: Common-law proponents claim that their system puts the poor on an equal footing with the monied. While authorities play catch-up trying to cope with the threat of the antigovernment movement's militias, common-law courts have surged past the militias as the most influential and rapidly growing element of the antigovernment phenomenon.

In January 1997, I saw the name Darrell Frech in the *Daily Oklahoman* under the headline "Common Law Advocate's Federal Trial Underway." Frech hadn't been charged with a crime, but the article said that a search warrant had been issued for his home. The way things are going for Darrell Frech, it seems possible that he may eventually complete the metamorphosis from farmer to inmate—just as Gideon Cowan and scores of other rural residents have done. The charges against these antigovernment proponents are varied, but their real crime is the same—they can't adjust to the changing world that's being created by the corporations that run this country.

The Posse Model

Regarding your response to the Lake Co. Sheriff's Posse Comitatus, that was your signature to your death warrant. You will hang shortly if you live long enough.
—**Death warrant issued to a U.S. Senator by the Americans Concerned for Freedom and Liberty, 1976**

Today's common-law court system is an exaggerated version of the Posse Comitatus system created in the 1970s–1980s. The Posse was the first of the antigovernment groups to incorporate common-law courts into its structure. The Posse based its common-law philosophy on a combination of the old English common law, the Magna Carta, and the belief that people are born with certain God-given rights. According to radical Right expert Daniel Levitas of Atlanta, the Posse believed that the supreme power in the land rested with the county sheriffs. The sheriff's job is to enforce the common law, which is based upon a particular county's local custom and precedent. In the Posse's court system, no crime had been committed unless there was an injured party. On the one hand, the Posse system would eliminate our prison overcrowding by decriminalizing things like drug infractions. But on the other hand, the Posse courts had their own brand of violence and abuse.

The Posse's courts met infrequently in only a few states and were therefore never very consequential. These early common-law courts would send out arrest warrants to public officials who they believed were guilty of one crime or another—usually something related to a farm foreclosure—but that was about the extent of it. The sentences passed by these Identity-influenced Posse courts were stiff but rarely, if ever, carried out. The Posse's code of justice, laid out in a manual known as the *Blue Book*, spelled out the basic sentence for nearly all crimes: "He shall be removed by the Posse to the most populated intersection of streets in the township and at high noon hung by the neck, the body remaining until sundown as an example to those who would subvert the law."

Today's common-law courts are different from the Posse's earlier versions in a number of ways. They are considerably more widespread than the Posse courts ever were. For example, some of the forty-odd states where the common-law courts are now operating are literally saturated with the quasi-legal groups. According to Thomas Moyer, the chief justice of Ohio's supreme court, common-law courts are now active in sixty of Ohio's eighty-eight counties, and other states are equally blanketed. In Oklahoma, Richard Wintory, chief deputy of the attorney general's criminal division, has said, "We can't identify any part of the state they are not in."[5]

Technology is a big factor in the spread of the movement's common-law justice. Want to start a common-law court in your town? It's easy: Just get on the Internet and download one of the many available common-law "how-to" kits. Within days, you, too, can be costing the federal government millions of dollars and thousands of man-hours. As Wintory laments, "They are tying up our court system. They are causing hundreds of thousands of dollars in legal fees."

One of the goals of today's common-law movement is to bring the U.S. judicial system to a screeching halt by filing more paperwork than the system can handle. In some places, the plan is already working. Ilse Bailey, an assistant attorney in Kerr County, Texas, reported that she was spending as much as 40 percent of her time just dealing with paperwork filed by common-law courts in her county.[6]

Another function of today's common-law courts is to grant sovereignty to citizens. Common-law practitioners claim that once their courts grant sovereign status to someone, that person can legally stop paying taxes. And people are coming forward by the thousands for such an opportunity. As you can imagine, those attending a common-law court for the purpose of escaping their tax obligations aren't among the wealthiest 10 percent of Americans. In my experience, those who use the common-law courts for such purposes are generally in the lower third of the economy. Besides, people at the top of the money ladder don't need common-law courts. They have the current system to ensure that they can bypass the vast majority of their tax burden.

Sovereignty

I am of private status and not a subject of the United States nor subject to its jurisdiction, as it has no constitutional jurisdiction except in the District of Columbia and its possessions. Absolutely no contracts exist where I have knowingly, will-

ingly, or intentionally refused my common-law rights or gave up my private status to become a federally privileged person.

—Thomas Gipson, testifying before
a common-law court in Texas, 1996[7]

Antigovernment behavior in rural America is becoming increasingly tied to the idea of the sovereignty of the individual—the belief that citizens can take certain steps to legally remove themselves from the authority of the current federal government. The idea is that if the federal government won't help rural America, then rural America will simply govern itself by ignoring federal authority.

These self-designated sovereigns claim that their actions are political, but as with many of the movement's beliefs, they're more rooted in economics. If not, then it's a huge coincidence that the majority of sovereigns I've met owe back taxes, can't afford to have taxes taken out of their paychecks, or have had a run-in with the IRS at some point.

Rural Americans are having trouble making ends meet. One-fourth of them cannot even afford to properly feed their children. If these people did not have to pay taxes—which the movement claims is a benefit of becoming a sovereign—their limited financial resources would go further. Sovereignty is a complicated, contrived argument designed to free people from the federal system that they can no longer financially afford to support.

In most instances, the movement's sovereignty concept is derived from a hyperliteral interpretation of the Constitution. Sovereigns claim that there are two types of citizens described in the founding document: Fourteenth Amendment citizens and "natural" citizens. Fourteenth Amendment citizens are those who received their citizenship from the federal government through the Bill of Rights. Those in the movement view this type of citizenship as second class, because people granted citizenship by the federal government must therefore abide by its rules and regulations, including its taxes.

Natural citizens are those born in this country who are thereby the citizens of the state in which they were born, with no obligation to follow any laws established by the federal government. Sovereigns claim that the federal government's true jurisdiction covers only a ten-square-mile area around Washington, D.C., plus U.S. territories like Guam and Puerto Rico, and that its authority pertains only to Fourteenth Amendment citizens.

Sovereignty disciples say that most "natural" citizens have been duped into Fourteenth Amendment status by establishing a contractual relationship with the federal government. The contracts to which they refer are such things as social security cards, driver's licenses, car registrations and tags, birth certificates, and marriage licenses. But according to the movement, "natural" citizens can be "unduped."

Sovereigns teach that people can reclaim their "natural" status by rescinding all their "illegal" contracts with the government. Those wishing to be sovereign must renounce their U.S. citizenship (federal citizenship) and get rid of their social security number, driver's license, and so forth. Once this is done, sovereigns need only follow the rules of common law.

What Is Common Law?

Defining common law can be pretty challenging. That's because common law, like religion and constitutional interpretation, is a malleable idea that tends to vary from group to group. One theme that is echoed throughout the movement is that common law is simple. But it seems that it's simple only because it can't be rigidly defined and, therefore, misinterpreted. One group told me that common law is synonymous with the Old Testament laws in the Bible. Another group claimed that these are the laws that God has placed on everyone's heart, written down nowhere. Yet another faction bases its common law on the Magna Carta, in conjunction with the Bible. And finally, a man in Texas told me that common law is whatever people in a particular county want it to be. This last description of common law seems to be the most accurate in that it incorporates all other definitions.

Common-law advocates such as Dr. Eugene Schroder realize that for this new judicial system to evolve and be taken seriously, it must become uniform. Schroder and Florida common-law leader Susan Mokdad have been actively pushing to create a uniform national structure for common-law courts. "It's a learning process," says Schroder. "It's gonna take some time to transition."[8]

Schroder, who claims that the government has illegally suspended the Constitution through enacting the emergency war powers (as described in Chapters 7 and 8), recently got his day in court—common-law court, that is. A grand jury was convened at the Wichita, Kansas, convention center in June 1995. In case you were wondering just how many people are involved in this newest level of antigovernment activity, consider that over one thousand people traveled to Wichita to participate in this single common-law event. The grand jury concluded with the jurors demanding that the defendants in the case—President Clinton, the nine Supreme Court justices, and Congress—must "show cause" as to why the Constitution has been suspended.

The size of the Wichita event and the enormous growth of the common-law court system is evidence that rural America is no longer willing to take a purely defensive posture in its growing discontent with government. Common-law courts have provided antigovernment adherents with a means to take action, something that the militias couldn't offer. The only direct action a militia member could take was to start shooting people or blowing things up, something the majority of antigovernment people are not yet willing to do. The common-law courts, however, give antigovernment adherents a nonviolent way to attack the government through "paper terrorism"—the filing of liens and other documents against those found guilty by their courts.

The purpose of paper terrorism is to cause one's enemies as much trouble as possible without physically harming them. Once a person has been found guilty by one of these renegade courts, the paper starts to fly. It's not uncommon for those found guilty to have millions of dollars' worth of bogus liens filed against them and their property. The documents look authentic, so they generally make it through the clerk and recorder's office. If a recorder in a particular county refuses to file the common-law court's papers, they themselves become the targets of the renegade court. Several county clerks have been tried and sentenced to death for their lack of cooperation. The court clerk and county recorder are critical functionaries in the heartland war, and their role has therefore been transformed from glorified secretary into frontline soldier, a role many are reluctant to play. Many of them avoid the difficulty by turning a blind eye to the movement's tactics, which may explain why so many of these bogus documents make it through the system.

Another form of paper terrorism is the filing of lawsuits accusing public officials of a multitude of injustices, usually on the grounds of their failing to keep their oaths of office. Frivolous lawsuits by the thousands are being filed at a pace faster than the system can dismiss them. Just to get a suit dismissed costs the person being targeted by the common-law court a great deal of money, and that's precisely the goal.

But this bulletless technique for confronting the government is quickly coming to an end, as state and federal governments have started to crack down on the common-law courts. As of January 1997, authorities were prosecuting or investigating people accused of paper terrorism in twenty-three states.[9] And several states have now passed laws with harsh penalties pertaining to the filing of common-law liens. The question is: How will the antigovernment movement react to the loss of this nonviolent outlet for its frustrations? The short answer is this: poorly.

Common-law advocates see this crackdown as further proof that the government places itself above the law. Conspiracy theories are being spun to explain why the government is refusing to recognize the authority of common-law courts, which advocates say is derived from the Constitution. These theories usually revolve around the belief that the federal government has suspended the document. If the crackdown on common-law courts continues, which is inevitable given the pseudo-courts' illegal activities, the paper terrorism that has been a trademark of these common-law courts may be transformed into real terrorism. There is growing evidence that this metamorphosis from paper to physical violence has already been completed in some renegade courts.

From Paper to Pipe Bombs

Understanding the rural culture helps explain the growth of common-law courts. In the same way that the movement uses religion as an excuse to fight a fabricated holy war that substitutes for its real economic struggle, common-law courts allow rural people to feel justified when they take action against their enemies—whether through the filing of liens or by means of terrorist bombings. The rural culture doesn't allow people to simply attack the government because they are frustrated with their own situation. But if a common-law court can transform such an action into a perceived act of justice, then a person is psychologically freed up to commit illegal acts that would otherwise be indefensible in the rural world. In that sense, common-law courts are just a contrived excuse to fight.

William Dressel, a district court judge in Ft. Collins, Colorado, has felt the intimidation of common-law courts that have moved beyond paper weapons. "It hasn't been pleasant," says the judge, who has received numerous warrants for his arrest as well as death threats. At one point, men came to Dressel's door to arrest him. He was eventually forced to hire round-the-clock protection. Ohio Attorney General Betty Montgomery received a "petition for redress of grievance" from an Ohio common-law court that stated, "The degree of your crime is capital in nature as set forth in the U.S. Const. 5th Amend., and anyone committing a capital offense is to be executed."[10]

Judge F. Dennis Alvarez of Hillsborough County, Florida, has also had to change his lifestyle because of threats from the common-law courts, among them numerous death threats. The judge told reporter Emily Barker of *The American Lawyer* that at one point, he decided to sit down and talk with the antigovernment people who were attacking him. As Alvarez put it, "When you meet with them and deal with them, these are just very, very scary people."

In Montana, the Justus Township Freemen were known to have sentenced numerous county and state officials to death by hanging. At the time of their arrest in 1996, federal authorities claim that the Freemen were about to carry out the kidnapping and hanging of several public officials. Nicholas Murnion, the prosecutor in Garfield County, Montana, was one of those officials.

Murnion's first experience with the Freemen was when he was hit with a $500 million lien payable in gold or silver. Murnion had refused the demands of the Freemen to prosecute the FHA for its role in several ranch foreclosures in the area. Shortly after the lien incident, Murnion found his name posted on bulletin boards around Jordan, Montana, along with a promise of a $1 million bounty for his arrest. The posters read, "The sum of one million dollars of money will be tendered over to any Freeman or other person who successfully causes the arrest and subsequent conviction of the following named suspects." Sheriff Charles Phipps of Garfield County was also named on the poster. Phipps and Murnion had both been involved in a foreclosure on one of the Freemen's property. The poster didn't state what sentence the officials had received in the Freemen's common-law courts, so Phipps called William Stanton, the Freemen's constable, to inquire about the sentence. Stanton flatly told Phipps that those convicted were to be hanged.

As the antigovernment movement evolves, it's becoming increasingly complex and well organized. It's beginning to take the form of a government in which different branches of the movement perform separate tasks. It's becoming clear that the common-law courts have joined forces with the militias. The obvious purpose for this merger has federal authorities extremely concerned. The courts pass the sentences—and the militias carry them out. And the sentences we're talking about aren't prison terms.

In Idaho's Madison County, the court-militia merger has become all too real. County Magistrate Mark Rammell received a "notice of felony" from a local common-law court because he had presided over a case involving a sovereign who was driving without a permit. The common-law court accused Rammell of acts of "subversion to the United States." At first Rammell received the usual death threats and hate mail, but the intimidation escalated. On Thanksgiving, while running some family errands, Rammell noticed that he was being followed. Since that time, his house has been continually staked out by these antigovernment intimidators, who often park their cars at the end of his driveway. Rammell says that "they scream religious scriptures and go on about the wages of sin is death."[11] Like thousands of others targeted by the common-law courts, Rammell wonders how long it will be before the groups act on their threats. As Tim, the man in the Oklahoma farmhouse, told me, certain cells within the militias are getting ready to start carrying out the death sentences. As he put it, "You should start seeing it soon."

Sarah Lowe, the first lady of the Republic of Texas, a large group that believes that Texas is a sovereign nation, told me that the courts are a natural progression springing forth from the militia movement. Lowe comments, "A lot of men became involved on the militia level because they didn't believe they had a remedy at law, and they feared the federal government. But that's [militias] the most basic reaction. They started with militias but they are moving beyond it to establish a legal system." In the Republic of Texas's legal system, the common-law courts pass the sentences, and the "Texas Rangers," the group's enforcement arm, carry them out.

In Wisconsin, the common-law courts have announced that their sentences will be carried out by a Christian militia group headed by Donald Treloar, who says, "We promise to go after every last one of them [attorneys, judges, and politicians] who have violated the Constitution." Susan Mokdad's court in Tampa, Florida, has also joined forces with a militia. The Florida court sent out an arrest warrant to Judge Alvarez, stating that he should turn himself in to the common-law court in order "to avoid physical arrest at your home or workplace by the militia, which could result in a dangerous confrontation."[12]

The Ohio common-law courts are also known to have militia ties. In Oklahoma, a group called the United Sovereigns shares a post office box with the militia. Richard Wintory, the deputy of the Oklahoma attorney general, says that common-law courts all over the nation have turned to the militias for enforcement of their orders: "That is the link we have been concerned about. Are they just going to give up when everybody ignores their pleadings?"[13] Unfortunately, that's not likely to happen.

Kenneth Toole of the Montana Human Rights Network puts it bluntly: "If we see common-law courts beginning to direct the activities of the militias, watch it. I think you're going to see some of these wacky warrants enforced."[14] The truth is, we're likely already seeing it in the form of bombings at IRS buildings and abortion clinics. Several of my sources have told me that at least some of these violent actions are originating from common-law court sentences. Not all of the common-law court sessions being held in America are public events. There's an underground, military-style court system in operation around the country, and it's possible that these military courts are responsible for much of the nation's terrorism—from church burnings to the slaughter in Oklahoma City.

I have never attended one of these military courts, but several of my antigovernment contacts have. In August 1996, I heard about a man who had been the presiding judge in several of these closed-door courts. The man, who wishes to be known only as "Arthur," was considered by many in the movement to be its authority on legal matters such as banking, common law, and sovereignty. I had also heard that Arthur was surrounded by armed guards at all times because antigovernment patriots feared that the government would assassinate him. In November 1996, I went looking for Arthur.

Six Flags over Reality

I'd been on the road for several weeks, moving from one antigovernment group to another. In some ways, I was feeling the effects of the community psychosis that rural counselor Glen Wallace had warned Congress about in 1989. There's a segment of our society that is at war with the federal government, and if you're immersed in that stress-filled culture long enough, it takes its toll. I began to look in my rearview mirror constantly to see whether I was being followed. Sometimes I was, but I never knew which side of the conflict was tail-

ing me. Nearly every antigovernment group I've encountered believes that it has been infiltrated by the government—a belief that
goes a long way toward fostering paranoia.

Sometimes the folks I'd meet would tell me that they thought I was
a government agent posing as a reporter. Usually, after they discovered that I was more interested in their personal stories than in their
future plans to fight the government, they would open up, despite my
questionable employment. Paranoia has always been the Achilles' heel
of revolutionary movements. The government understands and exploits this vulnerability whenever possible.

In the 1970s, the FBI used paranoia to attack the American Indian
Movement (AIM). If the government wanted someone out of the
picture, all it had to do was give that person a very public ride
through town in a government vehicle. When revolutionaries see one
of their own in the company of the FBI, bad things happen. This gov-
ernment-enhanced fear of informants is usually enough to produce a
corpse. The government wins without ever firing a shot.

Many of the people I meet in today's movement believe that the
government is only a few hours, days, or weeks away from launching
a full-scale attack against them. Consequently, they can't sleep or eat
properly, which only intensifies their paranoia. Even though I was
acutely aware of these things, it didn't protect me from the effects of
the stress. After weeks of watching people grab weapons and scurry to
windows every time they heard a car door slam in the night, I, too,
began to have a Pavlovian response to such everyday events. It's a
hard way to live. You don't even realize it's happening until some
chunk of reality jumps up and hits you between the eyes.

For me, that needed dose of reality came in the form of a simple
roadside attraction. I was driving through Texas on my way to meet
Arthur, the common-law guru. While negotiating the highway between Dallas and Ft. Worth, I came across the brightly lit, year-round
festival known as "Six Flags over Texas." At any other time in my life,
I would have flown right past this orgy of capitalism, but the juxtapo-
sition of this festival against my recent antigovernment investigations
and my coming meeting with Arthur sent my head reeling. I pulled
onto the shoulder of the highway and got out of my car. I can only
guess how I must have looked to passers-by, as I stood there on the
shoulder of the highway staring up at a giant Ferris wheel as if I'd
never seen one. In between the trucks flying past me, I could hear the
sounds of children screaming for joy and garbled traces of carnival

music. "How could such a thing be taking place," I wondered, "right in the middle of a war?"

It was then that I realized I'd spent the last few weeks in what felt like a different country, on what might as well have been a different planet. In the light of that Ferris wheel, the rural world I'd been living in seemed so dark and apocalyptic that I shuddered. The sounds of joy emanating from the park made the people I'd been living among seem so stressed, poor, angry, frustrated, and most of all, sad. In that moment, the distance between where I was and where I'd been seemed infinite.

As I pulled my car back onto the highway, I wanted to turn north and go home. Instead, I headed for another armed compound filled with economic and political refugees—a place where the conversation would be about death sentences, not amusement parks. It was like deciding to go for a walk in quicksand.

Arthur

As I reached the top of Wild Rose Pass, my tires straddled a giant tarantula that was slowly making its way across the lonely highway. It seemed an appropriate introduction to the prehistoric-looking setting that surrounds Ft. Davis, Texas, a small town located north of Big Bend National Park. This is a beautiful and sparsely populated area where every rock formation looks like a fortress, and as I drove the empty highways through open range, it seemed the only abundant crop in this harsh land was the shattered foundations of abandoned homesteads.

Ft. Davis is a western town. It still has hitching posts in front of the courthouse. Its ancient wooden storefronts have been somewhat restored in an effort to attract the tourists that pass this way on their journey to Big Bend. But on the whole, the town has been bothered little by the modern world.

My motel room was phoneless, so I walked to a pay phone to get my final directions to the compound, or rather, the "embassy," as the people in the Republic of Texas like to call it. The Republic is the antigovernment group that was offering its protection to Arthur at the time of my visit, in exchange for his unique knowledge. The pay phone was occupied by a half-dozen young Hispanics, so I sat down on the curb to wait my turn. My wait was shortened by the sudden appearance of a Border Patrol vehicle that sent the young men scurrying to the rear of the gas station for cover. The vehicle slowed, then drove on by. I heard whoops and hollers of relief from behind the station.

The next morning I drove the last fifteen miles to the embassy. When I reached the final turn that begins the last five-mile stretch over washboard dirt roads, a pickup truck parked at the turnoff pulled in behind me and escorted me on my final approach. The Republic of Texas folks are more than a bit jumpy these days. Their "paper" battles with state officials have been escalating for several years. By the time I arrived, surveillance planes had been buzzing the embassy—a brown, rectangular metal building—for several days in a row. People at the embassy were convinced that an assault on their sheet-metal fortress was imminent, so stress was abundant.

I pulled up to the front of the building, and a man with sandy blond hair and a mustache, holding a rifle, pointed me toward a parking space. As I stepped from my car, he politely greeted me. "Mr. Dyer," he said, "Arthur and Ambassador McLaren are busy right now, but I'll take you inside as soon as I can."

There were four more men in front of the building, each with a rifle. As I approached, a man with a beard suggested that I be frisked. After being searched, which included making sure that my tape recorder wasn't a bomb, I decided that it was time to chain-smoke. By the third cigarette, things had settled down. The men with rifles turned out to be like most of the people I had met in the antigovernment movement—rural people treading the water of hard times.

One of the guards said he became involved with the Republic when he couldn't afford to pay the fine imposed on him for driving without a seat belt. He explained: "They issued a warrant for my arrest over a seat belt. I didn't know what to do. I was driving around one day and heard a guy on the radio talking about the Republic of Texas and how people in the Republic didn't have to obey laws like speed limits and stuff like that. So I started making phone calls and here I am. Now I'm a Texas Ranger."

Another guard told me how he'd lost custody of his kids:

My wife's family is rich. They never liked me because I was always making $5 or $6 an hour. When my wife and I were having troubles, my in-laws went to court to get custody of my kids. They had lawyers and they knew the judge. When it was over the judge said I had to pay most of my income for child support. They knew I couldn't live on what they left me. I was giving all my money to my millionaire in-laws. As soon as

I missed a payment they got the judge to cancel my visitation. That's what they wanted all along. That's the kind of courts this country has, and that's why I'm fighting for the Republic. Down here, nobody can take away your children because you're not rich.

Finally, it was time to go inside. The embassy is basically one big open room with four or five desks and a dozen or so file cabinets scattered throughout. There are computers, printers, fax machines, and telephones. It would have looked like any high-tech office if not for the stack of rifles—both assault types and older models—behind the front door and the various ammunition clips and boxes of ammo scattered around on the desks, file cabinets, and even on the back of the toilet.

Arthur was sitting at the desk that held the main computer. In another setting, he would have looked like any computer geek. He had black hair and beard, a dark complexion, and an accent that combined Kansas with Tennessee. But instead of a half-dozen pens in his pocket, Arthur had an occupied shoulder holster.

We shook hands and I sat down next to him at the desk about three feet away. Arthur pulled his pistol from its holster and looked at me with an odd grin. He set the gun down on the desk between us and rested his right hand on top of it, the barrel pointing just to the left of me. "So what can I do for you?" asked Arthur, still looking sheepish. I responded like the addict I had suddenly become, "Can I borrow your ashtray?" You see, I was raised in one of those gunless homes where you're repeatedly told that if you ever so much as look at a gun, it will miraculously discharge and kill you instantly. It was going to be a long day.

Arthur had recently arrived in Texas from the Freemen's compound in Montana. I asked him how he had managed to leave the Justus Township compound while it was surrounded by hundreds of FBI agents. His answer was more than a little mysterious. "Certain information is controlled information," replied Arthur. I asked him if the FBI had just let him walk out. "I wouldn't say that," he responded. "Why I survived and they didn't, I don't know. We were all issuing warrants. Some people in the militia pulled me out." Ultimately, Arthur attributed his evaporation from the Montana siege to divine intervention: "A couple of weeks before they were hit they placed a woman in authority over men. They appointed a woman as deputy clerk, and the Bible says that's wrong. That's why I left, and that's why they fell."

Arthur's religion seems to be a mix of Identity and fundamental Christianity, though it was hard to pin down. I knew that he was from St. Mary's, Kansas, where a unique strand of Catholicism—one that teaches that the pope is the Antichrist—is practiced by some antigovernment adherents, but I wasn't sure if Arthur was influenced by that or not. There seemed to be several theologies at work in Arthur.

Arthur grew up in the hills of Tennessee. His formal education stopped at the eighth grade. Arthur says that was a blessing, as it prevented the government from "brainwashing" him. As we talked, it became clear that Arthur's raw intellect is substantial. He told me he owns over four thousand books—primarily pertaining to the law and written during the 1700s and 1800s—and that he has read them all. Arthur quoted case law and sections of the Uniform Commercial Code like a second language, which made it difficult to follow his explanations and presumptions regarding legal matters. He seemed to know what he was talking about, but who on earth would know? It was like a firebrand preacher weaving his way through the complexities of the Old Testament scriptures: As long as he sounds authoritative, people just nod their heads in agreement. I nodded a lot while listening to Arthur.

Arthur used to be a prison guard. That was how he became interested in the antigovernment movement and the law. It all started when a man was sent to his prison to serve a year-long sentence. "That guy had seven kids," said Arthur. "His only crime was he couldn't afford to pay the tickets he'd gotten. First, they took his license away, but the guy had to drive to feed his family. They kept arresting him and finally they gave him a year in prison. That man hadn't harmed anyone. It was completely unjust." Arthur said he started to drive without a license to prove a point. He claims he had a number of heated run-ins with local authorities and judges that culminated in his being jumped and severely beaten by a group of men. That was when he started studying the law.

Arthur believes that the Constitution is an illegal contract that pertains to only those people who are not sovereigns. He claims that the Fourteenth Amendment didn't free anyone but rather made us all slaves—which is his way of saying he adheres to the theory that there are two types of citizens. It was while discussing the Constitution that

I started to get a feel for Arthur's radical, religion-based views. "They've [people in government] signed on the dotted line and sold their souls. You can't sovereign unless you have one of these," he shouted, as he waved his pistol in front of my nose. "If you can't be as cold-blooded as they are, then you'll lose."

Arthur and I simultaneously chain-smoked through several hours of brain-deadening conversation concerning contract law before we finally arrived at the subject of the antigovernment movement's military courts, a subject about which Arthur was very candid. "The militias across the country didn't have a court that they could go to. . . . Finally, they realized there was a court to go to and they picked me because I understand the law. I understood military law." According to Arthur, military law is reserved for individuals who break their oaths of office—people like judges, ATF and FBI officers, sheriffs, and the like. "You don't deal with these people on the civilian side," he said.

Militias in a number of states have called on Arthur to preside over their nonpublic military courts. It seems unlikely that people would go to the time, trouble, and expense of bringing Arthur in to preside over a military court that passes death sentences if they weren't serious about carrying out the court's orders.

Arthur handed me a file containing warrants he issued from the military courts. He said that hard-core militia people understand that they can arrest those named in the warrants and hang them, or they can just shoot them dead when the party is located. Several of the warrants in Arthur's files were for persons found guilty of being informants for the FBI.

One of the military-court warrants was for a man whose name I won't disclose because it might put his life in danger, a man who had tipped off authorities to a 1995 bombing plot by Willie Ray Lampley and several members of his Oklahoma Constitutional Militia. Lampley and his cohorts were planning to blow up the offices of Morris Dees and the Southern Poverty Law Center as well as an Anti-Defamation League office in Texas. According to the FBI, the bomb Lampley and the others were constructing was similar to the one used in the Oklahoma City bombing. Arthur related the story as follows:

> That guy [the alleged informant] had a real nice position. He was the owner of an Army/Navy surplus store. So guess where the militia came to get their gear. He just sat in there and gathered information and passed it along for a measly $1,700 a month [the amount Arthur says

the man was paid by the FBI]. Thieves and whoremongers come cheap.
That's why you need a military court. If agents are in violation, they've
committed treason. And the sentence for that is death . . . death! It's a
rope in a tree.

Considering all the judges and government agents, including those
involved in the Waco and Ruby Ridge standoffs, that the movement
believes are guilty of treason, it seems that the list of people to execute could be quite long. But Arthur doesn't see that as a problem.
He told me that "ropes go a lot further than lead does. You can hang
a lot of people with one rope." Arthur admits that military courts
around the country will probably get carried away with their death
sentences:

> Coming out of this chaos, there's going to be a lot of venting.
> . . . That's the reason the government would like to shoot me. I'm
> bringing stability to the courts. If a judge made a mistake accidentally, I
> offer him repentance. If they break their oath intentionally you hang
> them right there after they're tried in a military court. That judge the
> Freemen were going to hang had been warned for three years. He was
> involved with Clark's foreclosure. He should have been hanged, and
> that's what they were going to do. . . . Same thing with that attorney
> Murnion. He owned the bank, the telephone company, the house he
> lived in he'd stolen through foreclosure. He was taking land left and
> right. If it had been up to me, I'd have shot him [Murnion]. If these
> guys won't abide by the law you shoot 'em.

Having spent several hours with Arthur, I now suspect that Attorney Murnion was more fortunate than he'll ever know. Had a woman
not been placed in authority over men in Justus Township, Murnion
might not be around.

I asked Arthur if the sentences being passed by the military courts
are to be carried out now or in the future, when the movement will
presumably be stronger. He gave a biblical response.

> God told them [the Israelites] to go into a country and slaughter every-
> body right then. If they waited, God punished them for not obeying his
> orders. When you take in filth, it's like fleas. You have to get rid of
> them.
>   People eventually get to the point where they're sick and tired and
> they're going to slaughter somebody. When they're sick and tired
> they're going to pick up something [Arthur grabs his pistol] and shoot

somebody. We're slaves, and the only way to lose the chains is through force.

Referring to the people he had sentenced to death, Arthur said:

> If the one enslaving you has dogs that are keeping you from undoing your chains, what are you going to do to that dog? You're going to clean it out. Now if you want to give yourself time before you go in to fight the war—a stability and foundation from which to operate under —that's a good idea. Just wars are fought that way. You need to have a reasonable chance for success.

It seemed that Arthur was now advocating waiting until the movement was stronger before taking violent action, but that was not what he was saying. As he pointed out, it is all in the way you define "success." Arthur believes that

> success can be measured in two different ways. Success in this world or success in the next world. It's the success in the next world that counts. So one against a hundred or one against a million doesn't matter. My family knows it, my children know it, and they're ready to give their lives. That's why they shot Mrs. Weaver, because she was ready to give her life. And they had some filthy little Jap do the job for them.

Arthur told me that there are other military courts besides his around the country and that many of them are out of control. But he isn't worried about it because he believes that all bloodshed furthers the cause. It's on this point that Arthur's beliefs seem to be in line with those of the most radical Identity factions that teach that starting a war will benefit them, no matter what the odds of winning are. As he views it,

> If you're not willing to die then you're going to be a slave. People are being killed over this right now and it's only going to take a few more to water the tree, and then we'll have a full-blown confrontation. The other side thinks that they can just shoot a few and it will go away. But the tree gets watered no matter what happens. It's like the Christians who died in the Colosseum. They thought they could kill a few and it would go away—it tripled. Ruby Ridge, Waco, the Freemen, they all feed the tree of liberty.
>
> Those who have all the property are going to lose their lives. The enemy thinks they can win because of technology—their massive killing

machines. But they forget about divine intervention. All I can say is that eternity is a long time to spend in Hell. It's better to die than to live in chaos.

Finally, I asked Arthur how long he thinks America has until the antigovernment confrontation becomes full blown. His tribulation-based answer reflected the perception of many in the movement. It's impossible to overstate the impact that the upcoming turn of the century is having on the antigovernment movement. We saw the power of apocalyptic thinking in March 1997 when thirty-nine people belonging to the Heaven's Gate cult committed suicide in California, and they were pacifists. Consider what could happen when a group's apocalyptic beliefs turn them toward terrorism rather than suicide.

Arthur's schedule for bloody confrontation is similar to what I've been hearing all over the United States: "You've got about six months before everything comes to pass. . . . I've been following prophecy for years. Between now and the year 2000, there's gonna be Hell to pay, literally. Things are getting into motion. They're going to turn Jerusalem over to the Vatican by pretending that the Pope needs to mediate. There's a window here now. He's [the pope] already been put on notice." I couldn't tell if Arthur was implying that someone is going to kill the pope or not, so I asked him directly. He looked at me with that sinister smile again: "Certain people are ready to do certain things."

Arthur's last words to me were more of a warning than anything else. He counseled:

> I suggest you better quit looking and get something done. You need to prepare yourself with food, water and provisions, and get away from the population or you'll spend three and a half years burying the dead. Anytime you rob people of that which is given them by God—their land, their sustenance—people are going to fight back. That's the law of nature. The Earth cries out for vengeance when you withhold the wages from the laborer. More will die, and more will be set free.

Secret Courts

The existence of out-of-control military courts may help to explain the violence America is now experiencing. Unlike the more straight-forward common-law courts that are attended by as many as four hundred people at a time, military courts can be convened by one small cell (five or six people) of antigovernment radicals in any basement or back room. By holding a military court, hard-core radicals can keep their violent plans a secret, while still using the idea of a court to cleanse their conscience. Based upon the movement's almost sacred need to justify its actions, we can assume that for many pipe-bomb incidents, assassinations, church burnings, and acts of paper terrorism, there is a cell of at least five people involved and that there was a common-law or military court trial that took place beforehand. This also means that for every arrest the federal authorities make, they likely leave behind several coconspirators, who thus become—due to the arrest of a comrade—even more agitated and motivated to strike again.

Did the cell of radicals who blew up the Murrah Building in Oklahoma City hold a military-style trial beforehand? I suspect the answer is yes. Many of my contacts within the movement have told me it's likely such a trial took place. But they deny having any firsthand knowledge of such an event. There have probably been dozens of military trials around the country concerning the actions of the ATF and FBI at Waco. I've been told about several of them, though not about any that involved any of the known suspects in the bombing. Waco trials have also been conducted by public common-law courts that issued arrest warrants for President Clinton and Attorney General Janet Reno. The Republic of Texas group has scheduled a public common-law trial for sometime in 1997 to deal with the government's actions against the Branch Davidians. Antigovernment activists who want to take action over Waco have a veritable smorgasbord of common-law court sentences to choose from—all designed to free violent radicals from any guilt they might feel over taking action against the government.

10

Little Countries

Five million to ten million people are prepared to take action to restore constitutional government to the United States.
—Colorado State Senator Charles Duke, 1996[1]

The antigovernment movement is in a constant state of evolution. The Internet, shortwave radio, and antigovernment publications have speeded up its evolution to such an extent that it's hard to keep up with the process. Following Ruby Ridge and Waco, the antigovernment movement focused on the creation of militias. With its military arm in place, the movement's next push came in the form of common-law courts. As the sovereignty concept took hold across the nation, antigovernment adherents began to form organizations that encompassed all of these antigovernmental elements—sovereignty, courts, and militias.

The goal is that each organization should become self-sufficient, able to fully govern its membership with no assistance from the outside world. It's as if there are thousands of independent countries operating within the borders of the United States. Some of these antigovernment countries have formed around Identity beliefs, whereas others get their inspiration from the U.S. or state constitutions. Some still follow the Posse Comitatus model, whereas others are driven by Christian fundamentalism. Regardless of their differences, which are substantial, these groups realize that they must ultimately support each other to avoid being crushed by the federal government—a lesson they learned at Waco.

These self-governing antigovernment bands range in size from a dozen people to several thousand. They represent the next stage in the evolution of the antigovernment movement—a stage that threatens to unleash even more violence and chaos. The actions of these supposedly sovereign groups are often in direct conflict with the laws of the United States, which they no longer recognize. The question is: How long can Washington afford to let this push for self-rule go on? The longer it exists, the stronger it grows, as more and more people are choosing to opt out of the federal system, whose taxes make the difference between a family's eating or sending its children to bed hungry.

No Alternative

The government's refusal to recognize the sovereignty of these pockets of patriots is understandable: That would lead to anarchy. But Washington must be ever so careful in how it deals with these nations within a nation. Eliminating the movement's nonviolent attempts to remedy its economically rooted problems, such as individuals declaring their sovereignty to avoid taxes, without providing a meaningful alternative to sovereignty, all but ensures the outbreak of widespread terrorism.

Telling paranoid, conspiracy-believing, antigovernment soldiers that their only alternative to bringing about change is to use their vote doesn't go very far. People are no longer willing to choose between one corporate-sponsored, millionaire attorney and another when it comes to electing their representatives. That's how we got into this mess in the first place. The federal government continues to offer rural America no solutions to take the place of the pseudosolutions being concocted by the movement. It has offered no hope that rural people's lives will improve. Washington's policy is to destroy the antigovernment movement without ever trying to understand why it exists.

General George Armstrong Custer used the same philosophy as the federal government is using now in his dealings with Native Americans. And we all know how Custer's story ended. In Custer's day, the government's shortsighted antics nearly caused the genocide of our entire Native American population. What price will we pay for Washington's lack of judgment this time? How many freedoms will we sacrifice to antiterrorist legislation? How many more events like Oklahoma City will we endure? Unfortunately, the government's policies toward rural America and the underclass as a whole—or rather, its lack of policies—seem hell-bent on giving us the answers to these questions before the turn of the century.

The Freemen Revolution

It's [foreclosures] what happened to the folks in Montana [Freemen] and it's what happened to me. That's why LeRoy [Schweitzer] was arrested. He was teaching people how to keep their farms and ranches. He was showing them that the government isn't constitutional.

—Tim, California Identity believer who attended
a course taught by the Montana Freemen, 1996

The evolution of the antigovernment movement has created a new genre of radicals known as Freemen. The most notorious group of Freemen is the one that was involved in an eighty-one-day standoff with the FBI at the Justus Township stronghold in Montana. But the Montana Freemen are just one small pocket in the growing Freeman network—a network that is constantly establishing new, self-governing pockets of antigovernment radicals.

The term "Freeman" applies to anyone claiming to be a sovereign. In some instances, a group of sovereigns will band together on one or more pieces of property that they believe have been removed from the jurisdiction of the United States. Once the Freemen have established a piece of property as their own "country," they create their own laws, courts, and militias. When I was staying at the Republic of Texas embassy, people were arriving there from out of state every few hours. I asked a guard why they were coming and going so frequently. He told me that they were people picking up documents and getting the information needed to set up their own sovereign townships.

Freemen townships can vary greatly in character. Some Freemen organizations are completely peaceful, whereas others compose the movement's most violent elements. In Oregon, Freemen claiming citizenship in the "Embassy of Heaven" are pacifists. These fundamentalist Christian Freemen drive without license plates, driver's licenses, and such, but their only goal is to be left alone. If they're arrested for driving illegally, they simply go on a hunger strike until they're released from jail. They never threaten to harm anyone but themselves. Unfortunately, pacifist Freemen are the exception to the rule. Freemen in Seattle were arrested for operating a bomb-making school. Freemen in Texas have been blamed for threatening to blow up the state capitol. And then there was the eighty-one-day Freemen standoff with the FBI in Montana.

It is this group, the Justus Township Freemen in Montana, that gave birth to the modern Freemen movement. Justus Township was used as a training center for people interested in establishing their own sovereign townships. The Montana Freemen, led by LeRoy Schweitzer, taught their antigovernment students how to establish a sovereign township, set up common-law courts, and create pseudo-banking systems designed to convert antigovernment justice into cash.

Authorities have estimated that approximately eight hundred people went through the antigovernment crash course at Justus Township, but my sources, some of whom were involved with training at the compound, tell me that over eighteen hundred people were trained by the Montana Freemen. That's eighteen hundred people who took their newfound wisdom back to their respective communities, where it was passed on to still more people.

As of January 1997, law enforcement officials were working on investigations involving 151 people from twenty-three different states who have ties to the Montana group. The Montana Freemen are being blamed for the nationwide proliferation of paper terrorism and common-law courts. Liens and money orders created by Schweitzer and his disciples are showing up in ever-increasing numbers all across the country, and many of the nation's common-law courts can trace their roots to Montana.

In Arizona, a dentist was arrested when he tried to use Freemen-style notes to purchase several four-wheel-drive vehicles. California has been saturated with pseudo-legal documents and bogus liens and money orders. Several Californians who passed through Justus Township are now holding their own seminars, ensuring that the Montana Freemen's philosophy will continue to spread, despite their arrest.

In Colorado, a woman was arrested when she tried to cash a $60,000 bogus check issued by Schweitzer. In Florida, common-law court advocate Susan Mokdad is said to have been in contact with the Montana Freemen. Another Florida organization known as the "American National Freemen" has been holding common-law court sessions guarded by as many as 150 militia members. It, too, is believed to have ties to Montana.

In Oklahoma and New Mexico, the United Sovereigns' seminars were based on the teachings of LeRoy Schweitzer, and seminar sponsors passed out newsletters created by the Montana Freemen. An analyst with North Carolina's State Bureau of Investigation says that antigovernment groups in her state have been sending people to Montana to take the Justus Township courses. In Kansas, eighteen common-law courts can be traced directly or indirectly to the Montana Freemen.[2]

The Montana Freemen are hard-core Identity believers, which accounts for their well-publicized tendency toward violence. We should assume that those they tutored in Montana departed their company sharing their radical beliefs.

But where did the influential Montana Freemen come from, and what forces chiseled their twisted thinking? The answer is simple: the same forces that created much of the rest of the antigovernment movement—economics, foreclosure, dominionist religion, and misconceptions regarding the Federal Reserve.

The Montana Freemen could serve as the poster child for the antigovernment movement: Hard times lead to a search for answers, a search that ends with the blame-shifting conspiracy theories and dominionist religion. The rural crisis took a heavy toll on Schweitzer's Freemen group. LeRoy Schweitzer himself lost his crop-dusting business to the IRS. The Clark family, which owned the farm that later became Justus Township, suffered through the devastating process of foreclosure. They converted their farm into a sovereign township as a last-ditch effort to save their land. Others in the group had tax problems; two were wanted by the law for their alleged participation in the We the People scheme, whose organizers claimed to have found an answer for people trying to save their farms and ranches.

Schweitzer and his followers were looking for answers to their economic woes when they attended a We the People meeting in the early 1990s. We the People was a patriot-for-profit group started by a man named Roy Schwasinger, who promised his victims that for a mere $300 they could receive millions from the government. Organizers of We the People claimed they had won a class-action lawsuit against the federal government that had resulted in a multibillion-dollar judgment. The lawsuit supposedly proved that the government had illegally abandoned the gold standard. Of course, no such judgment existed, and Schwasinger and his cohorts eventually made off with $2.5 million that has never been recovered.

The We the People antigovernment message was just what Schweitzer and the Montana Freemen wanted to hear. They would take the We the People teachings and expand upon them. They would make the government that had destroyed their lives pay for its actions. They would expose the Federal Reserve as a fraud and shut down the federal courts that they felt had treated them unjustly.

There has been a lot of confusion surrounding the Freemen's claims that their money orders and liens are legitimate. I once asked for an explanation of how their system worked. I was bombarded with huge sections of the Uniform Commercial Code (UCC), the Magna Carta, the Constitution, and an earful of confusing legalese. I tried to understand the Freemen's ideas by researching the nineteen-page document they had released to the FBI during the Justus Township standoff. The Freemen told the FBI that if the government could prove that the claims in the document weren't true, they would surrender peacefully.

I now understand why the government made no attempt to debunk the document. The nineteen pages are filled with a maze of bizarre pseudo-legal language that describes the two types of citizens found in the Constitution, agreements with foreign agents, and the penalties for fraud; it contains arguments concerning sovereignty and jurisdiction, quotes from Robert Bork, definitions of common law, and sections cited from dozens of court cases as well as from the constitution of Montana. It would have taken years to figure out what the Freemen were trying to say, let alone to dispute it.

After talking to several Freemen and asking a lot of questions, I finally came to understand their banking practice. It turned out to be a simple concept. The Freemen believe that the Federal Reserve's worthless paper money is backed by nothing more than the debts of the American people—which is basically the same argument put forward by Eugene Schroder, described in Chapter 7.

They decided that they would fight fire with fire by creating a banking system exactly like that of the Federal Reserve. They declared themselves to be a sovereign township, which separated them from the federal government. In their minds, being a separate country meant they could legally create a separate banking system. All they needed was something to back the money they wanted to print.

The Freemen decided to mix justice with banking. They convened common-law courts and found public officials guilty of treason. As part of their sentences against the guilty, they decided to impose, besides the death penalty, gargantuan liens against the property of the officials they had tried. Those liens would then back their money orders and checks in the new banking system. In other words, if they filed $10 million worth of bogus liens against people they had convicted, that entitled them to write $10 million worth of checks and money orders that, theoretically, were now backed by the property of the corrupt officials.

The Freemen sincerely believed that their banking system was just as legal as that of the Federal Reserve. If the United States had its own banking system, the Freemen's nation—Justus Township—could also have its own banking system. To the Freemen, the systems were the same. They adhered to all of the laws set out in the Uniform Commercial Code that are designed to regulate banking practices. In fact, they were fanatics when it came to following the letter of the law.

But if the Freemen believed the Federal Reserve system to be a fraud, then why did they establish a similar system? The Freemen were different than their We the People predecessors. The Freemen were motivated by their political and religious ideologies, not by money. The purpose of the Freemen system of liens and money orders was twofold: first, to take Federal Reserve Notes out of the U.S. system so that they could then be converted to gold and silver—the only form of money the Freemen actually recognize as legitimate—while simultaneously inflicting injury on their enemy, the government; and, second, to provide those people who were losing their property with a means to pay their debt and avoid foreclosure. The Freemen's banking system actually worked on several occasions. Credit card companies accepted Freemen documents as payment several times. The IRS accepted Freemen money orders written for two and three times the amount of the tax debt, and promptly sent the group a check for the overages.

But the Freemen's ultimate motive was politics, not greed. They ran their school as an effort to establish similar common-law courts and banking systems all across the country in the hope that they would eventually cause the collapse of what they believe is an unconstitutional totalitarian government. They believed that if that collapse occurred, their goal of a white America could finally be realized.

The Montana Freemen did more to further paper terrorism than any other group, but they didn't stop at paper. One of the reasons the government moved in on the Freemen when it did is that the group was preparing to carry out the death sentences it had passed on several local officials. Before the standoff, LeRoy Schweitzer said to his fellow Freemen: "We'll travel in units of about ten outfits, four guys to an outfit, most of them with automatic weapons, whatever else we've got, shotguns, you name it. We got a warrant on the sheriff. We got one on the deputy, on the judge and on the county attorney, and on the county commissioners. . . . We're going to have a standing order. Anyone obstructing justice, the order is 'shoot to kill.'"3

It's likely that many of the common-law courts established by the hundreds of people who passed through Justus Township are every bit as racist and violent as those run by the Montana Freemen. It's also quite possible that in the likely event that the Montana Freemen are convicted for their alleged crimes, their followers—many of whom believe Schweitzer and his group to be ordained by God—will retaliate with terrorism.

Lone Star Showdown

"We've gone proactive. We have taken a military target and we have prisoners." The voice on the other end of my telephone was beyond excited. I could hear shouting and what sounded like people running in the background. It felt like my stomach was trying to crawl up my throat. "Who is this?" I shouted into the receiver. "Lieutenant Richard Keyes," replied the caller. "The Republic of Texas is attacking and we wanted to notify you." April 27, 1997, was not going to be a normal Sunday morning.

Richard Keyes was one of the people I'd met in November 1996, when I drove to the Republic of Texas compound in Fort Davis and stayed with its members for several days. Since then, I had spoken with both Richard McLaren and Keyes on a fairly regular basis. The last I'd heard, Keyes was in Kansas. "Richard," I said, "what are you doing with McLaren? What have you guys done? If you took prisoners there's no way out."

In a suddenly calm, emotionless voice, Keyes said, "We are responding to the state of Texas's apprehension of Captain Scheidt [a Republic of Texas member who had been arrested]. We warned them we would respond if they continued to arrest our people. The two prisoners we have taken are informants and are therefore military targets. We will free them in exchange for our people. I understand the situation. It's time to separate the men from the boys. We're going to see this thing through to the end." I spent the next several minutes trying to talk Keyes into throwing down his gun and walking out. Though he appreciated my attempt, he never wavered. Keyes was ready to die.

That was the end of the first of several conversations I would have over the next thirteen hours with those who were involved in the Republic of Texas standoff near Fort Davis, Texas. At approximately midnight on that Sunday, Keyes called me again, but I was out. A few minutes after his attempt to contact me, the authorities cut the phone lines. I may never know what Richard Keyes wanted to tell me.

That morning, members the Republic of Texas had shot their way into the home of Joe and Margaret Ann Rowe. They had taken the Rowes hostage and told authorities that they would free the couple in exchange for two members of the Republic who were being held in the local jail on minor charges.

Twelve hours after abducting their hostages, county officials swapped Robert Scheidt for the Rowes. Keyes and two other members of the Republic then returned to the compound and dug in with six of their comrades.

It's been clear for quite a while that such a standoff had been brewing for some time. To understand why, we need to start at the beginning.

The Rebirth of a Nation

It is inevitable that one of these days the kids on the playground are going to stand up to the bully. . . . We have decided to stand up. One man or a million men, we will have our freedom or we will die. We've had enough.

—Archie Lowe, 1996

Archie Lowe is president of the Republic of Texas, one of the largest sovereignty movements in the country. Lowe and his organization in the Lone Star state have declared the state of Texas to be an independent nation, free from the rule of the federal government. It's like Justus Township, times a thousand.

As with most of the movement's legal claims, the Republic has gone to great lengths to prove its point. The Republic has taken its claim to sovereignty further than any other antigovernment group in the country. Its members have spent tens of thousands of hours researching their cause. With their incessant filing of documents, they have pumped literally hundreds of pounds of paper into the court system. They have sought and received international recognition as a nation. And as you might expect, they have irked state and federal authorities to a dangerous degree.

The short version of the Republic of Texas's claim to sovereignty as explained to me by Republic founder Rick McLaren goes like this: The group was founded in 1993, based upon its belief that the state of Texas was illegally annexed by the United States in 1845. Since the former Republic of Texas was the legal governing body in existence at the time of the supposed illegal annexation, members of today's Republic claim that the old Republic of Texas constitution is still in effect in full force. Many of the members of today's Republic of Texas have renounced their U.S. citizenship, have gotten rid of their driver's licenses, and have stopped paying taxes to the federal government. They have elected their own government based upon the constitution of the former Republic of Texas, and they have established a military force as well as a court system.

McLaren claims that the Constitution of the United States has no provision for annexing an existing, unconquered nation—which is precisely what the Republic of Texas was in 1845 when it entered the union. McLaren points to congressional records of the debates that took place in 1845 to prove his point. Many congressmen at the time were arguing that the annexation was illegal.

Since this discovery, McLaren has spent years creating exotic ways of trying to revive the Republic. He has filed lawsuits trying to prove his claims, and at one point, he established an environmental group in order to get federal jurisdiction over land use issues in his area. A person can talk to McLaren for hours and hours and only scratch the surface of the Republic of Texas argument for sovereignty.

But the real question is: Who cares? It was 150 years ago, and the United States isn't likely to give up the tenth-largest economy in the world to a bunch of antigovernment Texans who may have found an interesting historical snafu in the way Texas was brought into the union. So what's really behind this bizarre attempt at secession? Apparently, it's the same old story: Rural people in Texas are fed up with the government, and they desperately need an excuse to fight that is more acceptable than economics. And they will fight, one way or another.

It Could Have Been Worse

We've put them [the government] in a position that they're damned if they jump on us and damned if they don't. If we do have a situation where we have to call up the defense forces to defend the Republic of Texas, it will amaze people how many thousands upon thousands of trained men will come out of the woodwork.

—Dr. Ralph Turner, secretary of defense
for the Republic of Texas, 1996

As I cross the Red River into Texas, the hair on the back of my neck stands up. Having been born and raised in Oklahoma, such a reaction to Texas soil is to be expected—but today is different. I'm on my way to meet the Republic's secretary of defense, Dr. Ralph Turner. On the phone, I told him he'd recognize me because "my hair is longer than it should be." "I'll be the man with the shaved head and full black beard," Turner responded in a booming voice that obviously never left the military. If his shaved head was covered, he said he'd be wearing a hat that said something about guns or marksmanship or something equally appropriate. By the time Turner described the hat, my brain was too busy questioning my sanity to hear him.

I had just left a western Oklahoma farmhouse filled with Identity believers who had told me that the militia was getting ready to start carrying out death sentences against its enemies. This wasn't very encouraging news for a journalist, since the media are one such enemy. Now I was heading to Texas for a few weeks to hang out with another antigovernment group I knew little about. I always get a little apprehensive when I first get involved with new people. You never know exactly how they think and consequently how they'll react to a reporter's nosy questions. But time and again I have parted from such experiences with a great appreciation for the people I've met. It's not because I agree with what they believe but rather because I've discovered that they are just ordinary people who have been through very hard times. Once they realize that I'm not from the Connie Chung school of journalism and that I've never lived in New York City, they usually become warm and amazingly candid about why they're involved in the antigovernment movement. Using such thoughts to comfort myself, I roll toward my meeting with the Republic's head of defense.

As you might expect, Turner is easy to spot in the Plano, Texas, restaurant. After a few pleasantries and a bone-crushing handshake, we get down to business. I had heard that the Republic's military forces were substantial, so I asked Turner to describe his operation.

"We have over three thousand active defense forces and somewhere between fifteen thousand and twenty thousand people who are sympathetic to us should we need them," Turner explains.

> Each county—there are 253 counties in the Republic—will eventually have a county commander, an XO (that's an executive officer), his staff, and a few full-time military personnel. We're setting it up very much like Switzerland—a volunteer army but with paid personnel at the staff level. A typical county with a small population will have two fire teams. Each county has at least that. Members of the team will keep their weapons at their home. They keep them with them at all times, ready to go on alert at all times. We communicate through a system of radios which allows communication at all times.

Turner is a pleasant enough guy, though I wouldn't want to see him mad. This secretary of defense is as far from columnist Jack Anderson's description of the uneducated "Bubba" as you can get. Turner is former military and now teaches at the college in Gainsville, Texas. He claims to have written three books for the academic community and knows his military strategy like the back of his bone-crushing hand.

The interview was going well. I was feeling very comfortable with Dr. Turner—so comfortable, in fact, that I made a stupid mistake that I hadn't made in years. I referred to the Republic as a group. People within the movement hate words like "group," "movement," "faction"—anything that indicates that they are less than "the People." "Let me interject," thundered Turner:

> We are not a group. We're a nation. Everything lawful has been done to create the Republic of Texas as a free and separate nation. This is important. About eight weeks ago, I signed a document that went to every embassy in the world, all the military bases in the state, and all the governors in the United States. What that did was to declare the military defense forces of the Republic of Texas as a lawful military in the world community. We are a lawful military.

If Turner's description of the Republic's defense forces is even 10 percent accurate, it raises an interesting question. Has the Republic reached the magical "safe size"? Within the antigovernment movement, "safe size" is the point at which the federal government is no longer considered a threat. This doesn't mean that in an all-out war the federal government wouldn't easily destroy an antigovernment force. It means that the federal government can't afford the showdown.

Even one thousand troops would present an amazing challenge to the government, well beyond the ability of the FBI, ATF, or any other agency to handle. The only option for the government would be to send in the army or the National Guard, and militia leaders like Turner don't believe that Americans in the military will obey orders to open fire on Texans or anybody else on that grand a scale. And if they do, Turner has a warning: "We've reached safe status. It's beyond the point of them [the federal government] not being able to handle it. If they think they can, they need to remember Vietnam and other places where organized armies tried to go in and fight freedom fighters who were fighting for their country." Turner points out that many of his people are former military personnel and that a substantial number are former members of the Special Forces.

It's clear that the Republic of Texas is deadly serious about its status as a nation. It has taken its sovereignty claims much further than any other group. For example, it has sent out a resolution to the world's embassies declaring itself to be a neutral, nonaggressive nation on the order of Switzerland. It has sought and is starting to receive international recognition. It recently signed a treaty with the Washita Nation and says that it is close to gaining recognition from Syria.

The Washita Nation is an internationally recognized indigenous people. The Washita's recognition of the Republic means that the Texans now believe they can appeal to the international community in legal matters pertaining to the status of their Republic. This treaty business may not amount to anything in the long run, but it may force the state and federal agencies into a kind of paperwork hell.

Because of their perceived national status, citizens of the Republic believe that they are now immune to all state and federal laws. As Turner puts it:

If one of our people gets arrested for any reason, I'll file charges with Interpol. We're a nation. We don't have to follow anybody's laws but our own. We don't have to abide by their speed limits because the Republic of Texas doesn't have any. Our people have immunity. The whole concept of common law is responsibility. Now if a citizen of the Republic is going too fast and they harm someone, they'll come before a common-law court. And that's probably something they'll only want to do once in their lifetime. There are none of the deals and crap going on. Justice is swift and harsh.

This idea of immunity is just one of the issues that has the Republic on a serious collision course with the state and federal government. Turner told me that one of the Republic's people has been held in jail for the last five months. The man was driving without a license plate or driver's license. So far, the man has refused to identify himself to authorities except as required under the Geneva Convention. This is proof that antigovernment people such as those in the Republic are not just playing games: Stop and think about the sincerity it takes to waste away in a jail for months at a time over a simple traffic violation. These people are extraordinarily serious.

Turner says that the state has no right to hold the man. "I have a warrant for that sheriff's arrest," he says, "and he's [the sheriff] going to be in deep shit. I'm going to give Morales [Texas attorney general] seventy-two hours to release all our people. If Morales keeps this crap up, we'll arrest him and try him." Turner is not making an idle threat. I believe he would not hesitate to take whatever armed action is necessary to carry out his pronouncements. Turner, a longtime antigovernment warrior, has been openly refusing to file his federal income tax returns since 1971. He has been staring prison in the face for twenty-five years. He will do whatever it takes to win his war with the government.

In Turner's mind, all nonviolent remedies have been exhausted. He quotes Christian theologian and philosopher Francis Schaeffer, author of *The Christian Manifesto,* describing the three basic steps for regaining freedom: The first is through the legal system; the second is through civil disobedience; and the last is by leaving the particular country of which you disapprove. Turner says: "That last option is not available, and we've tried the other two. There's nothing left for us now but military action." Being somewhat familiar with Schaeffer, I suspect that if he were still alive, he would adamantly disagree with Turner's final solution.

While interviewing Turner, I listened for hints of the issues that bind the antigovernment movement's various factions into a single entity, and I heard them. There was the economic angle, in this case the tax issue. There was the religion—the common-law courts based on the Old Testament. He blamed the Gulf War on a plot between the Rothschilds and former president George Bush. There were also several comments about the international bankers who run the Federal Reserve, making it clear that conspiracy theories are driving the Republic's engine. The sovereignty issue is the Republic's excuse for armed confrontation—but all the other rural factors are its reason for existing.

Almost Populists

My next interviews were with the Republic's first family, Archie and Sarah Lowe. Once again, the "ignorant and uneducated" cliché can be tossed out the window. I'd first met Sarah at the "Third Continental Congress" meeting near Kansas City in late 1996. Since the Republic considers itself a separate nation, she could only attend the congress for a few hours as the representative of a foreign government. The Republic's First Lady is impressive. She graduated summa cum laude from SMU (Southern Methodist University) with a math degree and now runs her own computer business. Archie also graduated with a math degree.

President Archie Lowe is the best evidence that the Republic of Texas is different from many other antigovernment organizations—he's half Jewish and half Indian. The Lowes have worked hard to make the Republic an inclusive nation. As the interview begins, Archie is quick to point out that the Republic's vice president is black; one of the president's advisers is Vietnamese; one ambassador is Hispanic, and another is Jewish. That being the case, I point out to President Lowe that I had met citizens of the Republic who are also in the KKK.

Archie shrugs his shoulders, shakes his head, and says, "No matter what society you get involved with, you're going to have bigots. But we endeavor to present a strong enough picture of who we are as a provisional government that people will recognize honesty, integrity, and moral values, so we can at least minimize the bigots. You'll always have extremists."

The Lowes became politically active as Republicans, but Archie points out they also voted Democratic at times. Archie recalls,

We thought we could make a difference. We went to the precinct convention and I was elected chairman. Three weeks later I was elected as a delegate to the state convention. We thought we were making a difference until after the election when we found out that the Contract with America turned out to be a Contract on America. We were so disappointed we did a foolish thing, we picked up a copy of the Constitution and read it. We were ruined after that. Just look at things like the Brady Bill—they just legislated away the Second Amendment.

The last straw for the Lowes was when they witnessed a neighbor losing his house to foreclosure: "They send out agents by the thousands to regulate and tax us and torment us by taking away our property or our houses. The Texas attorney general, Dan Morales, who we call Moral-less, fined me $10,000 the day before yesterday. Yesterday he fined me $20,000 and today I was fined $40,000. All of this because I refuse to rescind a document I signed."

The document Archie signed is just another factor pushing the Republic toward a showdown with authorities. It's also a testament to the intentions of the Lowes and their followers. The Republic has filed a UCC lien against all of the assets of the state of Texas. The goal was to place the assets into an irrevocable trust in the name of the 18.5 million people who currently reside in the state. The Republic considers all of the state's residents to actually be citizens of the Republic, since the state of Texas has never legally existed. The Republic has also attempted to remove the state's $3 billion in monetary assets from 175 Texas banks and place that money into accounts owned by the people.

The attempted money transfer was an elaborate affair in its own right. With the help of Arthur, who had been flown in from Montana to create the necessary documents, the Republic was trying to move Texas's $3 billion from its banks into the Washita Nation's banking system by way of the international markets. The plan failed.

A Shift in Strategy

ROT [Republic of Texas] has issued yet another ALERT, ALERT, ALERT, THE FEDS ARE COMING. . . . The lawful authority of the Constitutional Militia is limited to: (1) Repel Invasion (2) Suppress Insurrection (3) Enforce the Laws of the Union. There is no lawful authority for the Constitutional Militia to intervene in the affairs of a "foreign nation." Despite the fact that ROT sovereigns do not recognize the United States Constitution, they are asking members of the Constitutional Militia to come to their defense.

—J. J. Johnson, Ohio Unorganized Militia,
E-mail correspondence to a Colorado militia regarding the
McLaren situation at the Republic of Texas embassy, March 1997

We can't just threaten and skirmish, in the long run, or we pass something on to our children that they will have no hope of resisting. With all the wisdom we have, we must find some way to stop this ever progressing beast, without just wildly flinging ourselves on it. We can't let them draw the best militia units into an open slaughter! Everyone must understand that! If it's to be war, it must be war on guerrilla's terms.

—Mike Chapman, E-mail correspondence to a Colorado
militia regarding the McLaren situation
at the Republic of Texas embassy, March 1997

The difficulty of trying to hold together a large antigovernment organization made up of every kind of person from Jews to Klansmen is becoming clear to those in the Republic. The group has already gone through three major splits. The most recent split has founder Rick McLaren in charge of a small faction of the Republic and the Lowes leading the other, larger portion. During the 1997 standoff, the main Republic of Texas group, the one controlled by Lowe, refused to support McLaren and those inside the Fort Davis compound. Had the larger group's defense forces been called out, the showdown would have escalated considerably. Even though McLaren and all but two of his followers surrendered after a week, the Republic's standoff had a major impact on the antigovernment movement as a whole.

A debate has broken out among the various militias all across the nation as to what should be done in response to the government's actions against McLaren. J. J. Johnson, leader of the powerful Ohio Unorganized Militia, has taken the position that he is obligated to defend the U.S. Constitution at all costs. Since McLaren believes that the Republic is a separate nation, the Ohio group feels no obligation to support him. Other constitutional militias around the country have also taken this position.

But many of the smaller militias composed of sovereigns believe that McLaren must be supported at all costs. They, like McLaren, believe themselves to be outside of federal jurisdiction. This national debate among the militias has become quite heated. But the real effect that the McLaren situation is having on the movement is much more serious.

The antigovernment movement has changed its strategy. Ever since Waco, the militias have insisted that if a similar situation were to happen again, they would come to the defense of those surrounded by the government and create a reverse Waco—by killing the federal agents. But as we saw in the Freemen and Republic of Texas stand-offs, that didn't happen. Few militia members have the desire to go to prison or be killed confronting the federal government in a head-to-head showdown. It appears that the militias are changing course, becoming more realistic and, therefore, more dangerous.

One militia contract states: "For every citizen of the Republic of Texas that is killed, five government agents will be assassinated." Welcome to the new antigovernment movement, the next step in the evolutionary chain. My contacts have told me that several militias have already signed on to the contract that made the above threat and that many others are expected to follow suit. This is the strategy that the government has long feared from the antigovernment movement. It's not new, being the same strategy that gave us the Oklahoma City bombing. Small radical elements of the movement have always been committed to blood for blood.

But according to my information, the people who are supporting this five-lives-for-one-life concept are in militias that until now have been opposed to terrorism. Considering that Republic member Mike Matson was shot to death by authorities after he and Richard Keyes—who is still at large as I write—refused to surrender, we can assume that the assassination contract is now in effect. The Internet discussions among militia members during and subsequent to the standoff have raised yet another concern. One militia member summed up the mood of the movement regarding the Texas standoff when he said, "Now we'll have barbecues in our own backyard"—implication being that antigovernment groups will retaliate for McLaren's showdown with authorities with acts of terrorism in different parts of the country.

The Republic's meddling with the state's banks has also increased the chance for future violence. On the day that McLaren and his followers surrendered, a federal fraud and conspiracy indictment was unsealed in Dallas. The indictment accused McLaren, his wife Evelyn, and five other members of the Republic of Texas of issuing more than $1.8 billion in bogus financial documents known as "warrants." Because the Republic's banking scandal predates the split between McLaren and the majority of the Republic, it's likely this indictment will spill over into the main group, substantively raising the potential for future violence all across the Lone Star state. We haven't heard the last of the Republic of Texas. If large segments of the antigovernment movement finally manage to knock down their mental barrier to terrorism, watch out. The tribulation will not be far behind.

Christian Reconstruction

*A Jural Society is an organized political community and a synonym of "nation,"
"state," and "country." It is founded in the general sense on the Law of God from
Whom it derives its authority and right to exist in the protection of life, liberty,
and property, in the preservation of the Christian way of life.*
—**An Introduction to the Christian Jural Society in California**

"The loss of the American union of states based upon the Constitution for the United States took place on April 15, 1861. Since that date, there has been no legal government in the United States." That's the claim of the Christian Jural Society, one of the least-known yet most significant organizations in the antigovernment movement to date.

The Christian Jural Society is the logical end product of dominionist Christianity. It's an attempt by dominionist Christians to "reconstruct" a Christian government throughout the United States by creating small pockets of self-governing Christians who are tied to a national Christian government through their chosen representatives. Jural societies believe that they are the only legitimate form of government now operating in America. As the jural societies proliferate throughout the country, they are doing more to pull the 10 to 15 million soft-core, dominionist Christians deeper into the antigovernment funnel than any previous manifestation of the antigovernment movement. If they continue to grow—and all indications are that they will—they could become the most powerful force within the movement.

I first heard about the Christian Jural Society in late 1994, shortly after its formation, but I had rarely met anyone who claimed to be a part of the organization. By 1996, that had changed. Every sizable "anti" function I attended was increasingly made up of people in jural societies. By the time I reached the Third Continental Congress meeting in Kansas City in 1996, it had become clear that the Christian Jural Society was growing like a weed and had become a dominant force in the movement. Several of the delegates in Kansas City were the representatives of jural societies.

Jural societies have, to a large degree, been flying under the radar of those who monitor the radical Right. One reason is that, unlike militias, they shun publicity. Jural societies have a hard-and-fast rule: Don't talk to the press.

The Christian Jural Society is the brainchild of a religious Right think tank based in California and known as the "King's Men." The society's leaders are John Quade, Randy Lee, and John Joseph. John Quade, an actor whose film credits include Clint Eastwood's *Every Which Way but Loose* and *Every Which Way You Can*, as well as *The Sting* and the miniseries *Roots*, serves as the society's front man. He travels the country, holding well-attended seminars on how to establish a jural society.

Regional jural societies are made up of approximately 100 families—that's the number recommended in the group's handbook, *The Book of Hundreds*. Each society becomes a self-governing entity, based somewhat on an updated version of the Posse Comitatus model. Their seminar information states: "Since the existing governments are *de facto* and without true law, once the jural society is formed it becomes the ultimate civil authority in the county. . . . It is a Christian body, based on God's Law, the *lex non scripta* (common law)."

The jural societies are completely self-sufficient. Their court system includes an ecclesiastical court to handle interpretation of scripture, a court of assizes to handle civil matters under common law, and a grand jury to investigate charges brought before it. Each jural society has its own enforcement arm, referred to as the lawful Posse Comitatus. The Posse Comitatus serves the courts as needed by bringing in witnesses or by enforcing sentences.

Jural societies elect officers who serve as their representatives at the state and national level of the jural society. The local or county jural society is considered to be the most powerful level of government, with the national being the least powerful.

As the name would imply, the Christian Jural Society is designed to be exclusively for Christians—non-Christians are not allowed to join under any circumstances. To be a voting member of a jural society, a person must file papers terminating all other voter registration. Once a person joins a jural society, as thousands have, it becomes the only form of government in his or her life.

The ultimate goal of the jural society is to create a national government for all Christians, with Jesus as the head of that government. Jural societies believe that this must be accomplished before Jesus returns to earth. As with the rest of the apocalyptic antigovernment movement, people in the jural societies feel a sense of urgency to accomplish their goal before the year 2000.

Jural societies are driven largely by end-of-the-world conspiracy theories. The mission statement for the American Jural Society of Cuyahoga County, Ohio, reads:

Our goal is to restore our Republic, as secured by the Constitution for the united states of America [sic] 1787, and the Bill of Rights of 1789, and the Ordinance of 1787, and the moral basis upon which these were founded, so that our children, and the generations not yet born, will know that they are the people of posterity, unencumbered by the oppression that is now at our front door. God bless the Republic. Death to the New World Order. We shall prevail!

Although it's still unclear just how violent the jural societies will become in their effort to be self-governed, there is evidence that the most radical forces in the antigovernment movement are already influencing them. Several of the jural society members I've met are Identity believers, whose concept of justice is a rope and a tree. When I telephoned the Cuyahoga Jural Society to follow up on an earlier interview, I was told that no one there could speak to me, and it was suggested that I direct my questions to Mark Koernke, one of the antigovernment movement's most radical leaders. Koernke was picked up by authorities immediately following the Oklahoma City bombing and is said to have ties to Timothy McVeigh. He was later released by authorities.

If the jural societies are being controlled by leaders like Koernke, who have long called for the execution of judges and other officials, then they may pose the greatest antigovernment threat to date.

The Cult Mentality

In many respects, individual antigovernment groups are, in fact, cults.
—Psychologist Glen Wallace

We have entered a unique time in the history of our country. People have become so disillusioned with our current corporate-controlled government that they've simply decided to create their own versions. Among the Freemen, the Christian Jural Society, and other sovereignty movements like the Republic of Texas, there are hundreds, if not thousands, of pockets of radicals numbering in the tens of thousands—all composed of people who no longer consider themselves to be under the authority of the federal government. Many of these people are willing to turn to terrorism in one form or another to defend themselves against law enforcement or to attempt to force society to adhere to their religion-based laws. Most, but not all, will escalate their violent activities over the next one thousand days because they believe that the turn of the century represents the end of the world. Time after time, antigovernment radicals have told me that everything is going to come down over the next three years.

Ever since the thirty-nine members of the Heaven's Gate cult committed suicide in San Diego in March 1997, the media have been interviewing experts who say that similar cult suicides are going to escalate dramatically between now and the year 2000. What no one seems to realize is that there are thousands of antigovernment "cults" out there that are on the same apocalyptic collision course with the turn of the century as the Heaven's Gate followers, but they have no intention of committing suicide. Just as Reverend Jim Jones was able to order over nine hundred of his religious followers to commit mass suicide, there are dominant personalities in the antigovernment movement who have the power over their followers to order them to commit mass terrorism.

Psychologist Glen Wallace has pointed out the cult mentality of antigovernment groups, observing that "it starts in the coffee shops."

> Sometimes the same ten or twelve fellows have been meeting each other in the same little restaurant for decades. They always bitched about the government, but now things have changed. I've sat in on some of these groups lately, and the conversation is much different. They talk about shooting the president or exterminating all the Jews, stuff they'd get arrested for if they said it on the street.

Wallace says eventually those involved in these coffee-shop sessions decide to meet in secret, to be more organized, and as he says, "That's when they enter a cult-like situation."

> The ones that are the most radical usually become the leaders. The longer they stay together the more they could be defined as a cult. The longer they share each other's stress and agitation, the more likely it becomes that they'll try and get even with the government. Eventually the whole group can become dominated by a single personality. At that point, there's no difference between an antigovernment cult and any other cult like Heaven's Gate.
>
> We think that people in a cult are so twisted and so abnormal, but they're not twisted and abnormal. We're all just as capable of getting mentally skewed as them. They have the same IQs as we do. They just fell prey to finding support in the wrong place. Once they enter the realm of the cult mentality, they can become convinced of anything. They can be convinced to do anything. It's very dangerous. The same

community psychosis that pulls people into the antigovernment movement in the first place can eventually lead to cult mentality.

All the signs indicate that between now and the year 2000, more and more antigovernment adherents will fall prey to the cult mentality as apocalyptic religion becomes an increasingly dominant force over their lives. Reasonably well-balanced people who I met just two years ago when they entered the movement have become completely obsessed with paranoid conspiracy theories.

In the case of Heaven's Gate, we tell jokes under our breath about weirdos who get castrated and then kill themselves in order to catch a flying saucer that was hiding behind the Hale-Bopp comet. In the case of the antigovernment movement, we laugh about their black helicopters and their claims that prisons for political prisoners are being built on the moon. We forget about the dark and powerful character of cults. The Heaven's Gate people are dead. The federal building in Oklahoma City was bombed.

We should learn to view crazy antigovernment conspiracy theories as a warning rather than as joke material. If people can, in all sincerity, believe that Jewish bankers have ordered the United Nations to attack their farms in order to control the food supply of Christians and if people can believe that the government has inserted microchips in their bodies so that satellites can track their every move, then they can also believe that they are supposed to blow up a building full of kids. Timothy McVeigh believed that the government had injected a microchip into his butt to track his every move. Enough said.

11

The Road to Oklahoma City

Hello, my fellow Americans and all my friends around the world.

When the government engages in terrorism against its own citizens, it should not be surprised when some of those citizens strike back and engage in terrorism against the government.

Terrorism is nasty business . . . but terrorism is a form of warfare and, in war, most of the victims are noncombatants.

Certainly none of us condone the killing of children. But in fact, it is the Clinton government that has led the way in killing children. The hatred one hears in [Clinton's and Reno's] voices when they talk about the Oklahoma City bombers is not because children were killed, it's because they know the bombing was aimed at them.

Americans haven't had a real war fought on their own sod for 130 years. . . . I think things are about to change. I suspect Americans will begin engaging in terrorism on a scale the world has never known.

—William Pierce, addressing his
radio audience (estimated at 100,000 listeners),
one week after the Oklahoma City bombing, 1995

When TWA flight 800 exploded over the Atlantic in 1996, news reports immediately raised the question of whether domestic antigovernment groups might have been involved. It was another example of the media's failure to understand the forces behind the movement. There would have been no reason for the antigovernment movement to commit such an act. The terrorism spawned by today's antigovernment movement is not without rhyme or reason. Its targets are carefully chosen as the result of its religious or political beliefs, or both.

Understanding the forces that make the movement tick makes it possible to discern which acts of terrorism belong to the movement and why a particular action was carried out.

Was the Oklahoma City bombing the result of the antigovernment movement? Of course, but the corpses from that deadly bombing shouldn't be laid at the feet of the movement as a whole. Most antigovernment zealots adamantly disapprove of such violent actions against the civilian population—most, but not all. The real ingredients of the Oklahoma bomb were more than fertilizer and racing fuel. The explosion in Oklahoma City was the result of the mixing of all the volatile elements described so far in this book—the rural crisis, community psychosis, conspiracy theories, sovereignty issues, the Second Amendment debate, and common law. Since this book is going to press as the trials of both Timothy McVeigh and Terry Nichols are beginning, I should point out that both men are innocent until proven guilty. With that in mind, I will explore the road that allegedly brought them to Oklahoma City.

"Inside His Head"

Timothy McVeigh was an ordinary kid from a typical blue-collar family. A lot has been made of the fact that his parents divorced when he was a teenager, but there's really no evidence that the divorce significantly scarred his life. His schoolmates and teachers remember him as a well-disciplined and smart kid. Childhood friends recall him as "intelligent," "a B-plus student who always took challenging classes," and "ordinary and straight." If McVeigh is indeed the bomber as the evidence suggests, something has to have changed him. A childhood friend told the *Rocky Mountain News*: "It would have been completely out of character for him [McVeigh] to blow up that building. Someone would have had to have gotten inside his head." As we shall see, someone did.

The first seed of influence to enter the life of Timothy McVeigh was the love of guns. McVeigh became a gun owner at age thirteen, when his grandfather gave him a .22-caliber rifle. When McVeigh turned sixteen, his father gave him his first shotgun. From the very beginning, McVeigh had an exaggerated affection for firearms. It was all he talked about. Also at age sixteen, McVeigh began to exhibit other behavior that was unusual for a boy his age—he began stockpiling food and large barrels of water in the basement of his home. We may never know what influenced the young McVeigh to adopt such survivalist behavior, but it was a theme that would play into many of his future decisions.

McVeigh's fascination for guns continued to grow. In 1986, after graduating from high school and subsequently dropping out of a business college, McVeigh and a friend, Dave Darlak, paid $7,000 for an undeveloped, ten-acre parcel of land near Olean, New York. The property was approximately ninety miles south of McVeigh's hometown of Lockport. The two young men converted the property into their own private shooting range or, more accurately, paramilitary training ground.

In 1988, a neighbor reported hearing what sounded like explosions coming from the Olean property. When the police investigated the call, they found several men, including Darlak and McVeigh, dressed in camouflage fatigues and wearing greasepaint. The officer reported that the men were well armed.

McVeigh continued his survivalist behavior. He would camp out on the property at night and practice his shooting from sunup to sundown. After a while, Darlak's interest in the shooting range waned, but for McVeigh, the hold that this lust for guns had on his life continued to swell, affecting nearly every major decision he made. After dropping out of business school, McVeigh got a job with an armored car company. Now he could make a living and wear a gun at the same time.

By all accounts, McVeigh was an excellent employee who did what he was told, that is, until the day he came to work with a sawed-off shotgun and bandoliers slung across his chest in an X-formation. Jeff Camp, McVeigh's partner at the company for eight months, described the scene this way, "It looked like World War III."[1] Coworkers say that McVeigh became angry when his supervisor refused to let him go to work looking like "Rambo." It was clear that McVeigh's passion for weapons needed a new, more extreme outlet. He found that outlet a few months later.

Boot camp at Fort Benning, Georgia, would be the next challenge for McVeigh. He joined the army in May 1988. McVeigh's excellent record as a soldier has been widely publicized: He volunteered for duty that nobody else wanted; he was always on time; he was quickly promoted to corporal and then sergeant; and he served in the Gulf War and received battlefield commendations. When McVeigh returned from the Persian Gulf, he tried to qualify for the Green Berets but quit after the first two days of the twenty-one-day qualification program. Many have speculated that this failure to make it in the Special Forces is what turned McVeigh against the government. But the evidence says otherwise.

Long before he'd washed out of the Green Berets, McVeigh had become skeptical of the government. He was an avid reader of survivalist and gun-related magazines. McVeigh was getting an earful of NRA rhetoric about how the government was destroying Second Amendment rights and the Constitution. Kerry Kling, a friend of McVeigh's, says, "He felt strongly about the right to bear arms and protecting the Second Amendment—he was fanatical about that."[2] McVeigh had entered the antigovernment "funnel," and his descent to the narrow end would be speeded by the words of the nation's most radical, racist ideologues.

McVeigh's literary taste went downhill from the gun magazines. He read *Spotlight*, the antigovernment and blatantly anti-Semitic newsletter put out by the Liberty Lobby. He was also an avid reader of a Christian Identity newsletter called *Patriot Report*.[3] These publications are filled with conspiracy theories about the government and the new world order. And then there was *The Turner Diaries*. Friends have said that it was McVeigh's favorite book. Some accounts have described McVeigh's appreciation for William Pierce's violent book of racist fiction as something more than literary zeal. McVeigh is said to have slept with the book under his pillow. After leaving the service, McVeigh sold the book at gun shows, sometimes for less than his own cost. Fellow gun-show merchants said it was as if the contents of the book were his religion and he was looking for recruits. *The Turner Diaries* apparently changed McVeigh's life, and consequently, should he be found guilty, the lives of thousands of others in Oklahoma City.

McVeigh wasn't reading these publications out of morbid curiosity. He believed what they were telling him. He sent copies of the newsletters and other antigovernment materials to friends. He tried to explain the movement's conspiracy theories to friends and family. McVeigh told his younger sister that members of the Special Forces were really assassins and drug runners for the CIA. He told Sergeant Albert Warnement that the military was now under the rule of the United Nations. He even claimed that the government had implanted a computer chip in his butt so he could be tracked. All of these seemingly bizarre beliefs are standard conspiracy fodder within the antigovernment movement.

No one knows how many people have become dysfunctionally paranoid due to prolonged antigovernment influence, but it's a significant number. Consider this: In 1995, I assigned my news editor, Wayne Laugesen, a story about the potential uses for the tiny microchips that veterinarians were implanting in people's pets. The chip's purpose was to help people locate lost animals. Laugesen talked to experts around the country about the technology's possible other uses, such as implanting them in prisoners or children. We had no idea what we were about to unleash.

The article became the topic of one of Bo Gritz's antigovernment radio shows. Gritz is an outspoken leader in the movement and was involved as a mediator in the Ruby Ridge and Freemen standoffs. The phone at my paper started ringing. People from all over the country were calling to either get copies of the story or to tell us that they had been implanted with such a chip. And it got stranger. People started asking us to help them pay for having their chips removed. One man wanted us to be present during the brain surgery he claimed to have scheduled to remove a chip from his head. After two years, that article still gets more hits on our web site than any other story we've ever written—to the tune of several thousand paranoid readers a month.

Sounds crazy, doesn't it? That's because it is crazy. There are people out there stockpiling food and weapons and watching the skies for the inevitable day when the Jewish bankers will send in the black helicopters full of United Nations storm troopers to attack their farms. These people aren't stupid; they're sick. Many have lost touch with reality to the point that they are no longer in control of their actions. Their potential for anger- and paranoia-induced violence is immeasurable. As psychologist Glen Wallace pointed out, there are only a few things that can happen when people reach this stage: They can get help; they can turn their anger inward and commit suicide; or they can turn it outward toward the rest of us. Oklahoma City was only the first shot in what promises to be a long and bloody period of psychotic discontent.

Another McVeigh acquaintance, Sergeant Royal L. Witcher, says that McVeigh began to complain that the NRA wasn't taking a strong enough stand against gun control. Another soldier, James Ives, says he heard that McVeigh had begun to associate with off-base antigovernment groups.[4]

McVeigh had become a paranoid antigovernment evangelist. But the conspiracy-laced literature that he was consuming was not the only influence on the young soldier. He had made a new friend at Fort Benning, a man named Terry Nichols. They shared their love of guns and their hatred for government. Through his relationship with Nichols, McVeigh would eventually be exposed to all of the elements of the rural crisis.

A Different Path

Terry Nichols's journey into the world of antigovernment radicalism took a more traditional rural path—one filled with financial failure, farm foreclosures, and Posse Comitatus influence. Nichols grew up on his father's Michigan farm. Over the years, according to neighbor Phil Morawski, Terry and his brother, James, had watched their father battle the banks to keep the farm. The two sons eventually became active in the radical farm movement, attending farm auctions where they would bid $25 in silver. The silver tactic was a Posse strategy to stop foreclosures. Terry and James believed that the Federal Reserve and its paper money were illegal—part of the new world order conspiracy—and that only bids made in gold or silver were legally acceptable.

In his book, *A Force upon the Plain*, Kenneth S. Stern examined the antigovernment behavior of Terry Nichols and his brother, James. Stern found that the two exhibited behavior consistent with that of members of the Posse Comitatus.

As early as 1990, James Nichols decided he should become a sovereign. He filed papers renouncing his U.S. citizenship and declaring that he was "a nonresident alien, nonforeigner, STRANGER!" James also got rid of his other "contracts" with government such as his driver's license and social security card. On the economic side, he stopped paying his taxes. Neighbors say that James considered himself to be a part of the militia. Terry Nichols would follow in his brother's footsteps.

Terry Nichols accepted the Posse and Freemen procedures for sovereignty as a legitimate way of opting out of the system he couldn't afford to live in. He destroyed his driver's license, passport, and voter registration card. His truck was unregistered and had a homemade license plate. On two occasions, Terry Nichols filed papers that claimed to dissolve his U.S. citizenship.

Economically, Terry Nichols was struggling. He worked dozens of menial jobs, though never for very long. Eventually, he found himself buried in credit card debt. The Chase Manhattan Bank sued Nichols in civil court over the $19,739 he had run up on his credit card. If there was ever any doubt about Nichols having swallowed the common-law court rhetoric hook, line, and sinker, it vanished during the Chase court proceedings.

Nichols told the court he had already paid the debt with a "Certified Fractional Reserve Check," a meaningless instrument similar to those the Freemen issue. Nichols described to the judge how the bank had created the debt out of thin air so it could repossess his property. It was the same argument made to me by Gideon Cowan from prison and by Sam Conners as he wept over his foreclosure notice. Nichols warned the judge that he, the judge, might be sued if the court found in the bank's favor, because Nichols was a "common-law individual" and the judge had no jurisdiction over him. Nichols lost the case.

Terry Nichols's financial problems continued. He was sued by yet another credit card company, and he was also hauled before Judge Donald Teeple for failure to pay child support to his first wife, Lana Padilla, with whom he had a son, Chase. Again, Nichols told the judge that he had no jurisdiction over him due to the fact that he wasn't a citizen of the U.S. or the corporate entity known as the State of Michigan. Nichols was sentenced to thirty days in jail over the child-support issue.

Terry Nichols told the world exactly what kind of "citizen" he considered himself to be in a letter to the Michigan Department of Natural Resources. In the letter, Nichols described himself as "no longer . . . a citizen of the corrupt political corporate state of Michigan and the United States of America. . . . I am a 'non-resident alien' . . . a natural born human being born in the area you call Michigan not the corporate state of Michigan." This letter makes it clear that Nichols believed in the antigovernment movement's "two types of citizens" theory (Fourteenth Amendment and natural), and he considered himself to be a sovereign.

The Syndrome

We have communities that are made up now of collectively depressed individuals, and the symptoms of that community depression are similar to what you would find in someone who has long-term chronic depression. This community depression could turn into a social and cultural psychosis, which is similar to delayed stress syndrome.

—Psychologist Glen Wallace, testifying
before a congressional subcommittee, 1989

These are the influences that Terry and James Nichols brought into their relationship with Timothy McVeigh. And as numerous people have pointed out, from rural psychologists to undercover government agents, if people are exposed to the stresses that give birth to these antigovernment beliefs for long enough, they will fall prey to them. After leaving the army, McVeigh spent months with the Nichols brothers on James Nichols's farm near Decker, Michigan. McVeigh also spent time with Terry Nichols in and around east-central Kansas, where the rural crisis is clearly the driving force behind the area's agricultural-based antigovernment movement.

This is not to say that if McVeigh did blow up the Murrah building he did so because of rural poverty and farm foreclosures—those are more likely influences for Terry Nichols's alleged participation. But the evidence does suggest that at least part of McVeigh's frustration with government was born out of the same conditions encountered by those suffering from the rural crisis: economics, international trade agreements, and political disenfranchisement. McVeigh was a product of the Rust Belt. The decent paying blue-collar jobs that had provided his father's generation with meaningful employment had disappeared. The growing economic frustration of the Rust Belt working class is being exploited by the antigovernment movement in the same fashion as the rural world. McVeigh had woken up from the American Dream. McVeigh wrote the following letter to the *Union-Sun and Journal*, in Lockport, New York, in 1992. Read his words closely and you will find nearly all of the elements described in the first eight chapters of this book:

> Crime is out of control. Criminals have no fear of punishment. Prisons are overcrowded so they know they will not be imprisoned long . . .
>
> Taxes are a joke. Regardless of what a political candidate "promises," they will increase taxes. More taxes are always the answer to government mismanagement. . . .
>
> The "American dream" of the middle class has all but disappeared, substituted with people struggling just to buy next weeks groceries. Heaven forbid the car breaks down! . . .

Politicians are out of control. Their yearly salaries are more than an average person will see in a life-time. They have been entrusted with the power to regulate their own salaries, and have grossly violated that trust to live in their own luxury. . . .

Who is to blame for this mess? At a point when the world has seen communism falter as an imperfect system to manage people, democracy seems to be headed down the same road. No one is seeing the "big" picture. . . .

What is it going to take to open the eyes of our elected officials? AMERICA IS IN SERIOUS DECLINE.

We have no proverbial tea to dump; should we instead sink a ship full of Japanese imports? Is a Civil War immanent? Do we have to shed blood to reform the current system? I hope it doesn't come to that! But it might.

McVeigh's letter reveals many of his frustrations, but not all of them. McVeigh had also become extremely angry over the government's handling of its standoff with the Waco Branch Davidians, in which over eighty men, women, and children burned to death. The government had originally stormed the compound over a minor weapons charge.

To people in the movement like McVeigh, Waco was seen as a government-sponsored slaughter, created out of its effort to destroy the Second Amendment. McVeigh repeatedly watched a videotape titled *The Big Lie* that was produced by antigovernment extremist Linda Thompson. *The Big Lie* became one of the movement's most successful conspiracy theories and consequently one of its most successful recruiting tools.

The video claims that the government tanks that were used in the final deadly assault on the Waco compound were really flamethrowers ordered to incinerate the Branch Davidians. McVeigh believed *The Big Lie*. He visited the site of the Waco massacre more than once. He is said to have traveled from Michigan to Florida in the company of antigovernment leader Mark Koernke, possibly as his bodyguard. McVeigh is said to have made the trip because surviving Branch Davidians were to be the featured speakers at a militia gathering. McVeigh and Koernke deny they know one another, but one of my sources was at this Florida meeting and recalls seeing the two men. My source said: "It looked like McVeigh was serving as his [Koernke's] bodyguard. That's how I remember it." At the time of

McVeigh's arrest on the day of the bombing, he was in possession of literature describing the government's role at Waco as a conspiracy to commit murder.

McVeigh may have seen Waco as the fulfillment of the prophecies of white supremacist William Pierce. The government's behavior at Waco seemed to parrot the actions of the fictitious federal government in Pierce's novel *The Turner Diaries*. Considering the hold that Pierce's book had over McVeigh and considering McVeigh's paranoid state of mind at the time, it's possible that McVeigh reacted to Waco in the same fashion that his hero—the book's central character Earl Turner—had reacted to the fictional government's crackdown against gun owners.

In Pierce's novel, Turner is an antigovernment patriot who is finally forced to take action after the government passes anti-gun legislation. What action did Earl Turner take? He blew up a federal building that housed the FBI, with a fertilizer and fuel-oil bomb that was concealed in a truck. The bomb in Pierce's book was almost identical in size and components to the bomb used in Oklahoma City.

The book even contains a passage in which Turner consoles himself over the deaths of the innocent people he has just blown up by explaining that the bombing was necessary to wake up America. *Time* magazine has reported that a photocopy of that very passage from *The Turner Diaries* was glued to the outside of an envelope in the car Timothy McVeigh was driving at the time of his arrest.

It's likely McVeigh had entered the realm of psychologist Glen Wallace's "community psychosis," a mental process dominated by prolonged exposure to secondhand depression and antigovernment rhetoric that ultimately manifests itself in a type of "delayed stress syndrome." The dictionary defines community as a body of people with a faith, profession, or way of life in common. McVeigh's community, like that of most antigovernment adherents, was a group of people who shared a hatred for the government. After leaving the service, McVeigh's community was located in Michigan, Kansas, and Arizona. The distances between the geographic locations of the pockets of radical antigovernment believers with whom McVeigh associated make it no less of a community, nor does distance lessen the effects of community psychosis.

There is evidence that after his military service, McVeigh went through a serious personality change that left him increasingly paranoid—the possible result of this syndrome. In late 1994, McVeigh returned to New York and visited with some of his old friends. A relative of David Darlak, the man who had purchased the ten-acre shooting range with McVeigh a few years earlier, described McVeigh's personality this way: "He had slowly deteriorated and turned into a paranoid person. He got stranger and stranger, more intense."[5] In a letter to his sister, Jennifer, McVeigh exhibited his paranoia by telling her that "he knew too much" and had become a "liability" to the federal government. He continued to tell people that the government was monitoring his every move by way of the embedded microchip. As his paranoia increased, McVeigh began to use methamphetamines (speed). He told his sister it enhanced his memory, but it's more likely that the drugs only enhanced his paranoia. In commenting on McVeigh's personality—as exhibited over the years in his letters to his sister—the *Rocky Mountain News* found "that by 1994, McVeigh had changed much from the man others had known before and after his Army service." And finally, McVeigh's mother put it simply: Her son Timothy had "totally changed."

An examination of McVeigh's travel habits and actions in the months prior to the Oklahoma City bombing are evidence of his troubled state of mind. During the six-month period leading up to the Oklahoma City bombing, McVeigh lived in his car and in cheap hotels and spent a lot of time on the telephone. *Denver Post* reporters Mark Eddy and Steven K. Wilmsen spent months sorting through over ten thousand pages of court documents and telephone logs in their attempt to document McVeigh's whereabouts during this time period. They came to this conclusion: "McVeigh was a man on the move, traveling from gun show to gun show. He may have had help driving, if not, it appears he needed little sleep. He didn't hesitate to drive a thousand miles, stay a short while, then start driving again."[6]

There is no evidence that anyone helped McVeigh drive. That fact, in and of itself, could be evidence that McVeigh's copilot was the amphetamines he was taking. Psychologist Glen Wallace says that many people suffering a personality disorder, such as paranoia brought on by long-term stress, practice self-medication.

McVeigh's cross-country travels were marked by seemingly bizarre behavior. He would drive from Michigan to Arizona, stay a short time, and then head back to Michigan. After a few days, he might then head for Kansas, the site of the Waco siege in Texas, or for New York. He would sometimes stop every fifteen minutes to make phone calls. Sometimes he would make calls one after another, for hours at a time. Phone logs show that McVeigh would check into a cheap hotel and call the same telephone number continuously for hours until he reached the party, usually a friend. It was as if he were in a constant state of panic to talk to someone.

Sometimes his pattern of travel and calls would have no rhyme or reason. He'd drive south out of Michigan, make a call, turn back north for two hours, then make another call, then drive back south the way he had just come. His phone calls were often to Michael Fortier, to one of the Nichols brothers, or to gun show acquaintances—in short, to his community. Sometimes he would call numbers that had taped messages espousing racist or antigovernment beliefs. It was as if he had to hear a voice, someone who understood him, even if it was only on a tape recording.

I've heard about this type of behavior before from those who ran the crisis hot lines. Suicidal farmers would sometimes talk to hot-line counselors for hours, hang up, and call back fifteen minutes later. Counselor Mona Lee Brock told me about a man who was attempting to drive across several states. The man was suffering from chronic long-term stress and was in such bad mental shape that he had to stop every twenty minutes or so and call a counselor throughout the duration of the trip. All of these are signs of long-term exposure to stress.

McVeigh also showed another characteristic of stress—an explosive personality. Fred Burkett, one of McVeigh's coworkers at a security guard company in Kingman, Arizona, recalled how McVeigh would be quiet for long periods of time and then explode into an unpredictable rage. McVeigh eventually left that job because he lost control after being reprimanded by a supervisor. Burkett also had a frightening experience when he accompanied McVeigh to a gun range. Burkett recalls, "[McVeigh] pretty much went crazy." McVeigh had been running through the course shooting at the targets when all of a sudden, says Burkett, he "began emptying clips on pretty much anything—trees, rocks, whatever happened to be there. The way he conducted himself right there quite frankly scared the hell out of me. I bet he went through three hundred rounds of ammunition in fifteen minutes."[7]

I described McVeigh's behavior in the six months leading up to the bombing to Dr. Wallace and asked his opinion. Obviously, having never seen McVeigh, such an opinion is purely speculation on Wallace's part, but I asked him to render his opinion as if he were profiling a suspect for police. After describing McVeigh's actions in much the same way as I have here, Wallace said, "It sounds like he would become nearly manic. His agitation when he was trying to reach someone by phone demonstrates his need for support. Part of dealing with his illness was the need for two things: a dialogue with somebody and acceptance from somebody."

Wallace also speculated that

> if he [McVeigh] had had a healthy set of people around him, he'd have been all right. Unfortunately, the people who did accept him kept him in his agitated role and his blame role. This behavior was his way of trying to be normal, but he never made it. His goal, like the rest of us, was trying to have a life with meaning. He wanted to have worth, and to do that, he had to be accepted. He knew he would be accepted by the people he was trying to call. He knew he would get positive feedback. He was in a state where he needed that feedback constantly.

I consider myself to be a reasonably lucid, well-balanced person, but even so, I thought I was being followed. The point is this: If I could become somewhat paranoid after only a few weeks of continuous exposure to the stress of the antigovernment lifestyle, I can't imagine what being immersed in that environment for years could do to a person's mind. Your heart stops every time there is a knock on the door. Every car in the rearview mirror looks sinister. Everywhere you go, there are suspicious-looking people wearing sunglasses who watch your every move. After even a short while, it becomes debilitating.

I'm not defending the actions of a man who may well have committed the most heinous crime in America's history. But we are supposedly a civilized people, whose judicial system is designed to seek justice. If McVeigh is indeed guilty, then we must take into account his state of mind at the time of the crime, particularly because the death penalty is involved in this case.

I don't make that suggestion lightly. I grew up in Oklahoma City. Most of my family still lives there, and each of them was directly affected by the bombing in one way or another. When I went home for Christmas, I visited the site of America's greatest tragedy. I cried as I made my way along the chain-link fence that surrounds what's left of the Alfred P. Murrah Building. The fence was stuffed with well-worn toys left in memory of the murdered children. The toys often had notes attached: "We still love you Tommy"; "I'll be in heaven with you someday"; "Mommy and Daddy will never forget you." I literally fell to my knees when I came across a beautiful white sweater that had been hung carefully on the fence. A card pinned to the sweater's lace collar said that it had belonged to a young woman who had been killed in the blast, and that it was her favorite. Then the note said: "If you need this sweater please take it. That's what Sherry would have wanted. That's the kind of person she was." The Oklahoma City bombing was a tragedy beyond comprehension.

But I have also seen the toll that stress and prolonged exposure to hate-filled religion, economic disaster, and conspiracy theories can have on what were once good and normal people. I have seen a good father and community leader—a deacon in his Baptist church—transformed into a prison inmate. I have seen lives completely destroyed as people are pulled deeper and deeper into the quicksand of the antigovernment movement.

We have a need to look on our enemies as if they were less than human. It's the same process soldiers go through during war. This is our mind's way of trying to protect our sanity when we're forced to shoot people we don't know for reasons we often don't understand. Hardcore antigovernment proponents have created a religion that eliminates the humanity of their victims. The rest of us use the same technique when we dehumanize criminals into animals so that we can feel good about ourselves as we execute them. The enemies that we should be executing are the economic, psychological, religious, and political forces that have transformed human beings into murderous antigovernment zealots.

"Unknown Others"

McVeigh and Nichols are not the only individuals said to be implicated in the Oklahoma City bombing. Another soldier who served with McVeigh and Nichols, Michael Fortier, has already pleaded guilty to knowing about the bombing plot and failing to warn authorities. Fortier lived in a small trailer on the outskirts of Kingman, Arizona, where he tried to make ends meet by working in a hardware store. He was a gun lover and an antigovernment patriot who had ties to militias in the Kingman area. There was a "Don't Tread on Me" flag in his front yard. Fortier has claimed that he drove McVeigh to Oklahoma City three months before the bombing to scout the Murrah building as a possible target, but he claims that was the extent of his participation.

McVeigh, Nichols, and Fortier are the three suspects the government has arrested. But even if all three are guilty, they are not the only people who were involved in the bombing. The government has tried to explain away eyewitness accounts of other suspects, but it's clear that the authorities know they exist. The indictment handed down in the bombing stated that McVeigh, Nichols, and "unknown others" had conspired to blow up the Oklahoma City federal building. During jury selection for McVeigh's trial, the prosecutor continuously asked prospective jurors if they would be able to convict McVeigh and sentence him to death even if they believed that there were other people, who have not yet been arrested, involved in the bombing. And when reporters Eddy and Wilmsen examined the thousands of pages of court documents pertaining to the trial, it became clear that the "unknown others" do indeed exist. What is not clear is where they are today.

In summer 1994, a blue truck with Michigan plates arrived at the small shack in Kingman where McVeigh was living. McVeigh's neighbor at the time, Robert Gohn, recalls that two men and a young woman in her early twenties were the truck's occupants. Gohn says that one of the men looked like Terry Nichols and that the other man was short and muscular "like a weight lifter." About the same time as this visit, federal investigators say that McVeigh left a message addressed to "S. C." attached to a utility pole near Kingman. The note read: "Seeking fighters not talkers." It's unclear who "S. C." is. If McVeigh did leave this message, he must have felt he needed more people to accomplish his goal. Also during this time in Kingman, McVeigh went to a local copy shop and produced several copies of antigovernment literature. Considering his past habits, the copies could have been made to mail to friends, but there is also a possibility that they were to be distributed to people in the Kingman area.

McVeigh's phone calls during the six months prior to the bombing were often to Nichols and Fortier, but he also made a substantial number of calls to James Nichols; to Kevin Nicholas, a Michigan man who had worked on the Nichols's farm; and to Dave Paulson, an Illinois gun dealer. Paulson told the grand jury that when he met McVeigh, they discussed weapons parts and explosives. Paulson said that a man was with McVeigh at the time and that it wasn't Fortier or Terry Nichols. FBI agents would later find a business card they claimed belonged to McVeigh. The card was for the military surplus store owned by Paulson's parents. On the back of the card was a note requesting "more five pound sticks of dynamite by May 1."

McVeigh and Nichols had rented several storage lockers in which the government claims they were storing the ingredients that would eventually be used in the construction of the bomb. One of those lockers was in Kingman; the others were in Kansas. James Rosencrans, one of Fortier's neighbors, says that McVeigh offered him $400 to drive a vehicle for about twenty hours—the approximate drive time from Kingman to Terry Nichols's home in Kansas. Rosencrans says that McVeigh never told him the purpose of the trip or what the cargo would be, and he says that he turned McVeigh down. Authorities have speculated that McVeigh may have needed a driver for a second vehicle in order to move bomb components from Arizona to Kansas. Nichols and Fortier didn't take time off from work during this period, so if McVeigh found a driver, it was someone unknown to authorities.

Meanwhile, back in Herington, Kansas, Terry Nichols had moved into a small house he had purchased. He was new in the neighborhood and had few visitors according to neighbors, so it seemed odd when one night, about three weeks before the bombing, several pickup trucks were parked in front of Nichols's home. One neighbor remembered that one of the trucks stood out—a full-size American-made truck that was rust-brown in color.

On April 5, two weeks before the bombing, McVeigh was in Kingman. Phone records show that on that day he attempted to reach the National Alliance, a white supremacist organization based in Mohave, Arizona. A few hours later a call was logged from Fortier's house to a residence in San Jacinto, California. On April 7, McVeigh called that same San Jacinto number from his hotel room. A few hours later, a call from the San Jacinto residence was made to Fortier's house. None of this phone activity proves anything. But it may shed light on who was in McVeigh's "community" at the time of the bombing.

Around noon on April 10, James Sargent, a sergeant in the army, went fishing for bass at Geary State Fishing Lake in Kansas—this is the lake where authorities claim the Oklahoma City bomb was assembled. As he stood fishing, Sargent noticed a Ryder truck parked directly across the water in front of him. There was no sign of activity. A short time later, says Sargent, a rust-brown pickup pulled up next to the Ryder truck. The pickup matches the description of the truck seen by neighbors in front of Terry Nichols's house a few weeks earlier. Then Sargent noticed still another vehicle arriving to join the Ryder truck—a white, midsize, family-style car. When Sargent went home, the car and pickup were still next to the Ryder truck.

The next day, Sargent drove past the lake in the morning and evening, and both times the Ryder truck was still at the lake. Another resident in the area, Herington real estate broker Georgia Rucker, passed by the lake during the next two days. Rucker claims that she, too, saw the Ryder truck each time she passed the lake. At the time of these eyewitness accounts of the Ryder truck, McVeigh and Fortier were known to be in Arizona and Terry Nichols was known to be in Michigan. The only thing known about whoever was present at the lake is that they are still at large.

According to neighbors, on April 12, a short, muscular man arrived at Terry Nichols's house, where he stayed for the next two days. Again, Fortier was in Arizona, and McVeigh had just begun the twenty-four-hour drive from Kingman to Herington.

On April 15, four days before the bombing, a man who has been identified by witnesses as McVeigh used a driver's license with the name of Bob Kling to put down a cash deposit on a Ryder truck at Elliott's Body Shop. This second Ryder truck is the one authorities claim housed the Oklahoma City bomb. There is speculation that the first Ryder truck—the one seen parked at the lake during the previous week—was used to transport the several tons of bomb components from the Kansas storage units to the lake. On this same day, someone in McVeigh's Dreamland motel room ordered Chinese food from the Hunan Palace restaurant under the name Bob Kling. Jeff Davis delivered the food to a man standing in the doorway of the room. Davis told the FBI that the man was short and muscular. Davis claims that the man was definitely not McVeigh, Nichols, or Fortier. This is likely the third or fourth time that witnesses have identified this short, muscular suspect.

On April 16, which was Easter morning, yet more witnesses—Rick Glessner and his family—saw the Ryder truck still parked at the lake. Later in the day, according to Dreamland motel owner Lea McGown, McVeigh parked a large Ryder truck in front of the motel. McGown is sure of the date because she had just returned from Easter dinner. She noticed McVeigh behind the wheel because he was having trouble backing up the truck. This event is extremely significant because April 16 was the day before McVeigh is alleged to have picked up the Ryder truck that eventually exploded in front of the Murrah building.

Therefore, the truck that McVeigh was parking on April 16 was probably the truck that witnesses had been seeing at Geary Lake.

Lea McGown went to work early on April 17. At 4 A.M. she says she saw McVeigh in the cab of the Ryder truck he had parked at the motel the day before. At 10 A.M., six hours after McGown saw McVeigh in the truck, Elwin Roberts passed by Geary Lake. Roberts says he saw the Ryder truck with a brown pickup parked close by. This is the last time anyone saw the first Ryder truck, which has never been located by authorities. At 4 P.M., a man identifying himself as Bob Kling and a short, muscular companion wearing a blue-and-white cap picked up the new Ryder truck from Elliott's Body Shop. Elliott's employees have identified McVeigh as the man claiming to be Bob Kling. The short muscular man became known as John Doe No. 2. For whatever reason, authorities now claim that John Doe No. 2 doesn't exist. But this was very likely the fifth time this man was seen. A short, muscular man was also with McVeigh when he was in Arkansas inquiring about a remote piece of property that had been advertised as a "perfect hideout."

On the morning of April 19, the day of the bombing, Tulsa banker Kyle Hunt saw a Ryder truck being followed by a yellow car matching the description of the vehicle McVeigh was driving at the time of his arrest making their way slowly through the streets of downtown Oklahoma City. Hunt thought they looked lost, so he pulled up next to the yellow car to see if he could offer directions. The driver of the car, whom Hunt later identified as McVeigh, shot him a nasty look, so Hunt didn't speak to him. Hunt says there were two men in the car with McVeigh, but he couldn't see who was driving the Ryder truck. Fortier and Terry Nichols were both in other states the morning of the bombing.

David Snyder was on a downtown loading dock waiting for a truck to arrive, so when a Ryder truck drove past, he tried to wave it down. Snyder has identified McVeigh as the passenger in the truck. Mike Moroz, a tire-store employee, says that a Ryder truck pulled into his store and asked for directions to the federal building. Moroz identified McVeigh as one of the men and claims a short, muscular man matching the description of John Doe No. 2 was with him.

Who owns the rust-brown pickup seen at the lake and also at Terry Nichols's home? Who was driving the white car that Sargent saw at the lake? Who was the man who ordered the Chinese food from

McVeigh's room? Who rented and drove the first Ryder truck to the lake at a time when all those now in custody were known to be out of the state of Kansas? Who were the three men seen with McVeigh the morning of the bombing at a time when neither Fortier or Nichols was in Oklahoma? These questions may never be answered. But the existence of "unknown others" is consistent with every aspect of the antigovernment movement.

Within the antigovernment movement, there's a standard operating procedure known as "leaderless resistance." Leaderless resistance gives the antigovernment movement the characteristics of a colony of single-celled animals—constantly growing, dividing, and growing and dividing again. This "leaderless" plan for organizing the movement was put forward by Louis Beam at the Estes Park, Colorado, Rocky Mountain Rendezvous. Leaderless resistance is practiced by those at the most violent levels of the movement and particularly by Identity-influenced groups. It's a strategy designed to guard against government infiltration. The idea is that all antigovernment adherents understand the common goal—overthrowing the government and, in Identity's case, starting a race war—so a top-down leadership strategy that can be easily disrupted by the government is neither needed nor desired. Groups of patriots, of five to six persons in size, recruit and grow until they reach ten to twelve members. At that time, they divide into two groups and start the process again.

The one hard-and-fast rule for a member of one of these dividing cells is that they can never discuss the cells to which they have previously belonged. Each of the tiny units has full authority to do whatever it deems necessary to further the cause. Some cells train together for purely defensive purposes, while others blow up buildings. And since the government can hardly supply an undercover agent for every five people in the movement, the plan works like a charm.

Antigovernment publications like *Spotlight* and *The Jubilee* and short-wave radio programs by movement leaders like Mark Koernke and William Pierce can, if they so choose, make sure that these small cells know exactly what is expected of them, without ever running the risk of direct communication. As terrorism goes, it's a brilliant strategy.

Understanding the forces that drive the antigovernment movement is important because it tells us what processes are likely to be involved before any act of terrorism is committed. People join the movement because they feel that the government has forsaken justice. Someone willing to take up arms over this issue isn't likely to commit an act of terrorism without first being given the blessing of a common-law court. People could just cut up their driver's licenses and social security cards, but they don't—not until a common-law court tells them to. People could file false liens against their enemies any time they desire, but again, they don't do it without going through some sort of pseudo-court process. If people in the antigovernment movement will not even carry out these simple procedures without a common-law court's approval, how likely is it that they would take on a significant task like blowing up a building without similar court authority?

In the months leading up to the bombing, McVeigh had a conversation with the owner of a copy shop in Kingman—and the topic was Waco. The owner, George Boerst, said he "mentioned something about an article [he'd] read [in a militia publication] about how an armed militia was supposed to have stormed Washington, D.C., to arrest politicians and try them in their own court." Boerst claims that McVeigh responded by telling him, "Well, that got canceled, but something else is in the making."[8]

This conversation reveals that the radical militia publications that McVeigh was known to read—the same publications that make leaderless resistance possible—were apparently calling for common-law courts to try officials involved with the Waco incident. Some of the ATF and FBI officials who had participated in the Waco operation had their offices in the Murrah building. McVeigh's response to Boerst may indicate that he was aware that the movement wanted trials for those responsible for the government's actions at Waco, and as a hard-core antigovernment adherent, McVeigh knew that a military court would dish out death sentences for those who had been involved in the deaths of the Branch Davidians.

"Something else is in the making," said McVeigh. Was he specifically talking about the Murrah building bombing, or was he saying that a different plan for trying officials had been determined, or both? Whatever he meant, it's clear that under the concept of leaderless resistance, McVeigh—or any other antigovernment zealot—had been given the green light to take action.

The End Results

For most of us, the end result of the Oklahoma City bombing is measured in corpses and sorrow—168 dead, over 500 injured. But for hard-core antigovernment soldiers, the bombing is measured as a success—federal law enforcement is backpedaling and the trumpets of war have been sounded. Mike Reynolds, an investigator for the Southern Poverty Law Center, attended a meeting of six hundred Christian Patriots who gathered in Branson, Missouri, on April 21, 1995, two days after the bombing. While sharing a sink in the bathroom with a Patriot from Oklahoma, Reynolds was shocked by what the man told him. The man said, "They've been taking this country from us piece by piece for years, but we got a piece of it back in Oklahoma City."[9]

Many of those who had been in attendance at the Estes Park, Colorado, Rocky Mountain Rendezvous were at the Branson gathering, and they made their sentiments clear. David Barley of America's Promise Ministries in Idaho spoke to the crowd, telling those assembled: "The media asks who are these evil cowards who were the perpetrators of this bomb? Well, I have another question. Who were the evil cowards who hid themselves and murdered those little children in Waco, Texas?"[10]

W. N. Otwell, a preacher who runs an antigovernment compound in Texas, told the crowd that the Oklahoma City bombing was God's retribution for the people killed at Waco. He said: "God did not mind killing a bunch of women and kids. God talks about slaughter. Don't leave one suckling. Don't leave no babies. Don't leave nothing. Kill them. Destroy them."[11] Those at the Branson conference understood why the bomb in Oklahoma City had exploded. They understood the concept of leaderless resistance that had made it happen. Oklahoma City was just the beginning.

But those gathered in Branson are not an accurate reflection of the entire antigovernment movement—they are only an example of those who have been sucked all the way through the antigovernment funnel. For the most part, people in the antigovernment movement choose to deal with the Oklahoma City bombing through denial. They distance themselves from the deadly blast by claiming that the government blew up the building, although many of them know better. Although not directly supporting such an inhuman act of terrorism, a few candid militia leaders are willing to admit that the bombing has benefited them.

"It changed the way they deal with us," says Ron Cole, Branch Davidian and commander of a Colorado militia. Cole makes it clear that he doesn't condone the bombing, even though he admits that it was likely exploded in retaliation against the government for its role in the deaths of eighty of his fellow Branch Davidians during the Waco siege. In Cole's opinion,

> At Ruby Ridge the government just opened fire on the Weavers. They didn't care how many people protested their actions. They turned right around and handled Waco the same way. They went in with a surprise attack, guns blazing. They're [the U.S. government] the single largest abuser of human rights on the planet. Congress did its investigations [of Ruby Ridge and Waco] and slapped them on the wrist, but that wasn't going to change the way the government deals with us. Look at the way they [the government] handled the Freemen in Montana—completely different. And the only reason it was different is because somebody blew up a building in Oklahoma City. Now, the government understands what happens when it abuses its power. They handled the Freemen situation properly, so nothing blew up in response. It [Oklahoma City bomb] was a terrible situation, but it's the only thing that got the government's attention.

There's no question that the government has changed its tactics regarding the movement. The eighty-one-day standoff with the Montana Freemen exposed a decisively different strategy for apprehending lawbreaking sectors of the antigovernment movement than those strategies exhibited at Waco and Ruby Ridge. Toward the end of the Freemen standoff, both the media and the general population were complaining that the government looked weak, that authorities should go in and apprehend the Freemen. But the government, unlike the public, realized what was at stake—one corpse in Montana could turn into a hundred innocent victims later on, when the next bomb exploded. Although the government would never admit it, Cole is correct in his analysis of the Oklahoma City bomb's impact on the behavior of law enforcement agencies. The truth is this: Terrorism works, and those who would commit such dastardly acts know it works. It's within the context of that disturbing reality that we must examine what the future is likely to hold for America between now and the year 2000.

12

A Thousand Days of Tribulation

"Could you watch my stuff for a minute?" I looked up into the face of a twenty-something man to make sure he was talking to me. "Sure," I said, still having forty-five minutes until my flight. As the man disappeared into the ocean of people that was surging through the crowded concourse, it hit me: We're not supposed to watch people's "stuff" anymore. I looked at the green duffel bag, then returned to my reading. A few minutes passed and the stranger hadn't come back. I started to feel uncomfortable sitting next to the bag. I was also feeling uncomfortable about feeling uncomfortable.

"When did the world get like this?" I thought. A few more minutes passed and still no sign of the guy, whose face was now causing me to flash back on every sketch I'd seen of John Doe No. 2, the mystery man in the Oklahoma City bombing. I stood up and searched the crowd—no sign of him.

I walked a few feet away and leaned against a concrete pillar, careful to place its thickness between myself and the giant bomb I was now convinced was ticking away in the bowels of the horrible green bag. A security guard walked past. I wondered if I should tell him about the bag. "No," I thought. "I refuse to live in fear." But I was living in fear. I decided to make my stand. I walked back to the bag and sat down nearly on top of it. People continued to hurry by, seemingly unaware that I was engaged in a life-and-death struggle for the soul of America.

For the next couple of minutes, I stared at the bag and thought about how times have changed. It wasn't just the Oklahoma City bombing. It wasn't the fact that bombs go off somewhere in the United States nearly every day. It was all of it: the identification requirement to get my boarding pass; the long lines at the metal detectors that are turned up so high they find the fillings in your teeth; and that damn computer voice saying, "Don't park here, don't set your bags there."

While reading my paper on the way to the airport, I found an AP wire story about a pipe bomb exploding in California; it was on page twenty-six. I remember when the farm crisis made its move from page one to page five, then to page twenty-six, and finally to nowhere. The crisis hadn't ended—we'd just accepted it as a fact of life, as no longer newsworthy. It's happening again with antigovernment terrorism. Big bombs with injuries still make the news, but little bombs have been relegated to the back pages, with all the other forms of political protest. How many bombs did we read about in the last year—five, ten? According to the Bureau of Alcohol, Tobacco, and Firearms, there were over six hundred pipe-bomb incidents in the United States in 1996. We've become numb to it.

A woman I know told me she refused to enter a store where she wanted to shop because there were unattended Christmas packages sitting near the front door. And here I am in an airport doing the tango with a concrete pillar, likely for no more reason than that some guy needed to hit the can. I try, but I can't remember what it was like when things didn't blow up.

"Thanks for watching it." I was startled by the man returning for his duffel bag. "No problem," I said, or rather lied, to him as he walked away.

You can feel it when you walk through an airport or a crowded shopping mall. You sense it when you read the daily paper or while watching the nightly news on TV. We don't talk about it—such verbal acknowledgment would interfere with our state of denial, but we all know it's there.

We've become vulnerable. We can die at the hand of a terrorist while shopping, going to work, visiting a friend, or dropping a child off at the day care center. We can have our property tied up with illegal liens and mountains of other equally bogus paperwork for no good reason. We can be tried and sentenced to death by a common-law court without ever uttering a word in our own defense. The antigovernment movement has turned our lives into a twenty-four-hour-a-day crapshoot, and we will never be the same. The harvest of rage is upon us.

History Repeats Itself

"What we're seeing now is recognized as the growing polarization of wealth in the country, with just 1 percent owning 40 percent of the wealth, with the middle class shrinking and becoming part of the working class and the working class shrinking as the people lose their jobs and become part of the homeless poor," says Howard Zinn, historian and author of *A People's History of the United States.* In 1996, I asked Zinn to compare the hectic times between 1880 and 1900 with what's happening today. I also asked him to gaze into his crystal ball and predict the possible consequences of today's heartland revolution. After pointing out that historians don't care much for predicting the future, he agreed.

As Zinn talks, he makes clear that the trend during the Reagan-Bush-Clinton era of less and less government regulation has been an attempt to return to the free enterprise system, a system in which the government doesn't do anything to help people in need. This is not the first time in history that corporations have been allowed to control their own destiny. Zinn also points out that rural America is often the loser when corporations are in control:

> When we go back to the 1880s and 1890s, what we see is a kind of unbridled capitalism. The country goes through a great industrial growth, but the poor and working-class people do not share in that growth and do not share in the profits from that growth. The middle class at that point was really the farming class. They were the people in the 1880s and 1890s that were being squeezed more and more. . . . They found themselves losing their farms and losing their livestock and being propelled into being tenant farmers or being forced into the cities to look for work.

Zinn's words paint an all-too-familiar picture. He could easily be describing the last two decades. And the comparison becomes even clearer:

> What you have in both eras is sort of capitalism at its worst, [which] means the impoverishment of both the middle class and the poor, until the distinction between the middle class and the poor becomes less and

less. Then the control of the country by the financial interests and by the politicians of both parties goes unchallenged. It's interesting that what you saw in the 1880s and 1890s was mergers. . . . There were monopolies in all of the industries like the railroads. Now, that's what we are seeing in the country today. We see it almost every day in the headlines: another giant merger taking place.

The labor struggles at the turn of the last century were a reaction to what the banks and corporations were doing to the farmers and the working class, and that is eerily similar to the effect that today's global restructuring is having on rural America. Corporate control of the system in the 1880s and 1890s ultimately gave birth to the Populist movement. So far, in the 1980s and 1990s, corporate control over government has only given birth to the antigovernment movement, but that may be changing. The recent popularity of third-party candidates may be the birth pangs of a new populist era.

Zinn notes another similarity between the two time periods, during which the Democratic and Republican parties grew to be almost indistinguishable, with a succession of Democratic and Republican presidents who resemble one another: "Grover Cleveland was the kind of Democrat that Jimmy Carter and Bill Clinton have been; that is, a Democrat who really played a very cozy game with the big corporations of his time." Zinn remarks that where this will all lead depends on the intensity of the attacks on the poor and middle class. It could lead to a new social movement and perhaps to new radical political parties.

In another parallel, the 1880s, like the 1990s, were not without their share of terrorism. On May 4, 1885, a bomb exploded in Chicago's Haymarket Square during a labor protest. I ask Zinn to compare the government's reaction to the Haymarket Square bombing with the Clinton administration's reaction to the Oklahoma City tragedy. He responds that "in both cases the government used the event as a way to denounce opposition to the existing order as terrorist and anarchist," remarking on the great irony that a government that engages in mass-scale violence in wartime should denounce "violence done by dissident groups within the United States and that [the government] should use those as an excuse for further oppression." He distinguishes between Haymarket Square, where the oppression was against the Left, and Oklahoma City, with its right-wing perpetrators. But Zinn thinks the Oklahoma City bombing "is the occasion for a very broad government action, not simply against the Left or

Right, but, for instance, against all immigrants. The so-called antiterrorism act enables the government to deport people who have legally come into this country who have been apprehended for one crime or another. It has nothing to do with terrorism."

Zinn believes that one of the great misconceptions by today's antigovernment movement is exhibited in their hatred of "big government." Most people in the movement express a desire to return to the good old days when the Constitution was written. According to Zinn, this longing for days gone by comes from failing to understand why the founding fathers created a central government in the first place:

> Big government started with the founding of the nation itself. . . . The whole idea of the Constitutional Convention of 1787 was to set up a big government, that is, a strong central government [in order to] help the bondholders, the slave owners, the merchants and manufacturers. Throughout our history, the business interests have needed a strong government to do what they needed done: to create high tariff barriers to help manufacturers; in the case of slave owners, to help them catch runaway slaves; in the case of bondholders to make sure their bonds were secure. A common thread running through from the founding fathers to today has been the security of bondholders and subsidies for corporations, which started way back.
>
> Big government can play a very class-conscious role on behalf of the rich—which it has throughout most of history—or it can, as it has done sometimes in this century, play a role on behalf of people who need help. If those distinctions are not made, then we are in danger of creating the kind of antigovernment movement that can sweep away whatever help has come to poor people as a result of the social legislation of the last thirty years.

The violence of today's antigovernment movement can also be put into historical perspective. According to Zinn, violence by the disenfranchised has often been a prerequisite of socially conscious government reform. If the country hadn't been swept by tenant movements, labor disputes, unemployment movements, and general unrest among the working class and poor, Roosevelt's New Deal reforms would never have come about. For example, the National Labor Relations Act (the Wagner Act) was enacted to counteract and put a stop to a wave of militant labor strikes. And the same was true of the social reforms of the 1960s. According to Zinn, John Kennedy was not planning to promote more civil rights legislation or to address racial segregation in the South, nor were Lyndon Johnson and Congress prepared to push for a voting rights act. But enormous demonstrations by black people in the South from the early 1960s through 1963 finally forced the government to address the problem.

Zinn says that this is the pattern throughout history. Reforms have come about as a result of protest: "It takes rebellion to move an otherwise sluggish system, a system that normally operates on behalf of the rich and powerful." Zinn points out that it's always helpful to have a president who is sensitive to the concerns of the working class and poor but oval-office sensitivity has never been enough on its own to bring about change. In fact, government inaction when it isn't confronting major social unrest is a formula for creating rebellion—as with the inaction that has given rise to today's antigovernment movement.

The fascistic forces behind today's antigovernment movement are also nothing new. According to Zinn, the problem is that

> in a situation like today where there is enormous alienation . . . that alienation and anger can be seized by demagogues of the Right, and this is what happened in Fascist countries like Italy and Germany. It could lead to a kind of American fascism. I have no doubt that it is easier to motivate people to violence than it is to motivate them to vote. If people become desperate enough and angry enough, they will take it out in various ways.

Clearly, that is exactly what has come out of today's economic hardships and rural fear of a changing world.

The Movement, Then and Now

The KKK is the granddaddy of today's antigovernment movement, and it has always been an accurate barometer of the rural psyche. After the Civil War, the Klan's numbers grew as the people of the South exhibited their uncertainty about a future controlled by carpetbaggers. In the 1920s, when the world entered a new technological age accompanied by a liberal shift in morality, the Klan's numbers again swelled, ultimately reaching 3 to 4 million members. The Vietnam War, love-ins, hippies, and civil unrest among blacks in the South during the 1960s once again spurred the radical Right. The 1960s differed from earlier right-wing resurgences in the sense that several different organizations came into existence; the Posse, the Minute-

men, the National Alliance, and the John Birch Society found a significant following.

The 1980s marked a change in the radical Right. Just as with the
rest of society, the violence of the antigovernment movement became
more random and ghastly. The Order, skinheads, and young neo-
Nazis composed the new generation of right-wing zealots. They had
no mental barrier to terrorism. Stomping an immigrant to death on a
public street was just something to do on a Saturday night. The old
guard, particularly the Aryan Nations, recognized the value of these
young warriors. If they could harness the uncontrolled anger of this
disenfranchised youth, they could use it to further their quest to start
an end-times race war. This new generation of hate would become
the bank robbers and assassins for the movement's most radical elements.

At the same time, another revolution was taking place. Society's
most conservative segment was being hammered by the worst economic crisis since the Great Depression. Farmers were suffering at the
hands of newly unbridled corporations that had managed to seize
control of both the food industry and American politics. In response,
the Posse Comitatus gained control of the farmers. The antigovernment movement grew all through the 1980s, but its ideological differences left it a divided army, as much at war with itself as with the
government.

The 1980s proved to be a difficult decade for millions of Americans. Corporate raiders purchased companies and pocketed the
worker's pension funds. They closed or downsized the factories that
working men and women depended on for their existence. Corporate
mergers cost millions of people their jobs. At times, unemployment
seemed to go down, but the real story was hidden by the statistics.
Jobs that had paid a decent wage were being turned into part-time
minimum-wage jobs. Benefits such as insurance and retirement funds
went out the window. Studies have shown that Americans at almost
every level of the economy had become insecure over their financial
future. History was repeating itself in the 1980s, but this time things
would be different. Technology would see to that.

The Internet has revolutionized revolution. A right-wing radical in
Idaho can recruit a laid-off textile worker in Alabama to his antigovernment cause. Depressed individuals can receive their "invitation to
live" from an antigovernment evangelist half a continent away. The
creators of antigovernment misinformation can spread their new con-

spiracy theories throughout the entire movement in less than twenty-four hours. And economic refugees of rural restructuring can find their needed psychological support from antigovernment adherents who are spread out over thousands of miles. Community psychosis has spread its devastating effects in a new and faster way—through cyber-psychosis.

In the 1960s and 1970s, improving technology made it possible for the antigovernment movement to exist in the form of dozens of somewhat interconnected organizations. But the technology of the 1980s has made it possible for thousands of antigovernment organizations to exist simultaneously. They are separate, yet in many ways they are more unified than at any time in history. It's ironic that the same improvement in global communications that have made it possible to ship rural America's jobs overseas has also become the weapon of choice for rural Americans who have decided to fight back.

Technology is polarizing the country. In government and antigovernment alike, everything is transpiring at warp speed. The gap between rich and poor no longer widens by small increments at a time; it's flying apart at such a rate that it's shaking the very foundation of our country. One of the reasons the antigovernment movement is growing so quickly is that everyone knows that it's growing quickly; that is, thanks to the Internet, the herd mentality is affecting every nook and cranny of America. For instance, a small band of sovereigns in a New Mexico compound no longer feels isolated and vulnerable to a powerful government. The group now sees itself as just one unit in a vast antigovernment force, and in many ways, technology has made that an accurate perception.

Futurists have predicted that the Internet will become the savior of our democracy by making it quick and easy for every American to vote. Their analysis of the Internet's political power is correct, but they have failed to consider the level of economic and political frustration that has afflicted well over one-half of the population. The Internet has indeed energized the long-apathetic voters of the underclass, but there's a twist.

Unfortunately, yet quite understandably, these newly politicized people have no desire to participate in the corporate-sponsored government that created their apathy in the first place. They have skipped right past the current federal government, opting instead to establish their own self-rule in the form of jural societies, sovereign townships, and the like. Votes are being cast daily in places like the Republic of

Texas, the Country of Kansas, the Nation of Hawaii, and Justus Township. We have entered a period of high-tech anarchy. It would be a fascinating turn of events, if it were not for the dark side of this technological phenomenon.

The new government being created by disenfranchised people in rural America is built upon their long-held dominionist beliefs; it's a theocratic government of apocalypse. This new antigovernment government that merges common-law courts, militias, and sovereignty doctrines is even less tolerant than the one it has been designed to replace.

In fact, the antigovernment movement is accelerating for more reasons than just improved communications. People in the movement have a sense of urgency. They must accomplish their lofty goal of toppling the federal government within the next 1,000 days, for the turn of the century marks the end of the world. If you don't believe me, just ask the experts—Hal Lindsey and his 30 million readers; Pat Robertson or any of his 5 million followers; the Montana Freemen and their thousands of disciples; Arthur; every post-tribulation believer who thinks the end-times have begun; or every Identity zealot who has declared war on ZOG. It's too late to ask the members of the Heaven's Gate cult. In the end, it will be the conspiracy theories and apocalyptic religions—and not the politics—of the antigovernment movement that will spill the blood of innocent Americans.

The Tribulation Begins

Between 1991 and 1995, there were 4,046 pipe-bomb incidents in the United States—and 3,160 of those bombs exploded. Over this same period, the most recent data available from the ATF say that there were an additional 900-plus bombing incidents that were not caused by pipe bombs (hand grenades, fertilizer bombs, and so on). There were over 5,000 Molotov cocktails thrown during the first half of this decade. The federal government has concluded that over 200 of the church burnings that took place in the last five years were the result of hate crimes. And we are only now entering what the antigovernment movement promises will be the final battle—the 1,000 days of tribulation between now and the end of the century, when they will make their presence felt by all.[1]

Ron Cole, Branch Davidian and leader of a Colorado militia, made a very disturbing statement to me in March 1997. He told me that the only reason pipe bombs were being used instead of bigger, more powerful explosives is because they are so simple to make:

> If they [the movement] could level buildings like they did in Oklahoma City, they would. Why would a person go to all the risk to throw a pipe bomb at a building knowing that it's just going to blow out some windows? They'll still get twenty years in prison if they're caught. If they're already running that kind of risk, I can promise you they'd much rather be flattening that building. People are getting more sophisticated and the bombs are going to get bigger.

In May 1997, a few weeks after making this statement, Cole was arrested in Denver after an FBI raid on his home produced illegal weapons and explosive materials. Cole may be right. The Freemen in Seattle were arrested for running a bomb-making school. A group of antigovernment zealots in Phoenix was arrested for allegedly planning to blow up a building. The main evidence against the Arizona group was a videotape showing them learning to make fertilizer bombs. Bomb-making literature is readily available to the movement through militias, gun shows, and the Internet. According to Cole, just as the movement is evolving politically, it is also evolving in its destructive capabilities.

One of my contacts—a man who travels the country teaching military tactics to militias and who spoke to me only when I agreed to keep his identity unknown—told me why we haven't already seen more incidents like Oklahoma City. He said that "it takes anywhere from twelve to eighteen months to pull off an attack like Oklahoma City. So if a group decides to seriously retaliate against the government for something it did, it might not happen till two years down the road." This source also told me how such tactical training takes place in the movement:

> Every militia has its share of idiots or informers. We'll teach a basic defense course for the whole group, where to shoot people when they kick down your door, guerrilla warfare, the tame stuff. The guys who are serious about changing things know that defense isn't going to do the trick. Later, usually the next day, we have another meeting with a few of the leaders who understand what's going on. We teach them offensive

tactics—how a small force can take on a larger military force and win. You can call it terrorism, but it's just being practical. If you're serious about changing things, it's the only option.

The antigovernment movement hasn't gone unnoticed by the rest of the world, particularly by those countries that view the United States as their enemy. Documents filed by McVeigh's defense team have tried to implicate foreign governments as being the masterminds behind the Oklahoma City bombing. The information I've seen in the Oklahoma City case leads me to believe that the defense team is just blowing smoke in an effort to create reasonable doubt in the minds of the jury, but the concept of foreign involvement in the antigovernment movement is on the verge of becoming a reality if it isn't so already.

Foreign financial support for Louis Farrakhan's Nation of Islam has been widely reported. Syria and Libya are said to have contributed substantial funds to the organization. If these countries are willing to support Farrakhan, it makes sense that they would be even more willing to funnel money to violent extremists in the antigovernment movement. Although most of those in the movement would never consider seeking money from such places, there are exceptions. There are two elements within today's movement that wouldn't hesitate to accept such support: hard-core Identity groups and a more disparate collection of groups I'll call the "new breed."

The hard-core Identity groups, whose only purpose is to bring about a race war, have shown that funding their cause by any means possible is acceptable. They have long funded their hate-filled agenda by robbing banks and other dubious means. In 1996, the Aryan Republican Army was charged with robbing twenty-two banks in its effort to fund the overthrow of the government and create a white America. In a chilling two-hour videotape that was used as evidence in the group's 1997 Ohio trial, the alleged leader of those accused of being white supremacist robbers, Peter K. Langan, looks into the camera and says: "Our basic goal is to set up an Aryan republic . . . Don't mistake us for cultists. We, ladies and gentlemen, are your neighbors."[2]

In Spokane, Washington, three gunmen linked to white supremacist groups are on trial for nine bank robberies designed to fund their religion-based agenda. The group allegedly used pipe bombs as diversions during the bank heists. In fact, the number of bank robberies has gone up nationwide, reflecting both the deteriorating economics of the underclass and the push by the antigovernment movement to secure the funds it needs for its final bloody showdown with the government. In Colorado, bank robberies increased by a staggering 65 percent during 1996 alone.[3]

There's no reason to assume that white supremacists who are willing to rob banks to further their goals wouldn't leap at the chance to get foreign cash for their cause. The benefit to foreign enemies of the United States is clear. They can supply the money to people whose goal is to destabilize the government through terrorism without running the risk of sending in their own agents. This is a match made in heaven—or more likely, in hell. In 1996, the government discovered that Iraq was sending at least small amounts of money to a neo-Nazi organization in Tulsa, Oklahoma. The foreign pipeline is only going to get bigger.

A new breed of other elements within the movement—representing perhaps yet another step in the movement's evolution—is also seeking foreign funding. One of my contacts, whom I will call "Tom" since he spoke on condition of anonymity, told me that he is actively seeking money abroad. Tom's antigovernment organization, which has established dialogues with Mexico's Zapatistas, South America's Shining Path guerrillas, and the Nation of Islam, is the antithesis of the Identity-driven groups. But don't mistake Tom for a leftist—he's not. His vision of America is similar to that of the sovereigns, with small pockets of self-governed individuals living in regions outside of any federal authority. "If blacks want to live separate from whites," says Tom, "they should have that right. I don't think that's necessary, but people should be allowed to choose how and where they live."

Tom says that the American government is responsible for creating the conditions worldwide that have spawned the sort of radical organizations his group communicates with in other countries, so it's only natural that today's antigovernment movement should consider them as allies. In line with this vision, he says: "Who knows? Maybe someday we'll have a standoff in Texas like the one with McLaren, and the Zapatistas will come to our defense. It could happen."

Ron Cole is another of the movement's new breed. He has long viewed the antigovernment movement as resulting from human rights abuses. Not surprisingly, Cole points to the deaths of his fellow Branch Davidians at Waco as an example of what the government has become. Cole, who is commander of the Colorado Light

Infantry Militia, has recently formed a new organization called the North America Liberation Army, with the goal of establishing international ties with organizations like the Zapatistas and the Shining Path guerrillas, groups that Cole views as springing forth from human rights issues.

Considering the hyperpatriotism and isolationist politics that permeate most elements of the antigovernment movement, it's highly unlikely that the international philosophy advocated by Tom or Cole will ever be embraced by the majority of antigovernment adherents. But that's not to say that establishing links between the Shining Path guerrillas, American militias, and countries like Syria can't have a serious impact on the antigovernment movement. We can only guess how these new international developments within the antigovernment world will play themselves out. It's just one more aspect of the "anti" situation we must consider as we head toward the turn of the century.

The Movement Divides

The antigovernment movement has always been a quagmire of infighting and unholy alliances among groups that fundamentally oppose any philosophy but their own. As we approach the year 2000 and the various components in the movement become more active in pushing their individual agendas, it's likely that the movement will divide into several more clearly defined factions. Ron Cole sees the future of the movement as composed of three forms: constitutional militias, human rights militias, and racist organizations.

Cole's analysis is a reflection of types of people who are currently involved in the movement. Based upon all of my experiences with the various groups, my best guess is that the coming split within the antigovernment movement will be more of a "who's in and who's out" scenario.

As the racist and religion-driven antigovernment factions intensify their terrorist effort to bring about a full-scale war before the year 2000, it will become more and more difficult for the moderate and soft-core elements to remain involved with the increasingly violent movement. The racist Identity factions believe that if they start it, others will join them. They point to the fact that less than 5 percent of Americans favored the Revolutionary War when it began, and they say that when blood begins to flow this time, the general population will once again fall in line with the patriots. It is this presupposition—coupled with their Identity belief that God has commanded them to start an all-out holy war—that gives them the confidence that they will actually be successful in toppling the government and establishing a white America. In reality, their efforts over the next 1,000 days will only serve to kill innocent people and divide the antigovernment movement. But to a small degree, they may be correct.

As the bloodshed increases over the next few years and the government is forced to react, both legislatively and militarily, many of those who have become brainwashed through years of existing in an antigovernment environment will join the racist radicals. But the opposite is also true. The majority of antigovernment adherents—those who comprise the moderate and soft-core elements of the movement—will be driven back to a more democratic means of attempting to deal with their economic frustrations. The effect will be a smaller antigovernment movement overall, but one that is much more prone to terrorism. William Pierce, who predicted that Americans are going to turn to terrorism in a proportion that the world has never seen before, will once again be proven a prophet.

Those who return to the democratic process could potentially become the driving force in an already growing Populist movement. Pat Buchanan's last bid for the presidency demonstrated that even a millionaire Washington insider could whip up a substantial following by throwing around enough Populist rhetoric, and there is other evidence that such a Populist resurgence is a distinct possibility.

In *The True and Only Heaven: Progress and Its Critics*, Christopher Lasch points to research that found that the vast majority of Americans favored some form of income redistribution. But much to the chagrin of progressives, the same research demonstrated that most Americans disapproved of the Democratic Party's stance on such issues as gay rights, sex education, abortion, and gun control. Studies also found that when it came to voting, these issues—income redistribution, morality, and individual freedoms—caused two things to happen: Either people stayed home because there were no candidates touting income redistribution combined with conservative morality, or they voted Republican because they placed moral issues ahead of economic concerns. This morally conservative and economically progressive segment of the population makes up the majority of voters. It also includes the majority of the middle class and the poor in this country. If the right candidate comes along, there may yet be a Democratic solution to America's heartland revolt.

The Point of No Return

My brothers let us be His battle ax and weapons of war. Let us go forth by ones and twos, by scores and by legions, and as true Aryan men with pure hearts and strong minds face the enemies of our faith and our race with courage and determination.

We hereby invoke the blood covenant and declare that we are in a full state of war and will not lay down our weapons until we have driven the enemy into the sea and reclaimed the land which was promised to our fathers of old, and through our blood and His will, becomes the land of our children to be.

—Aryan Nations' Oath of Allegiance

The Aryan Nations, many Freemen, the hard-core believers of the Christian Jural Society, and others in the religion-driven elements of the movement are beyond the reach of political solutions. Those who sincerely believe that their violent actions against the government are demanded by God and that the Antichrist or the Jews have taken over the American government will not seek democratic outlets for their frustrations, even if those outlets were to miraculously become available.

We've waited too long. Psychologist Glen Wallace and other rural counselors warned Congress a decade ago that the anger that was being created in the 1980s would not manifest itself for a number of years. In 1989, Wallace warned Washington that even if the government took drastic action to ease the pain of the rural crisis immediately, those who had already fallen prey to the restructuring would haunt us for decades to come.

Our elected representatives understood that the gap between rich and poor was making rural America and other segments of the working class restless, but they ignored it. They understood that these same people had lost faith in the democratic process, but again, they ignored it. And why not? Our politicians also understood that the fewer voters there are, the easier it is to target the remaining voters with the campaign ads purchased with money donated by corporations and wealthy constituents.

Poor people don't vote, so politicians can appeal to those who do by promising to cut entitlements. Immigrants don't vote, so savvy politicians are swept into office by promising more and harsher anti-immigrant legislation. Rural people still vote, but their numbers are insignificant, so would-be candidates can concentrate exclusively on the suburban agenda without fear of rural retaliation at the polls.

The only action the government took after Wallace's warning was to cut funding for rural programs, and now all of us are being forced to play pipe-bomb roulette at the hands of the antigovernment movement—a movement created by the failure of our democratic process.

The antigovernment movement has had an impact on our political process. Today, politicians realize that in order to get elected they must feign support for campaign finance reform, enforcement of antitrust laws, term limits, and antilobbyist legislation. But the lack of serious action on the part of our elected representatives exposes their insincerity when it comes to limiting their own power.

We didn't understand the role that apocalyptic religion was destined to play in the antigovernment movement until it was too late. The coming holy war being devised by religion-motivated antigovernment radicals—convinced that globalization represents the coming of the Antichrist and subsequently the end of the world—is as inevitable and unavoidable as the global marketplace itself. Technology and the psychological impact of the turn of the century have ensured that the next chapter in America's history will be a violent one.

But proper governmental reforms designed to make our democracy inclusive of all our citizens—rural and urban, rich and poor, minorities and the majority—would lessen the duration and intensity of the terrorism we must endure over the next few years. And if we don't reform the political process now, the long-term prognosis is increasing civil unrest and violence.

Futurists have predicted that in another twenty years, technology will make it possible for 60 percent of the world's population to fulfill 100 percent of the world's needs. These same visionaries have predicted that as a result, workweeks will be shortened to three days and people will use their newfound time to improve themselves and the world around them. I can't imagine what world these intellectuals are living in. It certainly isn't our world. It sounds like an episode of *Star Trek*.

History tells us that if 60 percent of the world can produce all of the needed goods, then 40 percent of the world will be left to starve. If you want proof, consider this example from the here and now: Haiti is only a stone's throw away from the United States. Many Haitians can't afford to eat; they die by the tens of thousands from malnutrition and easily curable diseases. At the same time, our farmers have been losing their farms because we have such a surplus of grain that the prices are kept lower than the cost of production. Why does Haiti starve while we drown in our excess? Because our government has stood by and allowed a handful of multinational companies to control the world's grain supply. And those multinational companies will not send grain to Haiti or any other economically strapped country because there's no profit in doing so.

I watched an Archer Daniels Midland commercial on TV in early 1997 that said the giant company was creating the technology that would make it possible to meet the world's ever-increasing food needs well into the next century. It would have been more accurate had the commercial said that the megacorporation was creating the technology needed to ensure surpluses and therefore cheap prices, which will allow them to continue to extract immoral profits from the wealthy nations of the world. "Hunger" is not in the vocabulary of the food monopolies.

So long as corporations run our government by providing the money that determines who can be elected and subsequently what legislation will be enacted, Haiti will starve, rural America will continue to race toward Third World status, our inner cities will continue to implode, and the gap between rich and poor will widen until all hell breaks loose. That's the corporate-controlled world we live in now, and that's the corporate-controlled world in which we will still be living in twenty years—unless we use the democratic process to instigate change designed to give a voice to those who have withdrawn from the system.

Rebellion usually leads to democratic reforms. The question is, how much rebellion? Apparently, five thousand pipe bombs are not enough. The Atlanta bombings weren't enough. Even Oklahoma City has changed nothing. We have continued doing business as usual, which has resulted in tens of thousands of disenfranchised Americans creating their own twisted and often violent versions of government.

Now is the time to create a democracy in which our elected representatives resemble the people they represent. Change must come soon—and it must be substantial—or we run the risk of becoming a country we can no longer recognize.

Bill Heffernan, dean of rural psychology at the University of Missouri at Columbia, shared his fears with me about the future of America. Heffernan compared our current rural uprising to several of the countries in South America where he's spent a fair amount of time. He said that unless something is done to stop the decline of rural America, there will come a time in the not-so-distant future when it will no longer be safe for people to move about freely. Heffernan sees a time when just driving across the country will be hazardous. He said that if the decline continues, we could become like other places where the gaps between rich and poor and urban and rural have become so large that people must fly from one city to another, knowing that if they drove through the rural areas they would be stopped by bandits or guerrilla factions composed of economically radicalized people. This is not an encouraging picture of rural America, but there is little in rural America that is encouraging these days.

I hope Bill Heffernan is wrong. I hope that Glen Wallace and the other rural counselors are wrong. I hope that William Pierce and all the radical antigovernment leaders who claim that the war has begun are wrong. For that matter, I hope that I'm wrong. We'll find out over the next thousand days.

Notes

Introduction

1. Pat Lewis, "Preventable Agricultural Deaths in Oklahoma 1983–1988: Self Inflicted or Suicides," Agriculture Engineering Department, Oklahoma State University, 1989.

Chapter One

1. Glen Wallace, "Rural Stress in Oklahoma," prepared for Oklahoma Dept. of Mental Health and Substance Abuse Services, unpublished, 1990, p. 1. See also Glen Wallace, "Rural Development," Testimony before U.S. House of Representatives, Committee on Agriculture, Amarillo, TX, August 9.

2. State Health Reports: Mental Health, Alcoholism & Drug Abuse. "Mental Health Services in Rural America," Intergovernmental Health Policy Project, The George Washington University, Washington, D.C., no. 58, June 1990, p. 1.

3. James Hansen, "When It Comes to Working Conditions, Nike Is No Sport," *Rocky Mountain News*, February 1997.

4. State Health Reports: Mental Health, Alcoholism & Drug Abuse, p. 1.

5. W. Sinclair, "Grief Is Growing on Farmland," *Washington Post*, May 24, 1987, reprinted in "Report of the National Action Commission on the Mental Health of Rural Americans," National Mental Health Association, Alexandria, 1988, p. 9.

6. "Report of the National Action Commission on the Mental Health of Rural Americans," National Mental Health Association, Alexandria, 1988, p. 10.

7. USDA Report quoted in ibid., p. 12.

8. Bob Herbert, "1 in 4 Kids Is Growing Up Poor," *The New York Times*, October 1996, quoting a Columbia University study titled "One in Four," by the National Center for Children in Poverty, October 1996. Subcommittee on Intergovernmental Relations, Committee on Government Affairs, "Governing the Heartland: Can Rural Communities Survive the Farm Cri-

sis?" Washington, D.C: U.S. Senate, sections reprinted in USDA Report quoted in "Report of the National Action Commission on the Mental Health of Rural Americans," National Mental Health Association, Alexandria, pp. 10–11, 1988.

9. Richard Gilmore, *A Poor Harvest: The Clash of Policies and Interests in the Grain Trade,* New York: Longman, 1982, pp. 8–9.

10. P. S. Armstrong and M. D. Schulman, "Financial Strain and Depression Among Farm Operators: The Role of Perceived Economic Hardship and Personal Control," *Rural Sociology,* vol. 55, no. 4, pp. 475–493, 1990. Peter G. Beeson, "Rural Mental Health Research: The Next Generation," *Outlook,* vol. 2, no. 3, October/November/December, 1992, pp. 2–5. D. Blazer et al., "Psychiatric Disorders: A Rural/Urban Comparison," *Archives of General Psychiatry,* vol. 14, no. 3, 1985. James T. Horner and Lavern A. Bartlett, "Personality Types of Farm Couples—Implications for Intervention Strategies," Department of Agricultural Education, University of Nebraska-Lincoln, Building Family Strength, 1987. See References, Chapter 1, for additional studies.

11. G. Garfinkle et al. "Stress, Depression and Suicide: A Study of Adolescents in Minnesota," Responding to High Risk Youth, Minnesota Extension Service, 1986. State Health Reports: Mental Health, Alcoholism & Drug Abuse, pp. 4–8.

Chapter Two

1. Mona Lee Brock, "State of Mental Health in the Heartland," Oklahoma City: Ag-Link, 1992; Charlene Finck, "The 80s Are Over But . . . Farmers Are Still Killing Themselves," *Farm Journal,* vol. 114, no. 12, October 1990, p. 38.

2. Mark Lee, "Study Shows Suicide High Among Farmers," *Tulsa World,* September 12, 1989; and Mark Lee, "High Suicide Rate Linked to Farm Financial Stress," *Tulsa World,* September 16, 1989. Pat Lewis, "Preventable Agricultural Deaths in Oklahoma 1983–1988: Self Inflicted or Suicides," Agriculture Engineering Department, Oklahoma State University, unpublished, 1989.

3. Val Farmer, "Grief over Loss of Farm Compares to Death in Family," *Iowa Farmer Today,* ca. 1989.

4. James T. Horner and Lavern A. Bartlett, "Profile of Rural Leadership," Paper presented at Thirteenth National Agricultural Education Research Meeting, Dallas, TX, 1986. James T. Horner and Lavern A. Bartlett, "Personality Types of Farm Couples—Implications for Intervention Strategies," Department of Agricultural Education, University of Nebraska-Lincoln, Building Family Strength, 1987.

5. Horner and Bartlett, "Personality Types," pp. 7–8.

6. William Greider, *Secrets of the Temple: How the Federal Reserve Runs the Country*, New York: Touchstone, 1987, p. 458.

7. K. A. Kettner et al., "Economic Hardship and Stress Among Farm Operators in North Dakota: The Buffering Effect of Social Support," *Great Plains Sociologist*, vol. 1, no. 1, 1988, pp. 69–88. Reprinted in Peter B. Beeson et al., "The Farm Crisis and Mental Health: A Longitudinal (1981, 1986, and 1989) and Comparative Study of the Economy and Mental Health Status," presented at The National Conference on Mental Health Statistics, Washington, D.C., June 1991, p. 9.

8. James Ridgeway, *Blood in the Face: The Ku Klux Klan, Aryan Nations, Nazi Skinheads, and the Rise of a New White Culture*, New York: Thunder's Mouth Press, 1990, pp. 145–146. Edited transcript of a telephone conversation between Arthur Kirk and police officials, 1984.

Chapter Three

1. Sidney M. Jourard, "Suicide, An Invitation to Die," *American Journal of Nursing*, vol. 7, no. 2, February 1970, pp. 269–275.

2. Lou Northcutt, "Oklahoma Farmer Suicides and Farm Foreclosure Actions: A Descriptive-Correlative Study," Texas Woman's University, unpublished proposal, 1989; Lou Northcutt, Transcript of testimony before the Subcommittee on Conservation, Credit, and Rural Development of the Committee on Agriculture, U.S. House of Representatives, Amarillo, TX, August 9, 1989.

3. Jourard, "Suicide," pp. 269–275.

4. Center for Mental Health Services, "Taking Rural into Account: Report on the National Public Forum," U.S. Department of Health and Human Services, June 24, 1993, p. iv.

5. Center for Mental Health Services, "Taking Rural into Account," p. 5.

6. State Health Reports: Mental Health, Alcoholism & Drug Abuse. "Mental Health Services in Rural America," Intergovernmental Health Policy Project, The George Washington University, Washington, D.C., no. 58, June 1990, p. 1.

7. Northcutt, Transcript of testimony, pp. 2–5.

8. M. J. Belyea and L. M. Lobao, "Psychosocial Consequences of Agricultural Transformation: The Farm Crisis and Depression," *Rural Sociology*, vol. 55, no. 1, 1990, pp. 58–75. W. Heffernan and J. Heffernan, "Survey of Families Leaving Farming for Financial Reasons: A Preliminary Summary," Columbia: University of Missouri, 1985. D. R. Hoyt, "Economic Stress and Mental Health in Rural Iowa," Ames: Iowa Department of Human Services, 1988. See References, Chapter 3, for additional studies.

9. Mona Lee Brock, "State of Mental Health in the Heartland," Oklahoma City: Ag-Link, 1992.

Chapter Four

1. Joint Economic Committee Congress of the United States, "New Dimensions in Rural Policy: Building upon Our heritage," Studies prepared for Subcommittee on Agriculture and Transportation, June 5, 1986, pp. 277–278.
2. Glen Wallace, "Rural Development," Testimony before U.S. House of Representatives, Committee on Agriculture, Amarillo, TX, August 9, 1989.
3. Wallace, "Rural Development."
4. William D. Heffernan and Judith Bortner Heffernan, Testimony before Joint Economic Committee of the Congress of the United States, Washington, D.C., September 17, 1985. William D. Heffernan and Judith Bortner Heffernan, "Survey of Families Leaving Farm for Financial Reasons: A Preliminary Summary," University of Missouri, 1985. Wallace, "Rural Development," pp. 175–176.
5. Jeanne DeBruyn and Morton O. Wagenfeld, "Salutogenesis: A New Perspective in Rural Mental Health Research," *Human Services in the Rural Environment*, vol. 18, no. 1, Summer 1994, p. 20.
6. Danny R. Hoyt, David O'Donnell, and Yagla Mack Mack, "Psychological Distress and Size of Place: The Epidemiology of Rural Economic Stress," *Rural Sociology*, vol. 60, no. 4, 1995, p. 718.
7. Hoyt, "Psychological Distress," pp. 707–720.

Chapter Five

1. Vicky Weaver was shot to death at Ruby Ridge, Idaho, in 1992, 19 months after writing these words. The quote is attributed to Robert Mathews, who also died in a shoot-out with the FBI in 1985. Lawrence W. Myers, "Chosen People: Inside the Mind of Christian Identity," *Media Bypass Magazine,* vol. 4, no. 7, July 1996, p. 20.
2. Morris Dees and James Corcoran, *Gathering Storm*, New York: Harper-Collins Publishers, 1996, p. 1.
3. William D. Heffernan and Judith Bortner Heffernan, "Survey of Families Leaving Farm for Financial Reasons: A Preliminary Summary," University of Missouri, 1985, as quoted in Cooperative Extension Service, "Can Churches Respond to Farm Crisis?" University of Missouri, June 17, 1985, p. 1.
4. Dees and Corcoran, *Gathering Storm*, p. 3.

5. Wayne Laugeson, "Terrorism from Within," *Boulder Weekly*, vol. 3, no. 31, April 4, 1996, p. 12.

6. Dees and Corcoran, *Gathering Storm*, pp. 50–51.

7. Bill Donovan, "Comet to Bring End of Time Hopi Says," *The Arizona Republic*, March 17, 1997.

8. Richard Abanes, *American Militias: Rebellion, Racism, and Religion*, Downers Grove, IL: InterVarsity Press, 1996, p. 55.

9. Dees and Corcoran, *Gathering Storm*, p. 5.

10. Dees and Corcoran, *Gathering Storm*, pp. 19–20.

11. Geraldo Rivera, "Interview with Gary Yarbrough et al.," *20/20*, ABC, circa 1985.

12. Dees and Corcoran, *Gathering Storm*, p. 21.

13. Dees and Corcoran, *Gathering Storm*, p. 58.

14. William Pierce, *The Turner Diaries*, Hillsboro, WV: National Vanguard Books, 1978. Quoted in James Ridgeway, *Blood in the Face*, New York: Thunder's Mouth Press, 1995, p. 112.

15. Heffernan and Heffernan, "Survey of Families Leaving Farm."

16. Cooperative Extension Service. "Can Churches Respond to Farm Crisis?" University of Missouri, June 17, 1985, p. 1.

Chapter Six

1. Richard Gilmore, *A Poor Harvest: The Clash of Policies and Interests in the Grain Trade*, New York: Longman, 1982, p. 24.

2. Lori Dodge Rose, "General Mills to Buy Chex Brand from Ralcorp for $570 Million," *Rocky Mountain News*, November 1996.

3. Missouri Rural Crisis Center, *Hog Wars: The Corporate Grab for Control of the Hog Industry and How Citizens Are Fighting Back*, Columbia, MO: Missouri Rural Crisis Center, 1996, p. 6.

4. Osha Gray Davidson, *Broken Heartland: The Rise of America's Rural Ghetto*, Iowa City: University of Iowa Press, 1996, pp. 67–68.

5. Mark Anderson, Transcript of speech before Western Organization of Resource Council's Public Education Forum, Indianapolis, Indiana, April 6, 1990.

6. Associated Press, "Restructuring, Mergers, Buyouts, Spinoffs Spark 1,471 Name Changes," *Rocky Mountain News*, January 5, 1997.

Chapter Seven

1. Thomas A. Bass, "The Future of Money," *Wired*, vol. 4, no. 10, October, 1996, p. 142.

2. Eugene Schroder and Micki Nellis, *Constitution: Fact or Fiction*, Cleburne, TX: Buffalo Creek Press, 1995, p. 25.

3. From the *Public Papers and Addresses of Franklin D. Roosevelt*, vol. 1, New York: Random House, 1938, p. 42. Reprinted in Schroder and Nellis, *Constitution*, p. 44.

4. William Greider, *Secrets of the Temple: How the Federal Reserve Runs the Country*, New York: Touchstone, 1987, pp. 228–229.

5. Pat Robertson, *The New World Order*, Dallas: Word Publishing, 1991, p. 216.

6. Greider, *Secrets of the Temple*, p. 50.

7. Greider, *Secrets of the Temple*, p. 49.

8. Greider, *Secrets of the Temple*, pp. 50–51.

9. Greider, *Secrets of the Temple*, p. 46–47.

10. Greider, *Secrets of the Temple*, pp. 123.

11. Senator William Proxmire, *Congressional Record*, October 19, 24, and 25, 1979.

12. Greider, *Secrets of the Temple*, p. 176.

13. Subcommittee of the Committee on Appropriations, House of Representatives, Testimony Concerning Wichita Land Bank, Agriculture, Rural Development, and Related Agencies Appropriations for 1997, March 21, 1986, pp. 492–1053.

14. League of Rural Voters Education Project, "Trading Our Future," slide show handout, Minneapolis, February 1990, p. 3.

15. Greider, *Secrets of the Temple*, pp. 163–164.

Chapter Eight

1. Jack Anderson, *Inside the NRA: Armed and Dangerous*, Beverly Hills: Dove Books, 1996, p. 13.

2. Morris Dees and James Corcoran, *Gathering Storm*, New York: HarperCollins Publishers, 1996, pp. 199–200.

3. Anderson, *Inside the NRA*, p. 83.

4. Dees and Corcoran, *Gathering Storm*, p. 218.

5. Richard Abanes, *American Militias: Rebellion, Racism & Religion*, Downers Grove, IL: InterVarsity Press, 1996, p. 67.

6. Abanes, *American Militias*, p. 67.

7. Witkin et al., Poll conducted by Celinda Lake of Lake Research and Ed Goeas of the Tarrance Group, May 7–9, 1995. Reported in Abanes, *American Militias*, p. 66.

8. John B. Donovan, *Pat Robertson: The Authorized Biography*, New York: Macmillan Publishing Company, 1988, p. 139.

9. Eugene Schroder and Micki Nellis, *Constitution: Fact or Fiction*, Cleburne, TX: Buffalo Creek Press, 1995, pp. 1–2.

10. Schroder and Nellis, *Constitution*, p. 86.

11. Merlo J. Pusey, *The Supreme Court Crisis*, New York: Macmillan, 1937, pp. 71–72.

12. Schroder and Nellis, *Constitution*, p. 108.

13. Pusey, *The Supreme Court Crisis*, p. 71.

14. Thomas Sowell, "The Founding Fathers Knew Best," *Rocky Mountain News*, January 1997.

15. Anderson, *Inside the NRA*, p. 75.

Chapter Nine

1. Emily Barker, "A Rule of Their Own," *The American Lawyer*, vol. 18, no. 4, May 1996, p. 56.

2. Barker, "A Rule of Their Own," p. 54.

3. Oklahoma Governor's Task Force on Rural Stress, various letters from rural residents in Oklahoma sent to Governor Henry Bellmon, 1989–1990.

4. Val Farmer, "'Justice' Seems Distant to Many in Agriculture," *Farm & Ranch Guide*, April 22, 1988.

5. Diana Baldwin and Ed Godfrey, "'Craziness' of Common-Law Courts Concerns Officials," *The Daily Oklahoman*, May 13, 1996.

6. Barker, "A Rule of Their Own," p. 57.

7. Barker, "A Rule of Their Own," p. 56.

8. Barker, "A Rule of Their Own," p. 59.

9. Thomas G. Watts, "Freemen Ties Spark Inquiries: Authorities in 23 States Study Links in Fraud Cases," *The Dallas Morning News*, January 11, 1997.

10. Barker, "A Rule of Their Own," p. 54.

11. Barker, "A Rule of Their Own," p. 57.

12. Barker, "A Rule of Their Own," p. 58.

13. Diana Baldwin, "Vigilante Courts Raise Concerns," *The Daily Oklahoman*, July 18, 1996.

14. Barker, "A Rule of Their Own," p. 58.

Chapter Ten

1. Howard Pankratz, "Senator Warns of Others Like Freemen," *Denver Post*, September 29, 1996.

2. Anti-Defamation League, "The Freemen Network: An Assault on the Rule of Law," 1996.

3. Ibid.

Chapter Eleven

1. Morris Dees and James Corcoran, *Gathering Storm*, New York: Harper-Collins Publishers, 1996, p. 151.

2. Kenneth S. Stern, *A Force upon the Plain: The American Militia Movement and the Politics of Hate*, New York: Simon & Schuster, 1996, p. 190.

3. Dees and Corcoran, *Gathering Storm*, p. 152.

4. Stern, *A Force Upon the Plain*, p. 190.

5. Stern, *A Force Upon the Plain*, p. 193.

6. Mark Eddy and Steven Wilmsen, "Who Bombed the Murrah Building?" *The Denver Post*, December 15, 1996.

7. Eddy and Wilmsen, "Who bombed the Murrah Building?"

8. Eddy and Wilmsen, "Who bombed the Murrah Building?"

9. Dees and Corcoran, *Gathering Storm*, p. 172.

10. Dees and Corcoran, *Gathering Storm*, p. 174.

11. Dees and Corcoran, *Gathering Storm*, p. 174.

Chapter Twelve

1. Interview with Special Agent Larry Washington of the Bureau of Alcohol, Tobacco and Firearms, Washington, D.C., April 21, 1997.

2. Michael Weber, "Race Warriors," *Columbus Guardian*, October 7, 1996.

3. John C. Ensslin, "Busy Bank Robbers Steal State Record," *Rocky Mountain News*, January 23, 1997.

References

This source list is by no means exhaustive. There are dozens of other studies that confirm the findings of those listed here. I would also like to acknowledge the many journalists who have added their insight to the antigovernment movement debate. Without their work, this book would have been much more difficult to write.

Introduction

Blazer, D., et al. "Psychiatric Disorders: A Rural/Urban Comparison," *Archives of General Psychiatry,* vol. 14, no. 3, 1985.

Brock, Mona Lee. Interview in 1996 regarding FBI investigation of those who attended meeting in Oklahoma City.

Lewis, Pat. "Preventable Agricultural Deaths in Oklahoma 1983–1988: Self Inflicted or Suicides," Agriculture Engineering Department, Oklahoma State University, unpublished, 1989.

_____Interviews in March 1990 and November 1996.

Morawski, Philip. Interview in 1996.

Powers, Josh. Interview in 1996 regarding FBI investigation of those who attended meeting in Oklahoma City.

Rosenburg, J. "The Personal Stress Problems of Farmers and Rural America," Rockville, MD: National Institute of Mental Health, 1986.

Schneider, Keith. "Oklahoma Suicides Show Crisis on Farm Has Not Yet Passed," *The New York Times*, August 17, 1987.

Sinclair, William. "Grief Is Growing on Farm Land," *Washington Post*, May 24, 1987.

Wallace, Glen. "Rural Stress in Oklahoma," prepared for Oklahoma Dept. of Mental Health and Substance Abuse Services, unpublished, 1990.

_____"Rural Development," testimony before U.S. House of Representatives, Committee on Agriculture, Amarillo, TX, August 9, 1989.

_____Over eighty interviews conducted between 1989 and April 1997.

Chapter One

Anderson, Don. Transcript of testimony before the Subcommittee on Conservation, Credit, and Rural Development of the Committee on Agriculture, United States House of Representatives, Amarillo, TX, August 9, 1989.

Beaver Herald-Democrat. "Bellmon Establishes Task Force," March 1, 1990.

Beeson, Peter G., and Johnson, D. R. "A Panel Study of Change in Rural Mental Health Status: Effects of Rural Crisis, 1981–1986," Lincoln, NE, Nebraska Department of Public Institutions and University of Nebraska, 1987.

Bjordahl, Hans, and Campbell, Greg. "Only in America," *Boulder Weekly,* vol. 4, no. 1, September 4, 1996.

Blazer, D., et al. "Psychiatric Disorders: A Rural/Urban Comparison," *Archives of General Psychiatry,* vol. 14, no. 3, 1985.

Burt, Pam. Interview, August 25, 1996.

Daily Oklahoman. "USDA Warns Pay or Face Foreclosure," August 14, 1989.

Davidson, Osha Gray. *Broken Heartland: The Rise of America's Rural Ghetto,* Iowa City: University of Iowa Press, 1996.

DeBruyn, Jeanne C., et al. "Salutogenesis: A New Perspective in Rural Mental Health Research," *Human Services in the Rural Environment,* vol. 18, no. 1, Summer 1994.

Farm News, and Views. Map titled "Rural Counties with Declining Population 1980–1985," April 1988.

Fitchen, J. M. "When Communities Collapse: Implications for Rural America." *Human Services in the Rural Environment,* 10, no. 4, and 11, no. 1, 1987.

_____*Poverty in Rural America: A Case Study,* Boulder, CO: Westview Press, 1981.

_____*Endangered Spaces, Enduring Places: Change, Identity, and Survival in Rural America,* Boulder, CO: Westview Press, 1991.

Hansen, James. "When It Comes to Working Conditions, Nike Is No Sport," *Rocky Mountain News,* February 1997.

Heffernan, William D., and Heffernan, Judith Bortner. "Social Consequences of the Economic Crisis in Agriculture," in Joseph J. Molnar, ed., *Agricultural Change,* Boulder, CO: Westview Press, 1986.

_____"Testimony Before Joint Economic Committee of the Congress of the United States," Washington, D.C., September 17, 1985.

_____"Survey of Families Leaving Farm for Financial Reasons: A Preliminary Summary," University of Missouri, 1985.

Herbert, Bob. "1 in 4 Kids Growing Up Poor," *The New York Times,* October, 1996.

Johnson County Capital-Democrat. "Hot-Line Available for State Farmers," Tishomingo, OK, June 8, 1989.

Kotter, John P. *The New Rules: How to Succeed in Today's Post-Corporate World,* New York, The Free Press, 1995.

Larson, Michelle, Beeson, Peter G., and Mohatt, Dennis. "Taking Rural into Account," U.S. Department of Health and Human Services, Lincoln, NE, June 24, 1993.

Mooreland Leader. "Economic Stress Cuts Wide Swath Through Rural Oklahoma," Mooreland, OK, September 7, 1989.

Morgan, Dan. *Merchants of Grain,* New York: The Viking Press, 1979.

National Mental Health Association. "American Dream or Nightmare: Unemployment and Mental Health in America," National Mental Health Association, Alexandria, VA, 1985.

_____ "Report of the National Action Commission on the Mental Health of Rural Americans," 1988.

Northcutt, Lou. "Oklahoma Farmer Suicides and Farm Foreclosure Actions: A Descriptive-Correlative Study," Texas Woman's University, unpublished, 1989.

Oklahoma Governor's Task Force on Rural Stress. Various letters from rural residents in Oklahoma sent to Governor Henry Bellmon, 1989–1990.

_____ Testimony from public meeting of governor's task force held in Ardmore, OK, March 27, 1989.

_____ Testimony from public meeting of governor's task force held in Tahlequah, OK, September 21, 1989.

_____ Testimony from public meeting of governor's task force held in Woodward, OK, March 1, 1990.

_____ Testimony from public meeting of governor's task force held in Tonkawa, OK, March 13, 1990.

Rosenblatt, P. C. "Farming Is in Our Blood," Ames, IA: Iowa State University Press, 1990.

Sinclair, William. "Grief Is Growing on Farm Land," *Washington Post,* May 24, 1987.

State Health Reports: Mental Health, Alcoholism, and Drug Abuse. "Mental Health Services in Rural America," Intergovernmental Health Policy Project, The George Washington University, Washington, D.C., no. 58, June, 1990.

Subcommittee on Agriculture and Transportation. "New Dimensions in Rural Policy: Building Upon Our Heritage," Joint Economic Committee, Congress of the United States, June 5, 1986.

Wallace, Glen. "Rural Stress in Oklahoma," prepared for Oklahoma Dept. of Mental Health and Substance Abuse Services, unpublished, 1990.

_____ "Rural Development," Testimony before U.S. House of Representatives, Committee on Agriculture, Amarillo, TX, August 9, 1989.

_____ Wallace, Glen. Over eighty interviews conducted between 1989 and April 1997.

Webb, Tom. "Farm Lender's Troubles Are Homegrown, Regulator Says," *Wichita Eagle-Beacon,* March 5, 1988.

Williams, Roger T. "The Farm and Rural Crisis: Developing Services for Farm Families and Rural Communities," Health and Human Issues Dept., University of Wisconsin–Madison/Extension, circa 1996.

Chapter Two

Anonymous undercover law enforcement officer. Interview, January 1997. This source requested anonymity as he is still working undercover in the antigovernment movement. .

Armstrong, P. S., and Schulman, M. D. "Financial Strain and Depression Among Farm Operators: The Role of Perceived Economic Hardship and Personal Control," *Rural Sociology,* vol. 55, no. 4, 1990, pp. 475–493.

Beeson, Peter G. Interviews, November 1996 and January 1997.

Brock, Mona Lee. "Testimony Before Subcommittee on Conservation, Credit and Rural Development of Committee on Agriculture, United States House of Representatives," Amarillo, TX, August 9, 1989.

_____ "State of Mental Health in the Heartland," Ag-Link farm crisis hotline, Oklahoma Conference of Churches, unpublished, 1990.

_____ Several interviews conducted between 1989–1996.

Brooks, N. L., Stucker T. A., and Bailey, J. A. "Income and Well-Being of Farmers and the Farm Financial Crisis," *Rural Sociology,* vol. 51, no. 4, 1986, pp. 391–405.

Conners, Sam. Four interviews in 1996–1997. This is a fictitious name assigned to protect the identity of the source. All accounts concerning Conners are accurate. He is not a composite character.

Corcoran, James. *Bitter Harvest: Gordon Kahl and the Posse Comitatus,* New York: Viking, 1990.

Covey, Bill. Interview, November 1996.

Dyer, Dr. Paul. Interview, January 1997.

Farmer, Dr. Val. "Advice on Helping a Family Grieving Over Loss of Their Farm," *Rapid City Journal,* June 19, 1988.

_____ "Grief Over Loss of Farm Compares to Death in Family," *Iowa Farmer Today,* circa 1989.

Finck, Charlene. "The '80s Are Over, But . . . Farmers Are Still Killing Themselves," *Farm Journal,* vol. 114, no. 12, October 1990, pp. 36–39.

Heffernan, William D. Interviewed twice in 1996.

Heffernan, William D., and Heffernan, Judith Bortner. "Social Consequences of the Economic Crisis in Agriculture," in Joseph J. Molnar, ed., *Agricultural Change,* Boulder, CO: Westview Press, 1986.

_____ "Testimony Before Joint Economic Committee of the Congress of the United States," Washington, D.C., September 17, 1985.

_____ "Survey of Families Leaving Farm for Financial Reasons: A Preliminary Summary," University of Missouri, 1985.

Horner, James T., and Bartlett, Lavern A. "Personality Types of Farm Couples—Implications for Intervention Strategies," Department of Agricultural Education, University of Nebraska–Lincoln, Building Family Strength, 1987.

Jourard, Sidney M. *The Transparent Self.* New York: Van Nostrand Reinhold Company, 1971.

_____ "Suicide, An Invitation to Die," *American Journal of Nursing,* vol. 7, no. 2, February 1970, pp. 269–275.

Kalimo, R., and Vuori, J. "Work and Sense of Coherence—Resources for Competence and Life Satisfaction," *Behavioral Medicine,* no. 16, 1990, pp. 76–89.

Kelly, Ed. "Former Farm Wife Takes Crisis Message to Capitol," *The Daily Oklahoman,* July 30, 1987.

Kohn, M. L., and Schooler, C. *Work and Personality: An Inquiry into the Impact of Social Stratification,* Norwood, NJ: Ablex, 1983.

Lee, Mark. "Study Shows Suicide High Among Farmers," *Tulsa World,* September 12, 1989.

_____ "High Suicide Rate Linked to Farm Financial Stress," *Tulsa World,* September 16, 1989.

Lewis, Pat. "Preventable Agricultural Deaths in Oklahoma 1983–1988: Self Inflicted or Suicides," Agriculture Engineering Department, Oklahoma State University, unpublished, 1989.

_____ Interviews in 1990 and 1996.

Madill Record. "Foreclosure Notices Could Add Mental Stress for State Farmers," September 9, 1989.

McCurtain Gazette. "Farm Groups Join Forces," vol. 85, no. 28, 1990.

Nesbitt, Jim. "Harvest of Discontent," *American Cowboy,* May/June 1996, pp. 36–40.

NewsPress. "Farm Safety Week: Suicides Top Death List," Stillwater, OK, September 13, 1989.

Ortega, Suzanne T., et al. "The Farm Crisis and Mental Health: A Longitudinal Study of the 1980s," *Rural Sociology,* Rural Sociological Society, vol. 59, no. 4, 1994, pp. 598–619.

Rivera, Geraldo. "Interview with Dolores Kirk," *20/20,* ABC, circa 1985.

Rosenburg, J. "The Personal Stress Problems of Farmers and Rural Americans," Rockville, MD: National Institute of Mental Health, 1986.

Schneider, Keith. "Oklahoma Suicides Show Crisis on Farm Has Not Yet Passed," *The New York Times,* August 17, 1987.

Sinclair, William. "Grief Is Growing on Farm Land," *Washington Post,* May 24, 1987.

Tally, Max. Interview, November 1996.

Wallace, Glen. "Rural Stress in Oklahoma," prepared for Oklahoma Dept. of Mental Health and Substance Abuse Services, 1990.

_____Over eighty interviews conducted between 1989 and April 1997.

Ward, M. C. "A Mental Health Crisis in Rural Oklahoma," *The News*, Tahlequah, OK, circa 1989.

Williams, Roger T. "Harvest of Hope Survey Summary of Results," Health and Human Issues Dept., University of Wisconsin–Madison/Extension, circa 1996.

_____"Public Policies and the Wisconsin Farmer," Health and Human Issues Dept., University of Wisconsin–Madison/Extension, circa 1996.

_____"The Farm and Rural Crisis: Developing Services for Farm Families and Rural Communities," Health and Human Issues Dept., University of Wisconsin–Madison/Extension, circa 1996.

_____"The Farm Crisis Persists: Responding to Farm Family Needs," University of Wisconsin–Madison, circa 1996.

Chapter Three

Baldwin, Diana, and Godfrey, Ed. "'Craziness' of Common-Law Courts Concerns Officials," *The Daily Oklahoman*, May 13, 1996.

_____"Common Law Overshadows All Others, Advocates Say," *The Daily Oklahoman*, May 13, 1996.

Beeson, Peter G. "Rural Mental Health in an Era of Reform," *Prairie Wind Productions*, September 12, 1994.

_____"Rural Mental Health Research: The Next Generation," *Outlook*, vol. 2, no. 3, October/November/December 1992, pp. 2–5.

Brock, Mona Lee. Several interviews conducted between 1989 and 1996.

Center for Mental Health Services. "Taking Rural into Account: Report on the National Public Forum," U.S. Department of Health and Human Services, June 24, 1993.

Cowan, Gideon. Several interviews between 1989 and 1996.

_____Letter from Cowan to author, December 29, 1996.

Daily Oklahoman. "Congressional Subcommittee Learns Plight of Rural Healthcare," August 15, 1989.

_____"Rural Mental Health Care Needs Cited," September 2, 1989.

Foster, Dick. "Militiaman Killed in Prison," *Rocky Mountain News*, January 18, 1997.

Horner, James T., Bartlett, Lavern A. "Personality Types of Farm Couples— Implications for Intervention Strategies," Department of Agricultural Education, University of Nebraska-Lincoln, Building Family Strength, 1987.

Hospital and Community Psychiatry. "State Program in Oklahoma Cuts Farm Suicide Rate by Reducing Stress, Increasing Support," vol. 42, no. 7, July 1991, pp. 761–762.

Jourard, Sidney M. *The Transparent Self*. New York: Van Nostrand Reinhold Company, 1971.

_____"Suicide, An Invitation to Die," *American Journal of Nursing*, vol. 7, no. 2, February 1970, pp. 269–275.

Morawski, Philip. "Affidavit of Facts" filed in Caddo County, OK, concerning the case of Gideon Cowan, July 6, 1996.

_____Interview regarding Gideon Cowan, November, 1996.

Northcutt, Lou. "Oklahoma Farmer Suicides and Farm Foreclosure Actions: A Descriptive-Correlative Study," Texas Woman's University, unpublished proposal, 1989.

_____Transcript of testimony before the Subcommittee on Conservation, Credit, and Rural Development of the Committee on Agriculture, United States House of Representatives, Amarillo, TX, August 9, 1989.

Oklahoma Department of Mental Health. "Memorandum Regarding Treatment of Poor Clients At State Facilities," July 7, 1989.

Schneider, Keith. "Oklahoma Suicides Show Crisis on Farm Has Not Yet Passed," *The New York Times*, August 17, 1987.

Stewart, Don. "Farmers Express Anguish," *Tulsa Tribune*, circa 1989.

Wallace, Glen. "Rural Stress in Oklahoma," Oklahoma Dept. of Mental Health and Substance Abuse Services, 1990.

_____"Farm Credit Agenda," prepared by Oklahoma Dept. of Mental Health and Substance Abuse Services for employees of Farm Credit Bank of Wichita, 1990.

_____"Letter to Chairperson, Enid Hearings on 1990 Farm Bill," 1990.

_____Over eighty interviews conducted with Wallace between 1989 and April 1997.

Williams, Roger T. "The Farm and Rural Crisis: Developing Services for Farm Families and Rural Communities," Health and Human Issues Dept., University of Wisconsin–Madison/Extension, circa 1996.

Chapter Four

Associated Press. "Cult Leader Sees Jesus Role," March 28, 1997.

Beeson, Peter G. Interview regarding community depression, 1996.

Blackwell Journal Tribune. "Economic Stress Spreads from Farm to City," circa 1989.

Brock, Mona Lee. "Testimony Before Subcommittee on Conservation, Credit and Rural Development of Committee on Agriculture, United States House of Representatives," Amarillo, TX, August 9, 1989.

_____"State of Mental Health in the Heartland," Ag-Link farm crisis hotline, Oklahoma Conference of Churches, unpublished, 1990.

Brock, Mona Lee. Several interviews conducted between 1989 and 1996.

DeCamp, Susan. Montana Association of Churches. Interviews on January 10, 1997, and February 27, 1997.

Dees, Morris, and Corcoran, James. *Gathering Storm*, New York: Harper-Collins Publishers, 1996.

Heffernan, William D. Two interviews in 1996.

Heffernan, William D., and Heffernan Judith Bortner. "Social Consequences of the Economic Crisis in Agriculture," in Joseph J. Molnar, ed., *Agricultural Change*, Boulder, CO: Westview Press, 1986.

———"Survey of Families Leaving Farm for Financial Reasons: A Preliminary Summary," University of Missouri, 1985.

———"Testimony Before Joint Economic Committee of the Congress of the United States," Washington, D.C., September 17, 1985.

Hoyt, Danny R., O'Donnell, David, and Mack, Yagla. "Psychological Distress and Size of Place: The Epidemiology of Rural Economic Stress," *Rural Sociology*, vol. 60, no. 4, 1995, pp. 707–720.

Northwest Oklahoman and *Ellis County News*. "Farm Stress Reaches All Levels of Economy," September 1989.

Stern, Kenneth S. *A Force upon the Plain: The American Militia Movement and the Politics of Hate*, New York: Simon and Schuster, 1996.

Wallace, Glen. "Rural Stress in Oklahoma," prepared for Oklahoma Dept. of Mental Health and Substance Abuse Services, unpublished, 1990.

——— "Farm Credit Agenda," prepared by Oklahoma Dept. of Mental Health and Substance Abuse Services for employees of Farm Credit Bank of Wichita, 1990.

———"Materials for Introduction to Suicide Prevention Including Lenders," prepared by Oklahoma Dept. of Mental Health and Substance Abuse Services, 1990.

———Over eighty interviews conducted between 1989 and April 1997.

Williams, Roger T. "The Farm and Rural Crisis: Developing Services for Farm Families and Rural Communities," Health and Human Issues Dept., University of Wisconsin–Madison/Extension, circa 1996.

Chapter Five

Abanes, Richard. *American Militias: Rebellion, Racism, and Religion*, Downers Grove, IL: InterVarsity Press, 1996.

Anti-Defamation League. *Beyond the Bombing: The Militia Menace Grows*, 1995.

Associated Press. "Cult Leader Sees Jesus Role," March 28, 1997.

———"3 Are Focus in Olympic Blast," *Rocky Mountain News*, January 27, 1997.

———"Bank Blast Follows Earlier Discovery of Separate Bomb," *Rocky Mountain News*, January 27, 1997.

_____"Bomb Like One Sent to FBI Is Found at Waste Firm," *Rocky Mountain News*, February 9, 1997.

_____"Mild-Mannered Ex-Professor Spreading Racist Message," *The Sunday Oklahoman*, July 7, 1996.

Berlet, Chip, and Lyons, Matthew N. "Militia Nation," *The Progressive*, June 1995, pp. 22–29.

Bock, Alan W. *Ambush at Ruby Ridge*, New York: Berkley Books, 1995.

Bynum, Russ. "Atlanta Abortion Clinic Blasts Hurt 6," *Rocky Mountain News*, January 17, 1997.

Calvo, Dana. "Authorities Find Third Pipe Bomb," April 1997.

Clay, Nolan, and Greiner, John. "Ruling Backs New Inquiry into Bombing," *The Daily Oklahoman*, January 1997.

Cohn, Norman. *Warrant for Genocide*, New York: Harper and Row, 1969.

Cooperative Extension Service. "Can Churches Respond to Farm Crisis?" University of Missouri, June 17, 1985.

DeCamp, Susan. Montana Association of Churches. Interviews on January 10, 1997 and February 27, 1997.

Dees, Morris, and Corcoran, James. *Gathering Storm*, New York: HarperCollins Publishers, 1996.

Donovan, Bill. "Comet to Bring End of Time, Hopi Says," *The Arizona Republic*, March 17, 1997.

Evens, Mark. "Arrest in California Blasts," *Rocky Mountain News*, February 3, 1997.

Gonnerman, Jennifer, and DuBowski, Sandi. "Anti-Abortion and Militia Movements Converge," *Front Lines Research, On the Issues, Censored 1997*, New York: Seven Stories Press, 1997.

Graham, Patrick. "Militia Member Gets 6-Year Term," February 1997.

Heffernan, William D., and Heffernan, Judith Bortner. "Social Consequences of the Economic Crisis in Agriculture," in Joseph J. Molnar, ed., *Agricultural Change*, Boulder, CO: Westview Press, 1986.

_____"Testimony Before Joint Economic Committee of the Congress of the United States," Washington, D.C., September 17, 1985.

_____"Survey of Families Leaving Farm for Financial Reasons: A Preliminary Summary," University of Missouri, 1985.

Laugesen, Wayne. "Terrorism from Within," *Boulder Weekly*, vol. III, no. 31, April 4, 1996.

Lindsey, Hal, and Carlson, C. C. *The Late Great Planet Earth*, Grand Rapids: Zondervan, 1970.

Media Bypass. "Shout It from the Mountain: An Overview of Christian Identity," vol. 4, no. 7, July 1996.

Pierce, William. *The Turner Diaries*, Hillsboro, WV: National Vanguard Books, 1978.

Reuter. "Magazine: Novel Key in Bombing Trial," *Rocky Mountain News,* March 24, 1997.

Ridgeway, James. *Blood in the Face: The Ku Klux Klan, Aryan Nations, Nazi Skinheads, and the Rise of a New White Culture,* New York: Thunder's Mouth Press, 1995.

Rivera, Geraldo. Interview with Dolores Kirk, et al., *20/20,* ABC, circa 1985.

Robertson, Pat. *The New World Order,* Dallas: Word Publishing, 1991.

Rocky Mountain News. "Intruder Shoots Up Abortion Clinic," February 3, 1997.

700 Club. Pat Robertson interview with William Bennett, February 4, 1997.

Spence, Gerry. *From Freedom to Slavery,* New York: St. Martin's Paperbacks, 1995.

Stern, Kenneth S. *A Force upon the Plain: The American Militia Movement and the Politics of Hate,* New York: Simon and Schuster, 1996.

Wallace, Glen. Eighty-two interviews conducted between 1989 and April 1997.

Chapter Six

An Adaptive Program for Agriculture, prepared by Research and Policy Committee, Committee for Economic Development, Library of Congress Catalog Card No. 62–19146, 1962.

Agriculture-Food Policy Review. "Perspectives for the '80s," U.S. Dept. of Agriculture, April 1981.

_____"U.S. Agricultural Policies in a Changing World: Food Security Act of 1985," U.S. Dept. of Agriculture, 1989.

Anderson, Curt. "Activist Groups Denounce Use of Pork Checkoff for Probe," February 15, 1997.

Anderson, Mark. Transcript of speech before Western Organization of Resource Council's Public Education Forum, Indianapolis, IN, April 6, 1990.

Associated Press. "Suing FBI Mole Could Backfire," *Daily Oklahoman,* December 28, 1996.

_____"Today's Business Motto: Merge or Die," *Rocky Mountain News,* January 1997.

_____"Restructuring, Mergers, Buyouts, Spinoffs Spark 1,471 Name Changes," *Rocky Mountain News,* January 5, 1997.

Burke, William K. Interview April 6, 1996.

Charter, Jeanie. Interview February 1997.

Cheeke, Peter R., and Davis, Seven L. "Where's the Beef? Factory Farm Operations Threaten Ranching . . . ," *The Oregonian,* October 18, 1996.

Cochran, Willard W., and Ryan, Mary E. *American Farm Policy, 1948–1973*, Minneapolis: University of Minnesota Press, 1976.

Cohn, Norman. *Warrant for Genocide*, New York: Harper and Row, 1969.

Cole, Ron. Interviews conducted in April 1997.

Davidson, Osha Gray. *Broken Heartland: The Rise of America's Rural Ghetto*, Iowa City: University of Iowa Press, 1996.

Dees, Morris, and Corcoran, James. *Gathering Storm*, New York: Harper-Collins Publishers, 1996.

Devine, Thomas. "Consumer Implications from Monopoly Control of the Livestock Industry," Government Accountability Project, April 6, 1990.

Diamond, John. "Boeing in Giant Merger," *Rocky Mountain News*, December 16, 1996.

English, Glen. Letter from Congressman English, Agriculture Committee, to Glen Wallace regarding export market, March 30, 1990.

Farney, Dennis. "A Town in Iowa Finds Big New Packing Plant Destroys Its Old Calm," *Wall Street Journal*, April 3, 1990.

Gilmore, Richard. *A Poor Harvest: The Clash of Policies and Interests in the Grain Trade*, New York: Longman, 1982.

Government Acceptability Project. "Fact Sheet on Streamlined Inspection System," August 16, 1989.

_____"Govt. Scientists Expose Animal Drug Residue Public Health Threat: FDA's Center for Veterinary Medicine Mishandling Drug Evaluations," January 19, 1990.

Green, G. P. "Large-Scale Farming and the Quality of Life in Rural Communities: Further Specification of the Goldschmidt Hypothesis," *Rural Sociology*, vol. 50, no. 2, 1985, pp. 262–274.

Hales, Donna. "Growers Say Funds Improperly Distributed," *Phoenix*, Tahlequah, OK, September 24, 1989.

Hightower, Jim. "Corporate Pledge of Allegiance," *The Progressive Populist*, vol. 3, no. 2, February 1997.

Hohler, Bob. "Black Farmers Press White House; Group Charges Race Bias in Loans Dispensed by Agriculture Department," *The Boston Globe*, December 14, 1996.

Kotter, John P. *The New Rules: How to Succeed in Today's Post-Corporate World*, New York: The Free Press, 1995.

Kramer, Farrell. " Boeing Deal Concludes Year of Massive Mergers," December 16, 1996.

_____"Companies Satisfied Urge to Merge in Big Way in '96," *Rocky Mountain News*, January 2, 1997.

League of Rural Voters Education Project. "Trading Our Future: Understanding Agricultural Trade and the GATT," February 1990.

McPhee, Mike. "No Hog Heaven: Yuma Pork Dream Ends as Pigsty," *Denver Post*, September 29, 1996.

Missouri Rural Crisis Center. "Natl. Pork Producers Council Uses Checkoff to Investigate Farm Groups," February 13, 1997.

———"Missouri Rural Crisis Center 1994 Annual Report," circa 1994.

———*Hog Wars: The Corporate Grab for Control of the Hog Industry and How Citizens Are Fighting Back*, Columbia: Missouri Rural Crisis Center, 1996.

Morgan, Dan. *Merchants of Grain*, New York: The Viking Press, 1979.

Nesbitt, Jim. "Harvest of Discontent," *American Cowboy*, May/June 1996, pp. 36–40.

Perry, Rhonda. Missouri Rural Crisis Center, interview February 24, 1997.

Pitnick, Richard. "Don't Fence Me In: Besieged Monterey County Cattlemen Fight to Preserve a Dying Way of Life," *Coast Weekly*, no. 852, July 18, 1996.

Progressive Populist. "Howling About Antitrust," vol. 3, no. 2, February 1997.

Ridgeway, James. *Blood in the Face: The Ku Klux Klan, Aryan Nations, Nazi Skinheads, and the Rise of a New White Culture*, New York: Thunder's Mouth Press, 1995.

Rose, Lori Dodge. "General Mills to Buy Chex Brand from Ralcorp for $570 Million," *Rocky Mountain News*, November 1996.

Rothschild, Emma. "The Politics of Food," *Foreign Affairs Quarterly*, January, 1976.

Shubin, Walter A. Transcript of testimony before the Committee on Agriculture, U.S. House of Representatives, concerning the Food Security Act of 1985, November 4, 1989.

Stafford, Jim. "Theories About Cattle Price Slump Abound," *Daily Oklahoman*, December 28, 1996.

Thompson, Sarah, and Roy. Interview in February 1997. The Thompsons were given this fictitious name to protect their identity. They feared that by speaking out they would lose any opportunity to sell their potatoes to ConAgra.

Waller, Helen. "You've Heard the Beef, Now Here's Something to Sink Your Teeth Into," Western Organization of Resource Councils, April 6, 1990.

Walsh, James. "Next Generation Says 'No Thanks' to Family Farm," *Minneapolis–St. Paul Star Tribune*, October 1996.

Chapter Seven

Bass, Thomas A. "The Future of Money," *Wired*, vol. 4, no. 10, October, 1996.

Beard, Charles A. *An Economic Interpretation of the Constitution of the United Sates*. New York: The Free Press, 1913.

Davidson, Osha Gray. *Broken Heartland: The Rise of America's Rural Ghetto*, Iowa City: University of Iowa Press, 1996.

English, Glen. Letter from Congressman English, Agriculture Committee, to Glen Wallace regarding export market, March 30, 1990.

Farm Credit Association Manual, 1986.

Farm Credit System. Testimony regarding Committee on Agriculture, Nutrition, and Forestry, September 17, 1986.

Greider, William. *Secrets of the Temple: How the Federal Reserve Runs the Country*, New York: Touchstone, 1987.

Hansell, Saul. "E-Money Making World's Bankers Fret," *The New York Times*, September 29, 1996.

League of Rural Voters Education Project. "Trading Our Future," slideshow handout, Minneapolis, February 1990.

Leuchtenburg, William E. *The Supreme Court Reborn: The Constitutional Revolution in the Age of Roosevelt*, New York: Oxford University Press, 1995.

Owen, Robert L. "National Economy and the Banking System of the United States." Washington, D.C.: United States Government Printing Office, 1939.

Perry, J. K. "Letter to Federal Land Bank Association Members," describing differential interest rate policy that took effect October 1, 1985. August 26, 1985.

Pritchett, Herman C. *The Roosevelt Court: A Study in Judicial Politics and Values*, New York: The Macmillan Company, 1948.

Reorganization of the Supreme Court. Compiled by Julia E. Johnsen, New York: The H. W. Wilson Company, 1937.

Robertson, Pat. *The New World Order*, Dallas: Word Publishing, 1991.

Schroder, Dr. Eugene, and Nellis, Micki. *Constitution: Fact or Fiction*, Cleburne, TX: Buffalo Creek Press, 1995.

Senate Resolution No. 0012. "Moratorium on Farm Foreclosures Pending Investigation of Banks and Farm Credit Service," Sixty-Eighth Session, State of South Dakota, 1993.

Shubin, Walter A. Transcript of testimony before the Committee on Agriculture, U.S. House of Representatives, concerning the Food Security Act of 1985, November 4, 1989.

Subcommittee of the Committee on Appropriations, House of Representatives. Testimony concerning Wichita Land Bank, Agriculture, Rural Development, and Related Agencies Appropriations for 1997, March 21, 1986, pp. 492–1053.

Webb, Tom. "Farm Lender's Troubles Are Homegrown, Regulator Says," *Wichita Eagle-Beacon*, March 5, 1988.

Chapter 8

Abanes, Richard. *American Militias: Rebellion, Racism, and Religion*, Downers Grove, IL: InterVarsity Press, 1996.

Alfange, Dean. *The Supreme Court and the National Will*, New York: Doubleday, Doran, and Company, 1937.

Anderson, Jack. *Inside the NRA: Armed and Dangerous*, Beverly Hills: Dove Books, 1996.

Boston, Robert. *The Most Dangerous Man in America? Pat Robertson and the Rise of the Christian Coalition*, Amherst: Prometheus Books, 1996.

Bovard, James. *Lost Rights: The Destruction of American Liberty*, New York, St. Martin's Press, 1994.

Cottrol, Robert J., ed. *Gun Control and the Constitution*. New York: Garland Publishing, 1993.

Davidson, Osha Gray. *Under Fire: The NRA and the Battle for Gun Control*, New York: Henry Holt and Company, 1993.

Dees, Morris, and Corcoran, James. *Gathering Storm*, New York: HarperCollins Publishers, 1996.

Donovan, John B. *Pat Robertson: The Authorized Biography*, New York: Macmillan Publishing Company, 1988.

Fong, Tillie. "Judge Tours Land in Dinosaur Monument Grazing Fight," *Rocky Mountain News*, October 12, 1996.

Goldwin, Robert A., and Schambra, William A. *How Democratic Is the Constitution?* Washington, D.C.: American Enterprise Institute for Public Policy Research, 1980.

Gun Control. Washington D.C.: American Enterprise Institute for Public Policy Research, 1976.

Helvarg, David. "Grassroots for Sale," *The Amicus Journal*, Fall 1994, pp. 24–29.

Leuchtenburg, William E. *The Supreme Court Reborn: The Constitutional Revolution in the Age of Roosevelt*, New York: Oxford University Press, 1995.

Nesbitt, Jim. "Harvest of Discontent," *American Cowboy*, May/June 1996, pp. 36–40.

New Mexico Citizens Action Committee. "I Pledge Allegiance to the Lamb," Corrales, NM, 1996.

_____ "A Call to Arms," Patrick Henry, distributed at Third Continental Congress, Kansas City, MO, 1996.

_____ "George Washington's Vision of America's Destiny," distributed at Third Continental Congress, Kansas City, MO, 1996.

Pierce, William. *The Turner Diaries*, Hillsboro WV: National Vanguard Books, 1978.

Pritchett, Herman C. *The Roosevelt Court: A Study in Judicial Politics and Values*, New York: The Macmillan Company, 1948.

Pusey, Merlo J. *The Supreme Court Crisis*, New York: The Macmillan Company, 1937.

Reorganization of the Supreme Court. Compiled by Julia E. Johnsen, New York: The H. W. Wilson Company, 1937.

Robertson, Pat. *The New World Order*, Dallas: Word Publishing, 1991.

Satchell, Michael. "Any Color but Green," *U.S. News and World Report*, October 21, 1991, pp. 74–76.

Schroder, Dr. Eugene, and Nellis, Micki. *Constitution: Fact or Fiction*, Cleburne, TX: Buffalo Creek Press, 1995.

Snow, Donald. "Wise Use and Public Lands in the West," *Utne Reader*, May/June 1994, pp. 70–82.

Southwell, Ray. Interview during Third Continental Congress, Kansas City, MO, October 27, 1996.

Sowell, Thomas. "The Founding Fathers Knew Best," *Creators Syndicate*, January, 1997.

Spence, Gerry. *From Freedom to Slavery*, New York: St. Martin's Paperbacks, 1995.

Stapleton, Richard M. "On the Western Front," *National Parks*, January/February 1993, pp. 32–36.

Sugarmann, Josh. *National Rifle Association: Money, Firepower, and Fear*, Bethesda, MD: National Press Books, 1992.

Third Continental Congress (TCC). Various materials issued by TCC. Attended from October 28–30, 1996, Kansas City, MO.

_____ "Mission Statement," TCC, October 30, 1996.

Will, George. "The Rationing of Constitutional Rights," *The Washington Post*, February 18, 1997.

Zimring, Franklin E., and Hawkins, Gordon. *The Citizens' Guide to Gun Control*, New York: MacMillan Publishing Company, 1987.

Chapter Nine

Abanes, Richard. *American Militias: Rebellion, Racism, and Religion*, Downers Grove, IL: InterVarsity Press, 1996.

Arthur. Interview conducted November 11–12, 1996. Arthur is a fictitious name created to protect the identity of this source.

Baldwin, Diana. "Vigilante Courts Raise Concerns," *The Daily Oklahoman*, July 18, 1996.

Baldwin, Diana, and Godfrey, Ed. "'Craziness' of Common-Law Courts Concerns Officials," *The Daily Oklahoman*, May 13, 1996.

_____"Common Law Advocate's Federal Trial Under Way," *The Daily Ok-lahoman*, January 9, 1997.

Barker, Emily. "A Rule of Their Own," *The American Lawyer*, vol. 18, no. 4, May 1996, pp. 53–63.

Black's Law Dictionary. St. Paul, MN, West Publishing Co., 1990.

Brock, Mona Lee. Interview in April 1996.

Corcoran, James. *Bitter Harvest: Gordon Kahl and the Posse Comitatus*, New York: Viking, 1990.

Farmer, Dr. Val. "'Justice' Seems Distant to Many in Agriculture," *Farm and Ranch Guide*, April 22, 1988.

Frech, Darrell. Letter to Oklahoma Task Force, November 4, 1989.

Jural Society. Study materials list from Christian Jural Society Press. Purpose statement, American Jural Society, Cleveland, OH. Biographies of Jural Society founders. Excerpts from *The Book of the Hundreds* by John William et al., Canoga Park, CA, Christian Jural Society, circa 1996.

Reuter. "Tax Protester Gets 97-Month Prison Sentence," *Rocky Mountain News*, October 11, 1996.

Sanborn, Hope Viner. "Courting Trouble: Emergence of Common-Law Courts Raises Concerns Among Critics," *ABA Journal*, November 1995, pp. 33–34.

Schroder, Dr. Eugene, and Nellis, Micki. *Constitution: Fact or Fiction*, Cleburne, TX: Buffalo Creek Press, 1995.

Soldier of Fortune. "Militias Court of Last Resort," vol. 21, no. 9, September 1, 1996, p. 82.

Stoner, James R., Jr. "Religious Liberty and Common Law: Free Exercise Exemptions and American Courts," *Polity*, vol. 26, no. 1, Fall 1993.

Watts, Thomas G. "Freemen Ties Spark Inquiries: Authorities in 23 States Study Links in Fraud Cases," *The Dallas Morning News*, January 11, 1997.

Chapter Ten

Abanes, Richard. *American Militias: Rebellion, Racism, and Religion*, Downers Grove, IL: InterVarsity Press, 1996.

Anti-Defamation League. "The Literature of Apocalypse: Far-Right Voices of Violence," 1996.

_____"Armed, and Dangerous: Militias Take Aim at the Federal Government," 1994.

_____"The Freemen Network: An Assault on the Rule of Law," 1996.

Arthur. Interview conducted November 11–12, 1996. Arthur is a fictitious name created to protect the identity of this source.

Associated Press. "Cult Leader Sees Jesus Role," March 28, 1997.

_____"2 Michigan Militiamen Charged in '94 Slaying," circa 1997.

Baldwin, Diana. "Without Driver's License, He's Running for Sheriff," *The Daily Oklahoman*, August 19, 1996.

_____"Ministries Leader Says God Wants Him to Get Rid of IRS," *The Daily Oklahoman*, August 1996.

Berlet, Chip, and Lyons, Matthew N. "Militia Nation," *The Progressive*, June 1995, pp. 22–29.

Brooke, James. "Right-Wing Freemen Use Courts as Their Stage," *The New York Times*, March 1997.

Churches' Center for Land and People. "Extremism: Concern and Challenge," Sinsiawa, WI, 1995.

Dateline. Interview with Rio DeAngelo, surviving Heaven's Gate cult member, NBC, April 8, 1997.

Freemen. 19 page document issued by the Montana Freemen during the Justus Township standoff with FBI, April 1996.

Gaines, Alayna A. "Militia Madness," *Emerge*, July/August 1996, pp. 28–31.

Lindlaw, Scott. "Cultist Awaited Spaceship," *Rocky Mountain News*, March 28, 1997.

Lindsay, Sue. "Jeffco Set to Prosecute Couple Who Surrendered: Pair Face Federal Charges over Freemen Standoff," *Rocky Mountain News*, June 23, 1996.

Lowe, Archie. Three interviews in 1996–1997.

Lowe, Sarah. Five interviews in 1996–1997.

McLaren, Rick. Two interviews in November 1996.

Morawski, Philip. "Causes and Effects of Where We Are—If the Foundations Are Allowed to Crumble," Decker, MI: FarmCare, 1995.

Pankratz, Howard. "Senator Warns of Others Like Freemen," *Denver Post*, September 29, 1996.

Parsons, Randall. Freedom Center, two interviews in November 1996.

Salter, Stephanie. "Complex Cultists Reduced to Cartoons," *San Francisco Examiner*, April 2, 1997.

Stern, Kenneth S. *A Force upon the Plain: The American Militia Movement and the Politics of Hate*, New York: Simon and Schuster, 1996.

Thomas, Judy L. "'Freemen' Using Fake Check Ploy," *Kansas City Star*, July 23, 1996.

Turner, Dr. Ralph. Interview in November 1996.

Wallace, Glen. Eighty-two interviews, conducted between 1989 and April 1997.

Watts, Thomas G. "Freemen Ties Spark Inquiries: Authorities in 23 States Study Links in Fraud Cases," *The Dallas Morning News*, January 11, 1997.

Wilkinson, Todd. "Big Sky," *The Denver Post*, August 25, 1996.

Chapter Eleven

Arthur. Interview conducted November 11–12, 1996. Arthur is a fictitious name created to protect the identity of this source.

Associated Press. "McVeigh Blames FBI for Waco in 1996 Letter," *Rocky Mountain News*, April 6, 1997.

_____"Jet Explodes over Sea," *The Daily Oklahoman*, July 18, 1996.

_____"Mild-Mannered Ex-Professor Spreading Racist Message," *The Sunday Oklahoman*, July 7, 1996.

Bacharach, Phil. "Citizen McVeigh: Sorting Through the Facts and Myths Surrounding the Bombing Suspect," *Oklahoma Gazette*, vol. XVIII, no. 46, November 21, 1996.

Cole, Ron. Interviews conducted in April 1997.

Dees, Morris, and Corcoran, James. *Gathering Storm*, New York: Harper-Collins Publishers, 1996.

Eddy, Mark, and Wilmsen, Steven. "Who Bombed the Murrah Building?" *The Denver Post*, December 15, 1996.

Flynn, Kevin. "McVeigh a Study in Complexity," *Rocky Mountain News*, March 30, 1997.

Kilzer, Lou, and Flynn, Kevin. "Special Forces Served as Drug Smugglers, Assassins, According to Bombing Defendant," *Rocky Mountain News*, April 3, 1997.

_____"Attempted Chemical Buy for Bomb Alleged," *Rocky Mountain News*, February 5, 1997.

Morawski, Philip. Three interviews in 1996.

Pierce, William. *The Turner Diaries*, Hillsboro, WV: National Vanguard Books, 1978.

Reuter. "Magazine: Novel Key in Bombing Trial," *Rocky Mountain News*, March 24, 1997.

Rocky Mountain News. "The Trial of Timothy McVeigh," March 30, 1997.

_____"McVeigh Letter Warned Sister 'Something Big' Would Happen," circa March 1997.

_____"McVeigh Tagged 'Most Talkative,'" March 30, 1997.

_____"Pool Members Usually Get Firm, Friendly Farewell," April 6, 1997.

Stern, Kenneth S. *A Force upon the Plain: The American Militia Movement and the Politics of Hate*, New York: Simon and Schuster, 1996.

Wallace, Glen. Over eighty interviews conducted between 1989 and April 1997.

Chapter Twelve

Abanes, Richard. *American Militias: Rebellion, Racism, and Religion*, Downers Grove, IL: InterVarsity Press, 1996.

Alcohol, Tobacco and Firearms (ATF). Interview with Special Agent Larry Williams, Washington, D.C., April 2, 1997.

_____ATF Arsons and Explosive Incident Report, May 1997.

Associated Press. "Cult Leader Sees Jesus Role," March 28, 1997.

_____"3 Are Focus in Olympic Blast," *Rocky Mountain News*, January 27, 1997.

Barlett, Donald L., and Steele, James B. "American Dream Turns into Nightmare for Many," *The Philiadelphia Inquirer*, September 22, 1996.

_____"1890s Issues Hauntingly Familiar," *The Philadelphia Inquirer*, September 23, 1996.

Berlet, Chip, and Lyons, Matthew N. "Militia Nation," *The Progressive*, June 1995, pp. 22–29.

Cohen, Sharon. "Trial Nears for Reputed Leader of Hate-Peddling Bank Robbers," *Rocky Mountain News*, January 5, 1997.

Cole, Ron. Interviews conducted in April 1997.

Dees, Morris, and Corcoran, James. *Gathering Storm*, New York: Harper-Collins Publishers, 1996.

Ensslin, John C. "Busy Bank Robbers Steal State Record," *Rocky Mountain News*, January 23, 1997.

Geranios, Nicholas K. "3 Arrested in Bank Heists," *Rocky Mountain News*, October 10, 1996.

Kilzer, Lou, and Flynn, Kevin. "McVeigh Team Tries Again for Delay," *Rocky Mountain News*, March 26, 1997.

Lasch, Christopher. *The True and Only Heaven: Progress and Its Critics*, New York: W. W. Norton, 1991.

Lindlaw, Scott. "Cultist Awaited Spaceship," *Rocky Mountain News*, March 28, 1997.

Lorant, Richard. "3% of U.S. Companies Account for 80% of Job Growth from 91–95: Study Helps Explain Job Security Anxiety," October 1996.

Militia of Montana. *Information Booklet*, Noxon, MT: 1994.

_____*Networking: The Nuts and Bolts*, Noxon, MT: 1994.

_____Catalog of materials for sale, Noxon, MT: 1994.

Pierce, William. *The Turner Diaries*, Hillsboro, WV: National Vanguard Books, 1978.

Pitz, M. "7 Held in W. VA. Bomb Scheme," *Pittsburgh Post-Gazette*, October 12, 1996.

Rather, Dan. "Report on Church Burnings," *CBS Nightly News*, January 14, 1997.

Reuter. "Magazine: Novel Key in Bombing Trial," *Rocky Mountain News*, March 24, 1997.

Ridgeway, James. *Blood in the Face: The Ku Klux Klan, Aryan Nations, Nazi Skinheads, and the Rise of a New White Culture*, New York: Thunder's Mouth Press, 1995.

Sniffen, Michael J. "FBI Investigating 200 Allegations: Domestic Terrorism Growing," *Rocky Mountain News*, February 1, 1997.

Spence, Gerry. *From Freedom to Slavery*, New York: St. Martin's Paperbacks, 1995.

Stern, Kenneth S. *A Force upon the Plain: the American Militia Movement and the Politics of Hate*, New York: Simon and Schuster, 1996.

Wallace, Glen. Eighty-two interviews conducted between 1989 and April 1997.

Weber, Michael. "Race Warriors," *Columbus Guardian*, October 7, 1996.

Zinn, Howard. Interview in 1996.

Index